OBAMA'S AMERICA

UNMAKING THE AMERICAN DREAM

DINESH D'SOUZA

Threshold Editions

New York   London   Toronto   Sydney   New Delhi

Threshold Editions
A Division of Simon & Schuster, Inc.
1230 Avenue of the Americas
New York, NY 10020

First Threshold Editions trade paperback edition July 2014

THRESHOLD EDITIONS and colophon are trademarks of
Simon & Schuster, Inc.

For information about special discounts for bulk purchases,
please contact Simon & Schuster Special Sales at 1-866-506-1949
or business@simonandschuster.com.

The Simon & Schuster Speakers Bureau can bring authors to your
live event. For more information or to book an event, contact the
Simon & Schuster Speakers Bureau at 1-866-248-3049 or visit our
website at www.simonspeakers.com.

Cover photograph © EKY Studio/Shutterstock

Manufactured in the United States of America

10 9 8 7 6 5 4 3 2 1

Library of Congress Cataloging-in-Publication Data

D'Souza, Dinesh, 1961–
  Obama's America / by Dinesh D'Souza.
    p. cm.
  1. Obama, Barack—Influence. 2. Obama, Barack—Social and political
views. 3. Political culture—United States. 4. United States—Politics and
government—2009- 5. United States—Foreign relations—2009- 6. United
States—Social conditions—21st century. 7. United States—Economic
conditions—21st century. I. Title.
  E908.3.D76 2012
  973.932092—dc23
                                                    2012027999

ISBN – 978-1-4767-7335-3

In memory of my father,
Allan D'Souza,
who taught me to dream my own dreams

That fellow seems to me to possess but one idea,
and that is a wrong one.

—Samuel Johnson, Boswell's *Life of Johnson*

CONTENTS

CHAPTER ONE

INNER COMPASS

*Starting today, we must ... begin again the work
of remaking America.*[1]
—Barack Obama, inaugural speech, January 20, 2009

The American Era, 1945–2016. This could well be the title of a chapter in a history book a generation or two from now. A future historian, contemplating the American era, might express surprise that a nation so young and robust, a nation whose power and prosperity was without rival in the history of the world, lost its preeminence so quickly. Previous great powers did much better. The Roman era, for instance, lasted nearly a thousand years; the Ottoman era, several centuries; the British era, nearly two centuries. Who would have guessed that America, the last best hope of Western civilization, would succumb this easily, pathetically, ignominiously. For future historians, the most incredible fact might not be America's decline and fall but the manner of it. Ultimately, history may show, this fall was achieved purposefully, single-handedly.

It was all the work of one man, a man who in two presidential terms undid a dream that took more than two centuries to realize.

I believe in the American dream. Born in India in 1961, I remember sitting on the floor of our verandah as a boy, thumbing through the *Encyclopedia Britannica*, reading about the great empires from the dawn of history. In every case there was a rise and a fall, as the Romans, then the Ottomans, then the British, and finally and ironically the Soviets all ended up on the ash heap of history. "Lo, all our pomp of yesterday," wrote Rudyard Kipling in his 1897 poem *Recessional*, "is one with Nineveh and Tyre." But there was one exception to the rule, or so I thought, and that was America. America wasn't so much an empire as it was an ideal, an ideal of freedom and prosperity and social decency, a dream that "all men are created equal" and entitled to a "pursuit of happiness," a universal dream, one that even a boy in Mumbai, on the outskirts of world power, could aspire to. And thus I conceived my own dream, the dream of coming to America. I wanted to move from the margin to the center, to be close to, if not involved in, the great ideas and decisions, the decisive movements of history. When I served as a policy analyst in the White House, it was the fulfillment of a lifelong aspiration. Finally, I thought, the dream is becoming real in my life. And it has been.

The dream started, of course, with the founders. Two and a quarter centuries ago, the American founders gathered in Philadelphia to come up with a formula for a new kind of country. They called it the *Novus Ordo Seclorum*—a new order for the ages. The founders were convinced that if this formula were adopted, the new country would over time become the strongest, the most prosperous, the most successful nation on the planet. They were right. America today is the richest, the most powerful, and the most culturally dominant country in the world. Not only is America a superpower;

it is the world's sole superpower. Americans live better, and have more opportunity, than their counterparts in other countries because they have the good fortune to be born and living in the United States. Historically this was also true of the citizens of other great powers: the Romans, the Ottomans, and the British all lived better, at the height of their empires, than did people in other countries.

But those empires ultimately declined, lost their dominance, and became irrelevant in the global arena. If Americans today are aware of anything, they are aware of the precariousness of their position as an economic powerhouse and world leader. Let's remember that America has only been a superpower for a couple of generations, since World War II, and America has only been the sole superpower for two decades, since the collapse of the Soviet Union in 1992. So far, America has been the shortest-lived superpower in world history. And history shows that once countries lose their top position, they never get it back.

So are we approaching the end of the American era? The International Monetary Fund thinks so; the IMF released a report saying that the Chinese economy will be larger than the American economy by 2016. Some have disputed the IMF's date, as well as its methodology, which uses purchasing power estimates rather than straight income data to reach its conclusion. But no one can deny that China, a country with three times the population of the United States, whose economy is growing at four times the speed of America's, will surpass the U.S. in the not-too-distant future. In a recent article, "The End of the American Era," Stephen Walt writes that "China is likely to overtake America in total economic output no later than 2025." Indeed, it seems reasonable to forecast that both China and India will have larger economies than America sometime in the twenty-first century. Consequently, we seem to be moving from the

American Century to the Asian Century. Not only is America falling behind, but Western civilization is losing the dominant economic and political position it has enjoyed for the past five hundred years. A great historical reversal is under way.[2]

While the seeds of American decline can be traced back to previous administrations and previous decades, the pace of decline has dramatically accelerated in the past four years. Ordinary Americans can feel this decline in their income, their net worth, and their standard of living. Here are some indices. In America, between 2007 and 2010, median net worth fell nearly 40 percent—wiping out more than a decade of savings and home appreciation. This is the biggest reduction in American wealth since the Great Depression. As America declines, the rest of the world gains; to take a single example, the number of American millionaires dropped by 129,000 in 2011, while the rest of the world gained 175,000 millionaires. Economic growth over the past four years has averaged less than 1 percent, the most anemic growth rates since the 1970s. More than 13 million Americans are out of work. The unemployment rate in America rose from 6.8 percent in January 2009 to around 8.2 percent currently; the percentage of working Americans is at its lowest in three decades. Unemployment has risen despite the expenditure of hundreds of billions of dollars in stimulus and bailouts and other evidently unsuccessful attempts to restore economic vitality. Even the 8.2 percent government figure for unemployment is misleading; the actual rate is closer to 12 percent, since millions of Americans have given up looking for a job and dropped out of the workforce, and thus they are not counted in the official data. The poverty rate has climbed from 13.2 percent in early 2009 to 15 percent, which means that 45 million Americans are living below the poverty line. Food and gas prices are markedly higher; for example, the average retail price of gas rose from under $2.40 per gallon in November 2008 to

$3.60 currently, a 50 percent increase. The federal deficit climbed from $500 billion in 2008 to over $1 trillion annually, and the country is now $15 trillion in debt, much of that owed to other countries, including some that are hostile to America. This figure refers only to debts accumulated by the federal government; it doesn't count credit card debt, consumer debt, or home mortgage debt. In sum, by virtually all objective measures, Americans are worse off than they were four years ago.[3]

Moreover, America has seen a dramatic erosion of its power in the world. America is out of Iraq and getting out of Afghanistan, though both countries seem unstable and not necessarily future allies. While it seems the world's sole superpower can win short wars against weak opponents, it cannot maintain the peace, even in small, impoverished Third World nations. America's huge nuclear stockpile, which provided deterrence during the Cold War, has been largely jettisoned. The current administration is reducing America's arsenal to a few hundred missiles and seeks to do away with nuclear weapons entirely. Finally, America has seen its influence diminish in South America, Asia, and especially the Middle East, where anti-American forces are on the rise and America's allies are increasingly isolated and endangered. Not since Jimmy Carter has America suffered such a stark decline of power and prosperity.

Who is responsible for this? At the center of the debate is one man, Barack Obama. There are those who think that he has nothing to do with any of it; that he inherited all the problems from previous administrations; that he has been gallantly restoring America's economy and America's position in the world; that he has faced unfortunate obstacles, mainly in the form of obstinate Republicans, but that success is just ahead; that if we only give him a second term, Obama will vindicate the hope and confidence that were placed in him in 2008. This is the liberal position, which I will show is dangerously delusional, utterly incongruent with the facts, although we still have to explain why intelligent people are so susceptible to such delusions. Then there is the mainstream Republican view, which is that Obama is a typical American liberal, a progressive bungler of the Jimmy Carter type. He wants to restore America's economy, but he simply adopts one misguided policy after another. He wants to bring down unemployment and gas prices, but doesn't know how markets work. He wants to repair America's standing in the world, but his efforts to do so thwart American interests, undermine our allies, and bring our enemies to power.

So the Republicans shake their heads and say: well, he has no experience of working in the private sector, he is unskilled in foreign policy, he just doesn't understand. We have witnessed four years of right-leaning pundits explaining to Obama that Iran and Syria are not our friends; that slashing our nuclear arsenal is not a way to make America stronger; that if we get rid of nuclear weapons Iran's mullahs aren't going to lose interest in acquiring their own bombs; that higher taxes don't foster economic growth; that if we drill for oil in America we will become less dependent on foreign oil; that debt is reaching a point at which the economy risks ruinous collapse; and so on.

I will show in this book that the mainstream Republican critique of Obama is no less problematic than the liberal hosannas. Obama is not merely the presiding instrument of American decline, he is the architect of American decline. He wants America to be downsized. He wants Americans to consume less, and he would like to see our standard of living decline relative to that of other nations. He seeks a diminished footprint for America in the world. He detests America's traditional allies, like Britain and Israel, and seeks to weaken them; he is not very worried about radical Muslims acquiring a nuclear bomb or coming to power in countries like Tunisia and Egypt. He is quite willing to saddle future generations of Americans with crippling debt; he has spent trillions of dollars toward this end, and if he had been permitted, he would have spent trillions more. He has shown no inclination, and has no desire, to protect America's position as number one in the world; he would be content to see America as number 18, or number 67, just another country seated at the great dining table of nations. The strength of my thesis is that it is completely congruent with who Obama is and what he does. We don't have to assume that he is always getting results opposite to what he intends; we simply have to see that he intends the results he is getting. He emphasized in his inauguration speech his goal of "remaking America"—and he is doing it, recognizing that in order to remake America he must first unmake America. The only question is whether Americans approve of their country being diminished and downsized, and whether they want to give Obama another four years to finish the job.

While the evidence is overwhelming that Obama's actions are accelerating America's decline, I can understand the reluctance of Obama's supporters, and even some of his critics, to believe that this could possibly be his objective. Never before in American history have we had a president who seeks decline, who is actually attempting to downsize his country. Presidents are elected to protect and strengthen their country, so why would a president weaken it? We cannot answer this question without understanding Obama himself, his background, and his ideology. Without such understanding, we are vulnerable to all kinds of crazy theories. I am certainly not one of those who say that Obama hates America, or that Obama is a traitor, or that Obama is a Manchurian candidate who is being manipulated by some secret cabal. Not so—Obama is doing these things because of who he is, because of what he believes. He subscribes to an ideology that says it is good for America to go down so that the rest of the world can come up. He wants Americans to be poorer so that Brazilians and Colombians can be richer. He thinks it would be beneficial to us and to the world for there to be many rich and powerful nations, with no single nation able to dominate or dictate terms to any other. Obama is a visionary for global justice. He wants to set right the ship of the world that, in his view, has been tilted to one side for nearly five hundred years, ever since Western civilization began to colonize and rule the nations of Asia, Africa, South America, and the Middle East.

So the key to Obama is his ideology, his inner compass. Here, however, we face an obstacle. Many conservatives and Republicans don't know Obama's inner compass, and there are some who don't want to know. "We don't really care what his background is," they say. "We are not interested in his underlying ideology." These conservatives fancy themselves as hard empiricists, carefully scrutinizing what Obama is saying and doing. Yet politics is a complicated business, where people say one thing and do another, where elected officials make strategic retreats so that they can advance their agenda under more opportune conditions. How can we tell the man's principles from his compromises? How can we predict where Obama will take us if he is given a second term?

A recent incident confirms that Obama has a hidden agenda. In late March 2012, Obama met with outgoing Russian president Dmitry Medvedev. The subject under discussion was America's missile defenses. Obama thought he was speaking just to Medvedev; he didn't realize the microphone was on. "This is my last election," Obama told Medvedev. "After my election, I have more flexibility." Obama urged Medvedev to give him "space," adding that he needed it "particularly with missile defense."[4] What can we make of Obama's remarks? Obama was saying that he wants to give the Russians more concessions, especially on missile defense, but he didn't want to have to defend such actions in an election year. The White House rushed to cover Obama's comments, saying that he just wanted negotiating flexibility. The incident undeniably shows Obama's concern that he cannot get re-elected if he actually tells the American people his second-term agenda.

We need to know the man's core beliefs to figure out that agenda. Peggy Noonan, who served with me in the Reagan administration, liked to say that even when Reagan wasn't around "the idea of Reagan ruled." What she meant is that we could all tell what Reagan believed in a given situation. We knew his compass, and it could guide us on specific issues even if Reagan were not consulted. Knowing a president's compass is a great advantage, not just for White House staffers but for the American people; it explains what a president is doing and what he intends to do.

All of this seems obvious, so why do some on the right refuse to examine Obama's ideology? I believe the reason is fear. These conservatives are scared of two words: "Africa" and "black." They are scared of being portrayed as racists if they go down this path. Thus when Newt Gingrich suggested that "Kenyan anti-colonialism" was responsible for Obama's actions, there was visible discomfort even among some conservatives. I could literally see it on their faces. They wanted to change the topic, to talk about health care, or the Solyndra case, anything except Kenya and anti-colonialism and black, black, black. This fear is understandable, and even noble. It is based on a desire to assess the first African-American president on his merits, to eschew any kind of a smear strategy. But the fear and qualms are misplaced.

I am the source of Gingrich's "Kenyan anti-colonialism" remark. He made it after reading my *Forbes* cover story on Obama. The story, titled "How He Thinks," was adapted from my book *The Roots of Obama's Rage*. In that book I drew on Obama's own autobiography, as well as his early actions as president, to advance the theory that the president is driven by a Third World, anti-American ideology that he got from his Kenyan father. While my thesis was embraced by Gingrich, Rush Limbaugh, Glenn Beck, and several other leading conservative figures, some of the conservative intelligentsia distanced themselves from it. For these pundits, "anti-colonialism" is a foreign word and "Kenya" a part of the "dark continent," and the thesis seems consequently tainted by racism, as if Obama was more African than American.

These apprehensions are based on a failure to understand the anti-colonial ideology. I know the term "anti-colonial" is obscure to most Americans. I have frequently considered substituting some other term, perhaps even coining a new phrase. But "anti-colonial" is the term that is used around the world; it is the way that this movement and ideology have been described over many decades. There is no getting away from it, and if Obama succeeds in remaking America we will become much more familiar with it.

Contrary to conservative suspicions, anti-colonialism is not some weird African thing, but rather an immensely important global movement. Anti-colonialism is the most powerful political force in the non-Western world in the past 100 years. Moreover, anti-colonialism has been exported to the United States—it arrived here as a consequence of America's close involvement in the last and bloodiest of the anti-colonial wars, the Vietnam War. Consequently, anti-colonialism is now embedded within Western liberalism, and you can learn its main principles at most leading colleges and universities. A familiarity with these principles is essential to comprehend the world we live in today. If you want to understand anti-Americanism around the world, you cannot attribute it to just Islamic radicalism; that can only explain anti-Americanism in the Muslim world, but not in Asia, Africa, and South America. This anti-Americanism is part of a larger anti-Western sentiment that derives from anti-colonialism.

Let's explore some of the main tenets of anti-colonialism, drawing on its leading thinkers. "The wealth of the imperial countries is our wealth too," writes Frantz Fanon in *The Wretched of the Earth*. Born in Martinique, Fanon fought in the Algerian revolution against the French; Obama says that in college he relished reading and quoting Fanon. Fanon adds, "For in a very concrete way Europe has stuffed herself inordinately with the gold and raw materials of the colonial countries—Latin America, China, Africa…. Europe is literally the creation of the Third World. The wealth which smothers her is that which was stolen from the underdeveloped peoples." These facts, Fanon concludes, lead to a "double realization—the realization by the colonized peoples that it is their due, and the realization by the capitalist powers that in fact they must pay."[5] As we see from Fanon's analysis, the core idea of anti-colonialism is theft. In other words, anti-colonialists believe that the wealth of the world has not been generated through work or effort or creativity. It has not been earned, but rather stolen. The rich countries became rich by invading, occupying, and looting the poor countries.

A second tenet of anti-colonialism is that exploitation continues even after the colonizing powers return home. This type of exploitation is sometimes called "neocolonialism." The basic idea, outlined in Kwame Nkrumah's book *Neocolonialism*, is that economic exploitation outlasts political exploitation, with former colonial powers continuing their economic piracy of their former colonies.[6] In other words, there remain powerful economic forces within the rich countries, such as banks, insurance companies, drug companies, and oil companies, that rob and exploit poor people, both within their own countries and across the world. Anti-colonialists demand that the stolen wealth be redistributed, not merely within the rich countries, but also from the people of the rich countries to those in the poor countries.

Anti-colonialism is not primarily about race. As the African writer Chinweizu puts it in *The West and the Rest of Us*, "We suffered indignities under colonialism not because of our color, but because we had become a powerless and conquered people."[7] Chinweizu recognizes, of course, that over time colonialism developed an ideology of national chauvinism and ethnic superiority. After all, when the British and the French established colonies around the world, they recognized they were white and the people they ruled were black, yellow, and brown. It was irresistibly tempting for the West to believe that race was the cause, or at least the distinguishing mark, of its economic and military predominance. In practice, a racial distinction was everywhere evident between ruler and ruled. But Chinweizu's central point is that the British didn't take over Kenya or India because the natives there were black or brown. Rather, the British established colonies all over the world to rule them and benefit from them. Thus exploitation, not racism, is and always has been the central issue.

Thirdly, it is a core belief of anti-colonialists today that America has replaced Europe as the main perpetrator of global theft and exploitation. Ali Mazrui notes with irony that "the United States, though a child of revolution late in the eighteenth century, has become the father of imperialism." The Palestinian writer Edward Said, one of Obama's teachers at Columbia University, adds, "America began as an empire during the nineteenth century, but it was in the second half of the twentieth, after the decolonization of the British and French empires, that it directly followed its two great predecessors." And Aimé Césaire in his *Discourse on Colonialism* insists that American domination is the worst kind of domination. It is, he writes, "the only domination from which one never recovers" because it involves "the gigantic rape of everything intimate, undamaged, undefiled that … our human spirit has still managed to preserve." America is "the machine for crushing, for grinding, for degrading peoples."[8]

Anti-colonialists seek radical change to remedy the situation. "Revolt is the only way out of the colonial situation," writes Albert Memmi in *The Colonizer and the Colonized*. Memmi argues that colonial exploitation is bad for both the colonizer and the colonized. "Colonization distorts relationships, destroys or petrifies institutions, and corrupts men, both colonizer and colonized." Memmi notes that colonialism "is a disease of the European, from which he must be completely cured and protected…. The cure involves difficult and painful treatment, extraction and reshaping of present conditions of existence." What is needed is what Fanon terms "a world of reciprocal recognitions." Chinweizu writes that since "European rule was entrenched … by means of a western Christian culture, a western political power structure, and a colonial economy," anti-colonialism "involves measures against all three." Chinweizu calls for a redistribution of political, cultural, and economic power. We must, he writes, "make the fruits of the earth available to all right here on earth."[9]

In terms of policy, anti-colonialism is a massive program of global reparations. Anti-colonialists want rich people to pay up so that poor people can improve their living conditions. Their definition of rich people, however, is not millionaires and billionaires. It is a global definition. Since the vast majority of Americans are rich compared to people in Asia, Africa, and South America, the anti-colonialists want to see a diminution in the American standard of living, even for the American middle class, so that people in Addis Ababa and Rio de Janeiro and Nairobi can see their living standards rise. Moreover, anti-colonialists want more than wealth to be spread

around; they also want a global redistribution of power. Consequently, they wish to see America lose its preeminent position in the
world to make way for a rough parity among nations. They seek a
multi-polar world in which power is shared by many nations—a
world similar to the one that preceded colonialism. For such a world
to exist, America must shrink and other countries must expand.

All these points will be elaborated and substantiated in this book.
In my earlier book *The Roots of Obama's Rage*, I had only Obama's
autobiography to go on, along with some news reports. Moreover,
since that book was published in the fall of 2010, I could report only
on the first eighteen months of the Obama presidency. Since then a
good deal of important information about Obama's background has
become available. I have traveled to many places, including Hawaii,
London, Indonesia, and Kenya, to capture the Obama story for a
documentary film. All this has given me first-hand insight into
Obama's world. Obama is now at the end of his presidential term,
leaving behind him a four-year record. So what I earlier offered as
a tentative hypothesis, I am now in a position to prove.

Obama is not a conventional liberal; he is not from the same
mold as Bill Clinton, John Kerry, Al Gore, Michael Dukakis, or
Jimmy Carter. Rather, Obama draws his identity and his values from
a Third World, anti-American ideology that goes by the name of
anti-colonialism. Obama's philosophy can be summed up in David
Gelernter's phrase: America the Inexcusable. Notice that this is an
affirmation of American exceptionalism, but exceptionalism of a
special kind. According to this ethos, America is exceptional in being
exceptionally militaristic, violent, greedy, selfish, and rapacious. For
Obama, America is the plunderer, and he is the restorer. Traditional
Democrats want to preserve American leadership and have America
be a model for the world; Obama wants to displace American hege-

mony and realign America in the world. Traditional Democrats want a bigger economic pie so they can redistribute income in America; Obama wants to curb America's growth and redistribute wealth globally so he can reduce the gap in living standards between America and the rest of the world.

Over the past four years, Obama has worked hard, within political constraints, to implement his anti-colonial ideology. He has met with considerable success. Yet his agenda is incomplete, because America, although poorer and weaker than when he took office, is still the richest and most powerful country on the planet. All that could change in the next four years; if Obama has his way, it will change. If we understand Obama's ideology, we can make sound projections about what America will look like in 2016 if Obama is re-elected.

For me, the boy from India all grown up now, this prospect comes with a bitter irony. I came to America, the greatest and most powerful nation in history, to be part of an American project, this new order for the ages. Yet it is entirely possible that in a very short time I will live through the eclipse of the American era. Something else will take its place. It is even possible that, as China supplants America, India will then supplant China as the world's economic and political giant. It crosses my mind now: Would I have been better staying in India and never coming to America? Was my American dream a mistake? I have thought hard about this, and I refuse to believe it. And I am writing this book because I do not want to allow one man with a very different vision to destroy the American dream that has sustained me and millions of others.

CHAPTER TWO

INVISIBLE MAN

I serve as a blank screen on which people of vastly different political stripes project their own views.[1]
—Barack Obama, *The Audacity of Hope*

For the past two years, since the publication of *The Roots of Obama's Rage*, I've been learning as much as I can about Barack Obama. I am not alone in this pursuit. Others are mining this territory, one seeking to invalidate Obama's birth certificate, another trying to prove that someone else wrote Obama's book, a third attempting to establish that Obama's real father was the Communist Frank Marshall Davis, and so on. Incredibly, there is very little mainstream investigation into Obama and his background. In this respect, as I journeyed to Hawaii and Indonesia and Kenya, following in Obama's path and understanding his life's journey, I feel that I have the territory almost to myself. As I unearth things, I have a sense of discovery, of a private world opening up between Obama and me. Not that I am a master sleuth, but no one else seems even to be looking. Moreover, I can see the world as Obama does, not through American eyes but through "global" eyes. Like Obama, I know how to switch back and forth between the American perspective and the global perspective. Obama has this bifocal vision because that's how he grew up, and he's been doing it all his life. As an immigrant who sees America from the outside and from within, I can do it, too. All of this helps me to "get" Obama and show him as he hasn't been shown before. And the subject is one of surpassing importance, because at a critical time for America, Obama seeks a second presidential term. If we didn't know and understand him before, we need to know him now.

Barack Obama is perhaps the most unknown figure to enter the White House. Columnist Charles Krauthammer observed in 2008, "Eerily missing at the Democratic convention this year were people of stature who were seriously involved at some point in Obama's life standing up to say: I know Barack Obama. I've been with Barack Obama."[2] Consider the following exchange between journalists Charlie Rose and Tom Brokaw near Election Day 2008.

> **Rose:** What do we know about the heroes of Barack Obama?
> **Brokaw:** There's a lot about him we don't know.
> **Rose:** I don't know how he really sees where China is.
> **Brokaw:** We don't know a lot about Barack Obama and the universe of his thinking about foreign policy.
> **Rose:** I don't know what Barack Obama's worldview is.
> **Brokaw:** I don't either.[3]

Much more surprising is that even with Obama in the White House, the mystery has not been cleared. Obama remains, as columnist James Fallows puts it, "the man we have become familiar with, without really knowing." Two years into his presidency, in 2010, Obama biographer Jonathan Alter could write, "Never before have we known so little about someone so intensely observed." Around the same time, columnist Richard Cohen noted, "There was never a question about who Reagan was and what he stood for. Not so Obama." A year later, in 2011, Bill Keller wrote in the *New York Times*, "He has in a sense failed to define himself. He is one of our more elusive presidents, not deeply rooted in any place or movement." Keller's column was titled "Fill in the Blanks." And even now, the blanks have not been filled in. Obama biographer David Maraniss writes, "As Obama approached the fourth year of his presidency, many people considered him more of a mystery than when he was elected. This seemed especially true for those who supported him and wanted him to succeed."[4]

Part of the Obama mystery is personal. There are still gaps in his personal story. I am not speaking here of the so-called birther issue, whether Obama was born in the United States. That issue is a distraction from other aspects of Obama's life that remain obscure. For instance, no one has revealed Obama's SAT score for getting into college, or his grades at Columbia University, or his LSAT score for getting into law school. We don't even know who Obama's friends and associates were at Columbia. "I spent a lot of time in the library," Obama told a student journalist in 2005. "I didn't socialize that much. I was like a monk." Even monks live in communities, however, and this monk also attended classes. One would expect that, with an unusual name like Barack Obama, several of his fellow students would recall him. When Obama was elected president, the *New York Times* sought to identify and interview people who knew and remembered him at Columbia. The *Times* found no one, and when reporters contacted Obama, "he declined repeated requests to talk about his New York years, release his Columbia transcript, or identify even a single fellow student, co-worker, room-mate or friend from those years."

Obama's romantic life, prior to meeting his wife, Michelle, also escaped public and journalistic attention for several years. Obama describes a serious relationship that he had with a white woman, even going for a weekend to her country home. This was no casual relationship: "We saw each other for almost a year." Finally journalist David Maraniss identified a woman who dated Obama in New York and suggested that she might be the missing girlfriend. Yet her description of their relationship did not match the one that Obama gave, and Maraniss quoted Obama saying that his account was based on a composite of several girlfriends. This only deepens the puzzle: Where are those girlfriends? Why haven't at least some of them come forward? Why has no journalist tracked them down and interviewed them?[5]

All of this is strange, not only that so much remains unknown about the president at the end of his first term, but also that reporters seem uninterested in chasing down the facts. Even Obama's critics, such as the right-wing press or the Republican National Committee, have not taken the time or trouble to pursue this missing information. Consequently, the Obama mystery isn't just about him; it is also about the peculiar incuriosity of our political culture. Why are we content to know so little about this president?

Here is a telling personal peculiarity about Obama: some of his closest relatives are living in desperate poverty, yet he refuses to help them in any way. His father's sister is Hawa Auma. This is how she describes herself: "I am the daughter of Hussein Onyango Obama and the sister of Barack Obama senior and the aunt of the president." Hawa Auma is a widow in her seventies, and you can find her on the streets of a small town in Kenya called Oyugis. There she sells charcoal by the side of the road, making barely enough to live on.

She says she would like to get her teeth fixed, but she doesn't have the money.[6]

Then there is George Obama, the president's half-brother. George is the eighth and youngest child of Barack Obama Sr., a son he conceived with his fourth wife, Jael Otieno. I first encountered George during the 2008 presidential campaign when I came across an article in a London newspaper saying that "George Obama, Barack Obama's long-lost brother, was tracked down living in a hut on the outskirts of Nairobi." In the article, George was quoted saying that he lived on a few dollars a day. He was reluctant to use the name Obama. "If anyone says something about my surname, I say we are not related. I am ashamed." A subsequent report on CNN showed George's six-by-ten-foot hut in the Huruma slums of Nairobi. One of George's neighbors, Emelda Negei, told CNN, "I would like Obama to visit his brother to see how he is living, to improve his way of life." But Obama never has, nor has he provided a penny to help George. We will meet George, and learn more about him, later in this book.[7]

Finally, there is the case of the Barack Obama Schools in the Kenyan village of Kogelo, where Obama's father grew up. Obama visited Kogelo as a U.S. senator in 2006, and he was given a hero's welcome. There are two schools in Kogelo, and both were renamed after him: Senator Obama Primary School and Senator Obama Secondary School. One third of the students there are orphans. Obama toured the secondary school and saw its dilapidated class-rooms that lacked electricity, sanitation, and running water. He told the people gathered there, including the Kenyan president, local politicians, and the press, "Hopefully I can provide some assistance in the future to this school." Later he assured Principal Yuanita Obiero, "I have said I will assist the school and I will do so." Two years later, in July 2008, Obiero told the London *Evening Standard*,

"Obama has not honored the promises he gave me. He has not given us even one shilling. But we still have hope."[8] I recently visited the school and was told that Obama has yet to contribute anything to help. One local resident told me, "We have completely given up hoping that he is going to do anything for us."

Most of the American press simply refuses to report this kind of information about President Obama. This is bizarre in itself, because the stories are both interesting and relevant. Obama's own conduct in these situations is odd, not only because Obama is a multimillionaire and the most powerful man in the world—it would take so little for him to help—but also because his entire political agenda seems to be based on asking people who are well off to pay more to assist those who are not so well off. Obama wants to force the rich to pay more taxes in order to benefit the poor and the middle class. Yet in situations where Obama is in a direct position to contribute and one would think has every reason to contribute, where a little assistance would go a long way, he doesn't provide any.

I think I can clear up some, although not all, of these personal mysteries. My focus in this book, however, is on the ideological mystery of Barack Obama. In deciphering the ideological mystery, I believe we will better understand why Obama has no interest in the school that bears his name, why he doesn't bother to help his needy relatives, and why he has taken such trouble to conceal important personal details about himself.

We can see the ideological mystery of Obama in the fantastically contradictory things that people say about the man. From the liberal side: he is the first African-American president. This is probably the most common way that Obama is understood. It is certainly the way that Obama biographer David Remnick understood him in his admiring book, *The Bridge*. Yet there are others who insist that Obama is not really black.[9] That's because he never sat at a segregated lunch counter, nor are any of his ancestors descended from slaves. This is in sharp contrast with Michelle Obama, who traces her roots back to a Carolina slave plantation. Her husband, however, grew up in Hawaii and Indonesia with multiple visits to Kenya, Indonesia, and Pakistan. By his own acknowledgment, he didn't live the typical black American experience.

Interestingly, as president Obama has shown virtually no interest in black issues, from affirmative action to hate crimes to inner-city poverty. He ignores those issues, raising the hackles of black activists like Tavis Smiley, Ishmael Reed, Michael Eric Dyson, and Cornel West. Reed charges, "It's obvious by now that Barack Obama is treating black Americans like one treats a demented uncle, brought out from his room to be ridiculed and scolded before company from time to time." West contends that Obama "doesn't care about the black poor.... His policies are generating misery among poor people, disproportionately black and brown." West terms Obama's policies "the new Jim Crow."[10]

It's not hard to see why these complaints are growing. African-Americans have suffered devastating economic losses during Obama's four years in office. The black unemployment rate is nearly 15 percent, almost double the white rate. Since 2008, blacks have seen their wealth erode, mostly due to plummeting home values. Black wealth used to be around $10,000, one-tenth that of whites. Now median black wealth is a mere $4,900, one-twentieth that of whites. Writing in *The New Republic*, Isabel Wilkerson grimly reports that "one out of every four black households has no assets other than a car." Many in the Congressional Black Caucus are angry and frustrated with Obama. At a recent Black Caucus meeting in Detroit, Representative Maxine Waters let loose. "Our people are hurting," she said. "The unemployment level is unconscionable." Yet she said that Obama was nowhere to be seen. "He's not in any black community." Waters confessed that she and other African-American leaders were scared to go after Obama. "If we go after the president too hard," she said, black voters would be "going after us." Obama seems confident that he has the black rank-and-file in his camp. Appearing before the Black Caucus in 2011, he pooh-poohed their concerns and gave them his instructions. "Stop complaining, stop grumbling, stop crying … take off your bedroom slippers, put on your marching shoes."[11]

Many liberals view Obama as a progressive champion, the bold challenger of Wall Street and the big, bad corporations. Yet these same liberals express puzzlement that Obama rails against Americans on top, but he doesn't express much concern or compassion for Americans at the bottom. Surely, say some, this is because Obama is an intellectual. He's just too cerebral, preoccupied with scholarly ideas. Maureen Dowd compares Obama to Mr. Spock and notes his "Vulcan-like logic and detachment." Jacob Weisberg remarks, "His relationship with the world is primarily rational and analytical rather than intuitive or emotional." A Harvard historian has a whole book, *Reading Obama*, devoted to those ideas. The book proclaims Obama a member of a "rare breed" of "philosopher presidents" and is supposedly focused on Obama's extensive writings.[12] But the book turns out to be unintentionally humorous because it leads to the revelation that there are no such writings. Obama was editor of the *Harvard Law Review*, but never wrote for it. Nor has he published any scholarly articles on any topic in any other publication. Obama's main attempts at "scholarship" can be found in two books, both autobiographies. Consequently, his intellectual output largely consists of two works about himself. I don't deny for an instant that Obama is smart, but the cerebral philosopher label doesn't quite fit him. If he doesn't seem to care about poor and ordinary Americans, that's probably because he doesn't really care about poor and ordinary Americans.

Some progressives recognize this, and they blast Obama. He's no progressive, they charge, rather he is a sellout to Wall Street. Writing in the *New York Times Magazine*, Frank Rich faults Obama with "failure to demand a reckoning from the moneyed interests." Commentator Robert Kuttner laments, "I cannot recall a president who generated so much excitement as a candidate but who turned out to be such a political dud as a chief executive." Even some union leaders criticize Obama for downplaying jobs and focusing on other issues. "Obama campaigned big, but he's governing small," says Larry Hanley, president of the Amalgamated Transit Union. AFL-CIO president Richard Trumka says that unions need a new strategy to build an independent voice separate from Obama and his Democratic Party backers. Other progressives, notably Ron Suskind in his book *Confidence Men*, say that Obama is a well-meaning but ineffective guy who has been manipulated by staffers who have sold out to Wall Street.[13]

From the conservative side, we hear that Obama is a socialist who wants the government to take over the private sector. Jonah Goldberg reflects this view in his article, "What Kind of a Socialist is Barack Obama?" This is a valid question. Certainly during Obama's tenure government power has expanded over banks, investment firms, insurance companies, and automobile companies. Yet Obama hasn't proposed a full-scale government takeover of the means of production, which is what true socialism is. Moreover, even if socialism could explain Obama's economic policy, it cannot explain his foreign policy.[14]

In conservative publications like *National Review* and the *Weekly Standard*, the prevailing take is that Obama is a mainstream liberal

Democrat, not very different from Bill Clinton or former Democratic presidential nominees John Kerry, Al Gore, or Michael Dukakis. Mitt Romney terms Obama a "big spending liberal" who "takes his political inspiration" from the "social democrats in Europe."[15] Yet the European Social Democrats have been imposing stern austerity programs, while Obama has been trying to discourage them from doing so. Moreover, Obama disavows any affiliation with Europe. In *Dreams from My Father*, he writes, following a trip to Europe, "It wasn't that Europe wasn't beautiful.... It just wasn't mine." Obama's European trip takes up just a few paragraphs in Obama's book, while his subsequent trip to Kenya takes up 130 pages. Perhaps Romney doesn't know better, but more likely he's just being polite. Romney doesn't like to say "socialist" and so he says "social Democrat." And he doesn't like to say "African," so he says "European." As for the other conservatives, they make accusations against Obama that refute the notion that he's just another progressive Democrat. "If Obama is re-elected," the *Weekly Standard* editorializes, "it's quite possible that Americans will never again enjoy the liberty, fiscal solvency, or economic prosperity enjoyed by our forebears." In this view, Obama is fundamentally endangering the American dream. But this could hardly be said of Clinton, Kerry, Gore, or even the hapless Dukakis; the person who would do this isn't a garden-variety liberal Democrat.[16]

A growing chorus on the right contends that Obama is, well, not very smart. "Over-Rated," reads one headline. "Obama's Learning Curve," reads another. A recent book terms Obama a "Bungler-in-Chief." This line of criticism was most cogently expressed by Brett Stephens in the *Wall Street Journal*. "The president isn't very bright," wrote Stephens, adding that Obama "makes predictions that prove false.... He surrenders positions staked in public.... Every time he opens his mouth, he subtracts from the sum total of financial capital." Stephens assumes that Obama does these things because he's stupid. "Stupid is as stupid does…. The presidency of Barack Obama is a case study in stupid does."[17] Yet if Obama is so stupid, how has he accomplished more than any Democratic president since Lyndon Johnson, perhaps since Franklin Roosevelt? He has fundamentally altered the relationship of the citizen to the state, and he has dramatically shifted America's position in the world, all in one term. Obama may not have been successful in achieving Bret Stephens's conservative agenda, but he seems remarkably successful in achieving his own agenda.

From less respectable quarters, we hear wilder accusations: Obama hates America, or he is a Muslim whose true commitments can be seen in his support for jihadists and Islamic radicals, or he is a wimp and a pacifist who is allergic to the use of military force. Obama's resolute action in ordering the killing of Osama Bin Laden has greatly undermined these charges, none of which was convincing in the first place. Obama doesn't hate America—he does what he does because he believes it is good for America, and for the world. Obama isn't allergic to the use of force, which he showed not only in the Bin Laden operation but also in Libya. There is no evidence whatsoever that Obama is a Muslim. His father Barack Obama Sr. and his step-father Lolo Soetoro were born and raised as Muslims; but eventually both men became atheists, as did Obama's mother, Ann. Obama was raised without any religious beliefs. I once asked a conservative Muslim friend if he saw anything in Obama that he recognized as Muslim. "Absolutely not," he said. Then he added, "Obama would be a much better man if he were in fact a Muslim."

There is a whole book, *The Manchurian President*, devoted to arguing that Obama is a radical acting on behalf of an anti-American cabal. The book shows that Obama behaves in apparently strange and incomprehensible ways, but it never reveals that anyone else is manipulating him. I was fascinated, however, to read an article by economist Kevin Hassett titled "Manchurian Candidate Starts War on Business." Hassett is a former colleague of mine at the American Enterprise Institute and the very opposite of a conspiracy buff. Hassett wrote, "Imagine that some hypothetical enemy state spent years preparing a Manchurian candidate to destroy the U.S. economy once elected. What policies might that leader pursue?" Hassett went on to argue that such a leader would pursue basically the policies that Obama has pursued. But then he concluded, "It's clear that President Obama wants the best for our country. That makes it all the more puzzling that he would legislate like a Manchurian candidate."[18]

That is the puzzle that this book seeks to solve. Hassett formulates the issue with utter clarity. If Obama is an American president who wants what's best for America, why is he doing things that clearly hurt America? If we can answer this question, we not only understand Obama, we even understand why so many critics say such disparate and sometimes manifestly foolish things about him.

Obama presents us with a unique challenge. We have to admit that never before has a president inspired such different and contradictory reactions, not only between ideological camps, but also within each ideological camp. With Bush or Clinton or Reagan or Carter, we might love them or hate them, but in general we knew what we were getting. Bush was a Texas cowboy and a right-winger of the swaggering, big-spending type. Reagan was an optimist whose Midwestern origins and California outlook gave him a cosmopolitan conservative flair. Clinton was a bit of a Southern moral reprobate who nevertheless governed, at least after the chastening 1994 midterm election, as a thoughtful centrist. Carter was a moralizing Southerner who proved ineffective in dealing with the issues of his

time. Both to their admirers and their critics, these men were rec-
ognizable American types.

Obama isn't. Writing in the *Wall Street Journal*, Dorothy Rabinowitz calls Obama "the alien in the White House." Rabinowitz goes
out of her way to distance herself from the birther allegation. And
yet, she says, Obama is "wanting in certain qualities citizens have
until now taken for granted in their presidents." Rabinowitz adds,
"A great part of America now understands that this president's sense
of identification lies elsewhere, and is in profound ways unlike
theirs. For example, Americans expect their leaders to take their
side, to champion their interests. Yet the Obama White House "has
focused consistently on the sensitivities of the world community …
of which the president of the United States frequently appears to
view himself as the representative at large." Even Democratic presidents, she notes, have consistently viewed themselves as supporting
and advancing American interests. Rabinowitz admits that attitudes
favoring global interests over national interests are hardly unique;
they are widespread abroad and can be found even in influential
precincts in this country. "They are attitudes to be found everywhere,
but never before in a president of the United States."[19] Obama, in
Rabinowitz's view, is not a traditional Democrat; there is something
foreign about his outlook. She's right.

Let's list some of the Obama anomalies that place Obama outside
the standard American political categories. Obama came to office
promising to unify America and to govern as a centrist. Go back and
read Obama's 2004 Democratic Convention speech, a speech that
could have been given by Ronald Reagan. Or, even earlier, Obama
wrote in *The Audacity of Hope*, "At the core of the American experience are a set of ideals that continue to stir our collective conscience,
a common set of values that bind us together.… We need a new

kind of politics, one that can excavate and build upon those shared understandings that pull us together as Americans." Yet Obama has governed as one of the most divisive presidents in American history. He shoved through health care reform without a single Republican vote. He denounces his opposition as not merely mistaken but greedy, selfish, and, in a word, immoral. At various times Obama has called his Republican opponents "enemies" and "hostage takers" and even likened them to terrorists. "They've got a bomb strapped to them and they've got their hand on the trigger." Even Obama supporters concede how inflammatory his rhetoric can be. Historian Sean Wilentz writes that the Obama presidency has "affirmed and deepened the partisan divide as never before."[20] Despite being repudiated in a midterm election—a result that caused Bill Clinton to become a dedicated centrist—Obama has dug in and refused to change course. A centrist Obama would almost surely be re-elected, but Obama seems to prefer risking setbacks and even electoral defeat in order to advance his ideological agenda.

Obama has added so promiscuously to the national debt that the United States risks bankruptcy and perhaps even economic collapse over the next four years, yet Obama seems unconcerned. If he had the chance, it's clear he would have spent far more. True, debt levels have been rising since the 1980s, yet as one economist put it, what used to be annual deficits under Reagan have now become monthly deficits under Obama. U.S. government spending rose from $2.9 trillion in 2008 to $3.7 trillion this year; currently the government borrows 40 cents of every dollar it spends. Much of this money is owed to foreigners and foreign governments, and according to economist Stephen Cohen and Bradford DeLong, "the money will not soon be coming back to America." In their book *The End of Influence*, they warn that debt will not only change America's economic place in the world but also its political, military, and cultural leadership role. The authors predict, "The American standard of living will decline relative to the rest of the industrialized and industrializing world" and "the United States will lose power and influence." Their conclusion: "The United States will continue to be a world leader, but it will no longer be the boss. The other countries, after all, will have the money." Obama seems fine with this; in fact, he recently spoke about how the American dream ought to be scaled back to more modest proportions: "raise a family," "not go bankrupt," "have health insurance that helps you deal with those difficult times," "put some money away for retirement." Obama concluded, "That's all most people want. Folks don't have unrealistic ambitions. They do believe that if they work hard they should be able to achieve that small measure of an American dream."[21]

While Obama has been blocking oil drilling in the United States, he has been promoting and even subsidizing it in other countries. Obama placed on hold the proposal for the Keystone oil pipeline even though the project would, at a time of economic hardship, create thousands of new American jobs. Many interpreted Obama's action as a concession to environmental groups, and this is consistent with the conservative view of Obama as a typical liberal, another acolyte of Al Gore environmentalism. Gore, however, is not like Obama. Gore believes the "earth has a fever," and he wants people all over the world to curb their energy use and their carbon emissions to help prevent global warming. This is not Obama's view. Case in point: On May 9, 2011, the Obama White House announced that it was providing $2.84 billion in American taxpayer money to finance oil drilling and oil refining in the South American nation of Colombia. The money goes to Reficar, a wholly owned subsidiary of the Colombian government. Now what rationale could there be for America giving money to the Colombian government to drill and refine oil? One might expect that oil to come to the United

States, but the U.S. Export-Import Bank, which cleared the transaction, clarified that this was not the case. The oil would be used for Colombia, and the Colombians could sell the surplus on the export market.[22] This raises the larger question: Why would Obama block drilling over here but promote it over there?

Obama routinely advances the interests of foreign companies over those of American companies. Currently the Obama administration is promoting in Asia a trade treaty called the Trans-Pacific Partnership. As drafted by the Obama team, the treaty would prevent any U.S. manufacturers who advertise "Buy American" from qualifying for U.S. government contracts covered by the treaty. Another provision would allow foreign companies doing business in America to appeal regulatory rulings on labor and environmental issues to an international tribunal. This international tribunal would have the authority to overrule American law and to impose trade sanctions on America for failing to abide by its rulings. When sixty House Democrats protested the impact of this on American sovereignty and American jobs, Obama officials refused to share with them the provisions of the treaty and said they were merely trying to be "non-discriminatory" in their contracting processes.[23] In 2011 the Obama administration was faced with two bids for a $1 billion military contract. The contract was between Hawker Beechcraft, an American company based in Wichita, Kansas, and the Brazilian company Embraer, which is owned by the Brazilian government. Hawker had worked closely with the Air Force for two years and invested more than $100 million preparing to meet the contract's requirements. But at the last minute, the company was informed in a letter that it would not be considered for the contract. No explanation was given. The contract was subsequently awarded to the Brazilian competitor. Industry analysts expressed surprise. Normally the American government tries to award contracts, especially in the defense industry, to American companies. Hawker Beechcraft's loss of the contract, the company confirmed, will now lead to layoffs, and of course it will make part of our national defense dependent on a Brazilian contractor. In another case, the Obama administration, once again operating through the Export-Import Bank, provided $3.4 billion in loan guarantees to Air India, the national airline owned by the Indian government. India used the subsidy to buy new planes and launch nonstop service between Mumbai and New York, undercutting Delta, which had pioneered nonstop flights between these two destinations two years earlier. Delta was forced to abandon its Mumbai-New York service, and the company has bitterly complained to the Obama administration, accusing it of subsidizing foreign carriers at the expense of American companies and American jobs. Obama, however, recently secured increased funding for the Export-Import Bank, and he has been praising its efforts to subsidize a loan program for Lion Air of Indonesia to purchase Boeing planes.[24]

Over the past two years, we have seen major uprisings in several Muslim countries, from Tunisia to Libya to Bahrain to Egypt to Syria. President Obama has responded in a very odd and inconsistent manner. First he dithered about using force in Libya; then, pushed by the French and the British (along with the Arab League, the United Nations Security Council, and NATO), he used force in Libya, finally ousting the dictator Muammar Gaddafi. Obama for the longest time, however, refused to provide any assistance to the rebels in Syria, who were attempting to remove the dictator Bashar Assad. What made Obama's conduct especially strange is that the American decision to use air strikes and other forms of military force in Libya was taken after Gaddafi had killed around 250 people; Obama raised the specter of genocide in Libya. The Syrians, however, had to kill thousands before the Obama administration, largely responding to international pressure, agreed to provide modest forms of assistance to the rebels while ruling out direct U.S. military involvement. How to account for Obama's conduct? Why intervene in one place but not the other? A similar inconsistency defines Obama's response to Egypt and Iran. In Egypt, Obama used diplomatic pressure to oust America's longtime ally Hosni Mubarak, clearing the way for the Islamic radicals, led by the Muslim Brotherhood, to win the subsequent parliamentary and presidential elections. Using the rhetoric of democracy, Obama allied himself in Egypt with the Tahrir Square protesters. Yet when there were equally massive democratic uprisings in Iran a year earlier, aimed at ousting the regime of the mullahs, Obama urged caution and restraint. He refused to embrace the protesters. Essentially, he did nothing. Eventually the Iranian police subdued the protesters and the Iranian rebellion dissolved. So we have a dual inconsistency here. We need an adequate account of Obama's selective involvement, using force here but not there, getting rid of one ruler but keeping others in place. With respect to the Muslim uprisings collectively known as the Arab Spring, what explains Obama's double standards?

More than any other president, Obama criticizes and apologizes for his own country and also takes sides against America's closest allies. An interesting example of this surfaced in a small portion of a cable that was published by the renegade group WikiLeaks. The September 2009 cable was from U.S. Ambassador to Japan John Roos. In the cable, he informed the Obama Administration that Japan didn't think it was a good idea for President Obama to visit Hiroshima or apologize for America using two atomic bombs on Japanese cities during World War II. Leave aside the fact that many military analysts believe the atomic bombs hastened the end of the war, saving American lives and possibly even Japanese lives (by preventing an Allied invasion of Japan). Isn't it odd for an American president to want to apologize for America to Japan, while the Japanese themselves don't want him to do so? Obama's dim view of America also seems to extend to America's allies, like Britain. Remember the Falklands War? The war was fought in 1982 between Britain, under Margaret Thatcher, and Argentina, under its dictator Leopoldo Galtieri, over the Falkland Islands. Britain won and retained the disputed territory. But Argentina still seeks possession of the islands it terms the "Malvinas." While previous administrations, Republican and Democratic, have sided with Britain on this one, the Obama administration has switched sides. It now backs the Argentine position, calling on Britain to enter into negotiations over the sovereignty of the islands. This is a position also supported by the Organization of American States, and it is one that the British government regards as completely unacceptable.[25]

These examples should suffice to show that, with Obama, we are dealing with a different kind of president. Where, then, do we begin the task of understanding him? We begin where Obama begins, with the dreams he got from his father.

CHAPTER THREE

ABSENTEE FATHER

It was into my father's image, the black man,
son of Africa, that I'd packed all the attributes
I sought in myself.[1]
—Barack Obama, *Dreams from My Father*

Y ou can get a meeting with Sarah Obama, President Obama's "granny," but to do so you have to bring her a goat. Our film team had taken the one-hour flight from Nairobi to Kisumu, and then made the one-and-a-half hour drive to Kogelo. We wanted to make sure we could get into the Obama homestead, so we brought three goats! Unruly animals they were, and I had difficulty yanking them up the dirt road to the farmhouse gate. But the old woman was delighted with the gesture, and there we were, sitting inside the Obama family compound, sipping Cokes and listening to Sarah Obama narrate the family history. While Obama calls her granny, Sarah isn't really Obama's grandmother; she is one of his grandfather's other wives. The man had five, and so by Obama's terminology he has five paternal grannies. I explained this to a member of the film team, and he commented, "I guess that's multiculturalism, Obama style." Sarah Obama is a woman of dramatic gestures, and she spoke in Swahili, while a translator made her meaning clear. But somehow I couldn't concentrate on what she was saying, most of which I knew anyway. My attention was raptly focused on the grave located just yards away from the main house. "That," I told my film crew, "is where the man himself is buried. That is where it all started."

As he tells us in his autobiography, Barack Obama stood before that grave in 1987, when he was twenty-six years old. He flung himself on the ground and wept. Later he recalled, "I had sat at my father's grave and spoken to him through Africa's red soil." The whole scene is a little creepy, because by 1987 Barack Obama Sr. had been dead for five years. Even so, Obama is almost literally trying to get the man out of the ground so he can talk to him. But he can't; his father is gone. Obama has also come to the bitter realization that his father was not the model figure that he once imagined him to be. He now knows that the man had terrible flaws and failings, as a husband, as a father, and also as a man. So Obama has an epiphany. "The pain I felt was my father's pain. My questions were my brother's questions. Their struggle, my birthright." Obama dries his tears, and he resolves then and there that he will not emulate his father's entire personality, but he will embrace his dream. Where the father failed in carrying out the dream, the son will succeed. Thus he will prove worthy of his father's love, even if he never got it.[2] This is the meaning of Obama's book title, *Dreams from My Father*. The book is about how Obama created his own identity and defined his core values by taking his father's dreams and making them his own.

I first noted this connection between Obama and his father in my earlier book, *The Roots of Obama's Rage*. The book was excerpted in a cover article in *Forbes*, and the article and the book produced a tremendous furor, including repeated and ferocious attacks by the Obama White House. To my knowledge, not since Watergate has the White House been so aggressive in attacking a critical exposé. Obama's point man in this was Robert Gibbs, the former White House press secretary, but the White House also dispatched Vice President Joe Biden to attack my thesis. Even Colin Powell went on national television to urge that we focus on Obama's policies, not on his family history. The White House barrage brought out the Obama attack dogs, such as Maureen Dowd in the *New York Times*, Keith Olbermann on MSNBC, and the activist group Media Matters. I am not so interested here in their wild accusations—D'Souza is a birther, D'Souza is a race baiter—which I have discussed and refuted in the introduction to the paperback edition of *The Roots of Obama's Rage*. Suffice it to say that I didn't get my facts wrong; nor am I (as Maureen Dowd tartly observed) "Ann Coulter-in-pants"; and I can hardly be considered, in Keith Olbermann's term, the second worst person in the world, although I am certainly working on it.[3]

The question that interests me is: Why all this bluster? Why would the White House accuse me of being a birther when I specifically said in my book that Obama was born in Hawaii, not Kenya? Why raise the race issue when I clearly say that, both for Obama and for me, race is not the issue? I wondered what was going on here—not just with Obama, but also with people who seemed oddly resistant to hearing Obama's own story. It was partly to answer those questions that I embarked on my journey to Kenya, tracing the path that Obama himself took, talking to people who knew him and his father, seeking to understand the truth about this elusive man in the Oval Office. My trip proved very illuminating. I was also helped in my quest to understand Obama's roots by new information that has become available about Obama's parents, teachers, and mentors. This new information and my own travels in Obama's footsteps have only strengthened my thesis. But they have also modified the story by making it more complex, more textured, and in many ways more riveting.

Let's begin with Colin Powell's question: Why even focus on Obama's background? The same issue was raised in a different way by *Newsweek* writer Jonathan Alter. Interviewing me on C-SPAN, Alter argued that it's un-American, yes un-American, to trace the formation of presidents to their flawed parents. Ronald Reagan's father was an alcoholic, Alter fumed, but we don't trace Reagan's character or views to his father. Yes, I responded, but Ronald Reagan didn't write a book called *Dreams from My Father*! It was Obama, long before me, who drew the close connection between father and son. Obama's autobiography wasn't a youthful escapade that he has subsequently repudiated; he first published the book in 1995 when he was thirty-four years old, then republished it in 2004 when he was a newly elected U.S. senator and addressed the Democratic Convention. The book was circulated as a campaign document in the 2008 presidential election. Besides, a large part of Obama's signature appeal is that he is different; he has a multicultural background. This defined him even when he ran for president of the *Harvard Law Review*; around that time, a Harvard humor magazine parodied Obama saying, "I was born in Oslo, Norway, the son of a Volvo factory worker and part-time ice-fisherman. My mother was a backup singer for Abba."[4]

The humor magazine didn't know the half of it. Here is a case where truth is more bizarre than fiction. Obama's actual background includes a pet ape and a transvestite nanny. He has relatives who, in keeping with Luo tribal custom, have their six front teeth removed; a father who has four wives and eight known children—none of which he looked after—and a mother who sent him to America at the age of ten while she lived the rest of her life as a bohemian academic in Indonesia. He has a half-brother who lives in a Nairobi slum, and an aunt who sells coal on the street. Most of his African relatives in the United States seem to have come here illegally, and his uncle was recently in trouble with the law. Yes, there is a great deal of "diversity" here, but there is also cruelty and abandonment and pain, and we have to understand that pain if we want to see how Obama's identity was traumatically forged. So the story I tell in this book is a multicultural story, but it is not simply a celebration of difference. Rather, it takes multiculturalism seriously and operates on the premise that if multiculturalism defines Obama's unique identity, there can be no reasonable objection to going beyond the Kumbaya rhetoric and actually examining Obama's own background, much of it set forth in his own words.

Everyone who knew Barack Obama Sr. testifies to how much the son resembles the father. They have "the same tall frame and gait," remarks Olara Otunnu, a longtime associate of Barack Sr. Otunnu also notes a similar "charisma, supreme confidence, and eloquence." Barack Sr.'s first wife Kezia told an African newspaper, "When I look at my stepson, he reminds me of his father. They share very many characteristics. Like father, like son, I would say." Obama's autobiography quotes his aunt Zeituni telling young Obama, "You sound just like your father, Barry." Obama's sister, upon meeting him, immediately compared him to their father. "You have the same mouth." She saw something that Barack Jr. wrote and observed, "The handwriting was startlingly similar to that of my father." When they go out, she tells her half-brother, "Agh, Barack! I see you're bossy like the Old Man as well…. It must be in the blood." George Saitoti, a former vice president of Kenya, recalls the Barack Sr. he knew as a young man. "He sounded just like President Obama does now." Neil Abercrombie, a longtime pal of Barack Sr. and now governor of Hawaii, is not reluctant to admit that "Barack Obama is carrying out his father's dream." And Obama's granny Sarah told *Newsweek* in 2008, "I look at him and I see all the same things. He has taken everything from his father. The son is realizing everything the father wanted…. The dreams of the father are still alive in the son."[5]

Obama himself repeatedly affirms his father's enduring influence. He told the *Washington Post* that thoughts of his father "bubble up at different moments, at any course of the day or week. I think about him often." Recalling his youth, Obama told a reporter, "The stories I heard about my father painted him as larger than life, which also meant I felt I had something to live up to." On another occasion Obama confided to journalist David Mendell, "Every man is trying to live up to his father's expectations or make up for his mistakes. In my case, both things might be true." Throughout his growing years, Obama writes in his autobiography, "My father's voice had … remained untainted, inspiring, rebuking, granting or withholding approval…. You must help in your people's struggle. Wake up, black man!" In his other book, *The Audacity of Hope*, Obama says, "My fierce ambitions might have been fueled by my father—by my knowledge of his achievements and failures, by my unspoken desire to somehow earn his love, and by my resentments and anger toward him."[6]

So Obama closely resembles his father and was deeply influenced by him. That seems well established, yet critics point out that Obama hardly knew his father. Their interaction was limited to a month-long visit to Hawaii by Barack Sr. when Obama was ten years old. Therefore, how could he have been strongly influenced by an absentee parent? Actually, Obama's interaction with his dad was not limited to a single encounter. Obama himself reports that he and his father regularly exchanged letters over a period of years. In one letter that Obama quotes, his father tells him that "the important thing is that you know your people, and also that you know where you belong."[7] Moreover, Obama says that despite the distance between them he maintained a strong emotional attachment to the man. Of his father, he writes, "Even in his absence his strong image had given me some bulwark on which to grow up, an image to live up to, or disappoint."[8]

We may ask, however, how such an attachment is possible. In the course of filming my Obama documentary, I raised the question with psychologist Paul Vitz, who has studied absentee fathers. Vitz noted that absentee fathers often have a very powerful impact on their children, especially their sons. Sometimes the impact is negative. In the inner city, for instance, young men grow up hating the fathers who abandoned them. They turn to gangs to find "family" and substitute father figures. Having written about civil rights, I knew about this literature. Yet Vitz told me something I hadn't thought of. During World War II, he said, there were hundreds of thousands of absentee fathers. They were in Europe or the Pacific, battling the Nazis and the Japanese. And in those situations the mother typically placed a photograph of the absentee dad on the mantel, and the kids grew up revering their fathers who were away fighting for freedom. Vitz remarked that those absentee fathers were positive role models, even in their absence, and in some cases because of their absence. In reality they may have been uninspiring fellows. But the real dads weren't around to dispel the myth. Like the beloved in Keats's "Ode on a Grecian Urn," they were forever lovely and forever fair. Even today the grown-up sons of World War II veterans remember their absentee fathers as the Greatest Generation.

In Obama's case, as with the sons of the World War II soldiers, the influence of the father was largely transmitted by the mother. We'll learn more about Obama's mom in the next chapter. She is the real author of the myth of Barack Obama Sr. She did her best to give her son a carefully edited portrait of her former husband. She also strenuously defended his character and his ideological principles, even blaming herself for his decision to abandon her and their new-born son. Barack Obama Jr. swallowed the story, and by his own account it sustained him while he grew up between the ages of ten and seventeen without either parent. But ultimately the son found out the truth about his dad, and the truth hit him very hard.

The truth was delivered to him, while he was a student at Columbia, by his half-sister Auma. She asked Obama, in effect: Why are you idolizing a man who was a chronic alcoholic and wife-abuser, who never looked after any of his wives or children? Auma told Obama how her father would come drunk into her room, wake her up, and rave and rant about everything from the evils of the white man to how he had been denied his rightful leading place in independent Kenya. Here is Obama's reaction: "All my life, I had carried a single image of my father, one that I had sometimes rebelled against but had never questioned, one that I had later tried to take as my own. The brilliant scholar, the generous friend, the upstanding leader.... He had never been present to foil the image. [Now] I felt as if my world had been turned on its head; as if I had woken up to find a blue sun in the yellow sky, or heard animals speaking like men."[9]

Around the same time, young Obama had a dream about his father that left a vivid impression. Obama writes of his father, "I met him one night, in a cold cell, in a chamber of my dreams." In Obama's dream, his father is in prison, and he has come alone to visit him. His father is "before me, with only a cloth wrapped around his waist." Barack Sr. looks weary and ashen. The prison guard steps aside, and the two of them embrace. "I began to weep," Obama writes, "and felt ashamed, but could not stop myself." Obama tries to talk to his father, but he "stared away from me, into the wall. An implacable sadness spread across his face." Obama writes, "I whispered to him that we might leave together." But his father "shook his head, and told me it would be best if I left." In Obama's account, he awoke from the dream "still weeping."[10] This dream, together with Auma's revelations, convince young Obama to go to Africa and learn himself about the man he never really knew.

We will rejoin Obama in Africa as he "finds" his father. But in the meantime, let's ask what is actually known about Barack Obama Sr. What kind of a man was he? Although he came from a poor background, he was a very stylish guy. He cultivated a British accent, and at the University of Hawaii he called himself "Bear-ick," not "Barack." He wore black-rimmed glasses and smoked Benson and Hedges cigarettes and also occasionally a pipe. His shoes were shined like glass, and later in life, when he could afford it, he wore silk suits, drove a green Mercedes, and employed house servants. When he returned to Kenya from America, he insisted on being called "Doctor Obama," even though he never completed a doctoral degree. He frequently corrected American students and later Kenyans on the proper British spelling and pronunciation of words, and reprimanded Kenyan bureaucrats who spoke in Swahili. He was gregarious and social and loved to order double shots of Johnnie Walker Black. Beer, he said, was a child's drink. Most of all he had a magnetic personality and was a great talker. When he spoke, according to Neil Abercrombie, who knew him in Hawaii, "He was the sun, and the other planets revolved around him." While Obama directly experienced his father's magnetism only once, during his father's visit to Hawaii when Obama was ten, he was clearly aware of his father's persuasive influence on others. "It fascinated me, this strange power of his," Obama writes in his autobiography. "I often felt mute before him." Young Obama consciously sought to emulate his father; he wanted for himself his father's charismatic power.[11]

While the persuasive power of Obama Sr. is undeniable, it was also based on very dubious foundations. Obama Sr. was a confirmed liar who often tried to look more important than he was. Even today many people believe that Obama Sr. was one of Kenya's "best and the brightest," who was selected to come on the famous Airlift to America, study at a major university here, and then return to lead his country. In fact, Obama Sr. took the competitive exam for the Airlift and failed. He needed a first-division score and he got only a third-division score. Robert Stephens, the cultural affairs officer at the U.S. Information Service, interviewed Obama and remembers him as a liar. "He really prevaricated about his school record," Stephens says. But Stephens had Obama's poor grades in front of him. "He was a very good talker and he tried to talk me out of it, but there was nothing I could do. He just did not have the grades."

Yet Obama Sr. was not done talking. He got on the Airlift by sweet-talking two missionary women into raising the money for him. One of the women was unmarried, and Barack Sr. charmed her by taking her out dancing a lot. "When I heard later that he'd made it to America another way," Stephens says, "I was pretty surprised." In America, Obama lied to young Ann Dunham; he didn't tell her he had a wife back in Kenya. They were married in 1961, and a few months later their son, Barack Jr., was born at Kapi'olani Hospital in Honolulu. We know Obama was born in America for three good reasons: first, Obama did finally release his birth certificate; second, two local newspapers published notices of his birth at the time; third, the young couple had no money and could not have afforded to go back to Kenya, have the baby, and then return to the United States. So the birther allegation is unconvincing.

Shortly after Barack Jr. was born, the father left Ann to go to Harvard. There he took up with another woman, Ruth Nidesand. Harvard officials and immigration authorities suspected Barack Sr. was a bigamist, but they could never get a straight story out of him. They finally canceled his scholarship, which forced him to return to Kenya. Back home, Obama Sr. embellished his Harvard experience. He tried to impress other Kenyan economists by saying he had studied at Harvard with Nobel laureate Ken Arrow, even though Arrow did not arrive at Harvard until 1968, four years after Barack Sr. left. For years Barack Sr. advanced economic theories that had been proven, he said, in his dissertation, but when someone asked him to produce the dissertation he could not; burglars, he said, had broken into his house and stolen it.[12]

At first, Obama Sr. was treated with great respect in Kenya. He was employed by a bank and then by the Kenyan government. But his career quickly went into a tailspin. Part of the reason was his arrogance, but a bigger factor seems to be that Barack Sr. got the reputation for making things up and saying anything to impress others or get what he wanted. "He would make wild exaggerations," said one of his co-workers, Nyaringo Obure. "One story he told over and over was about how when he was a boy he was looking after the family cattle. Suddenly a group of lions appeared and started to attack the cows. Barack pulls out a spear and kills the first lion by stabbing him in the chest. Then he goes for the rest, stab, stab, stab. Of course I knew it was a lie. Another time he said a buffalo attacked one of his relatives. Barack happened to be in the tree overhead and he dropped down on the buffalo's back and wrestled it to the ground. And so his stories went on and on."

Obama was frequently caught lying about expenses and other matters, and on more than one occasion he was demoted or fired. Yet even when real importance eluded him, Obama still found a way to get it. Later in his career he became known for impersonating important people so that he could be treated as a celebrity. On one occasion, he attended a conference in Ghana where he pretended to be Z. T. Onyonka, the Kenyan Minister of Economic Planning and Development. When the real Onyonka showed up, the organizers thought that he was the impostor. Needless to say, Onyonka was not amused and severely reprimanded Obama Sr.[13]

What can we make of all this? When I think of Barack Obama Sr., I am reminded of a woman who used to visit our house in India. The stories she told had us riveted as kids, and yet they seemed unbelievable, too fantastic to be true. She narrated them with such passion, however, that we felt they had to be true. In retrospect, I believe the woman was a fabulist, a spinner of fables. She was good at it, however, and this made her stories compelling. Barack Sr. was also a fabulist, and this is part of the magic that his son sought to learn from him.

Over time his personal failings brought down Barack Sr., whose personal life would today have surely qualified him for his own reality show. Barack Sr. turned down a full scholarship to the New School for Social Research in New York, even though the scholarship included funds to bring Ann Obama and young Barack Jr. with him. Instead he accepted a partial scholarship from Harvard that required him to leave his wife and child behind in Hawaii. The woman he took up with at Harvard, Ruth Nidesand, followed Barack Sr. back to Kenya. There he married her and had two children by her, while reuniting with his first wife and having more children with her. Ruth accused her husband of routinely abusing and occasionally beating her. She recounted a sample episode. "He shouted at me, 'You prostitute, I am going to take the children. I am going to kill you.' You know, on and on. It was drunken rages, and more drunken rages. He kept coming back every week, the same thing, shouting and calling me names." A neighbor, Gladys Ogolah, commented that "he would hit her about the shoulders and neck. Ruth would run screaming down the road to our house crying." A heavy drinker even at Harvard, Barack Sr. increased his alcohol consumption especially as his career declined. One of his friends, Leo Omolo, remarked that "he would drink in one night the equivalent of one month's salary."[14] Barack Sr. got into numerous drunk-driving accidents, in one case killing a man, in another hurting himself so badly that both his legs had to be amputated and replaced by iron rods. This did not, however, undermine his courtship style, because he impregnated his fourth wife, Jael Otieno, in that condition, thus producing his eighth child, George Obama. Finally, in 1982, Barack Sr. got drunk at a bar in Nairobi and drove into a tree, killing himself.

None of this sounds like Barack Obama Jr., who was horrified to discover this aspect of his father, and understandably vowed not to follow him in these destructive habits. What young Barack also knew, however, was that his father was a man of big dreams and big ideas. So far we have said nothing about those. Barack Sr. was, from his youth, an anti-colonialist, which is hardly surprising since he grew up at a time when Kenya was fighting for independence from the British. This was the 1940s and 1950s, and the anti-colonial juggernaut was spreading throughout the world. India became independent in 1947, and soon the freedom tide reached Ghana, which was the first African country to gain its independence ten years later.

While in Hawaii, Barack Sr. gave an interview to a local paper in which he discussed colonialism. "Many people have asked me, 'Are the people of Kenya ready for self-government?'" he said. "And to these people I say, 'Nobody is competent enough to judge whether a country is fit to rule itself or not. If the people cannot rule themselves, let them misrule themselves. They should be provided with the opportunity.'" I find it hard to disagree with this, but for Barack Sr. anti-colonialism was like a religion; he shunned people who held to different beliefs. Mark Wimbush was a white Kenyan with a Scottish mother and an English father; he arrived at the University of Hawaii around the same time as Barack Sr. Wimbush's attempts to befriend Barack Sr. were rejected. "We were the ugly colonialists," Wimbush said. "Part of the tension between Barack and me might have been that fact." Barack Sr. was also vehemently opposed to U.S. foreign policy, as well as to higher U.S. defense spending. In May 1962 he appeared at a Mother's Day peace rally in which he declared that "anything which relieves military spending will help us." Barack Sr. was a self-described socialist, a position he subsequently elaborated in his 1965 article in the *East Africa Journal*, "Problems Facing Our Socialism." And according to fellow student and future economist Naranhkiri Tith, Barack Sr. had a soft spot for Communism, regarding it as a modern version of the communalism of African tribes. "I did not believe Communism could save the world," Tith says. "I gave examples of what I had seen. Obama senior was the opposite. He was always glorying about how Communism had liberated Africa and Cuba. For him, Communism was going to save the world. Capitalism was going to collapse."[15]

In Nairobi I interviewed the journalist Philip Ochieng, who came to America to study around the same time as Barack Obama Sr., and who became a friend and drinking buddy of his. "Our generation was totally anti-colonial," he said. "And colonialism had very many faces—the economic face, the racial race, the religious face, there are so many." I asked Ochieng if he believed the West became rich by stealing the wealth from colonized countries. He replied, "This is almost a truism. The raw materials taken from the Third World are manufactured in Europe and America and then re-sold to us at very astronomical prices." Ochieng also said that "America has taken over from Europe in what we call the neo-colonial system. America has gradually taken over from Europe as overlord of the world." I asked about Israel. Ochieng described it as "a little Trojan Horse in the Middle East." I asked Ochieng if he still described himself as anti-colonialist, and if that characterization would apply to Barack Obama Sr. He said, "I am, I am still. Barack Obama was."

Even though Barack Sr. espoused anti-colonial ideals, he played a very small role in Kenya's freedom struggle. Kenya got its independence in 1963, and for the preceding four years Barack Sr. was in America. Even when he returned to Kenya, he became bitterly antagonistic to the leading figure of Kenya's independence struggle, Jomo Kenyatta. Kenyatta wanted self-rule, but he didn't hate the British. While occasionally calling himself a socialist, Kenyatta generally supported property rights and free markets. Barack Sr. roundly condemned Kenyatta as a hypocrite, insisting that true socialists are people who use state power to seize private property and bring down concentrations of economic power. Peter Aringo, a former member of Parliament, said of his friend Barack Sr., "He did not like the aggressive capitalism that Kenyatta was putting into place. This sharing of the crumbs from the table did not impress him and he said so."[16] Eventually Kenyatta lost patience with the left-wing socialists inside his government and got rid of most of them, including Barack Sr.

So we are back to the 26-year-old Obama in Kenya, trying to figure out the truth about his father and how to relate to him. For him, it is a basic question of his own identity. Everywhere he goes, he is haunted by his father. At the airport a woman asks him, "You wouldn't be related to Dr. Obama, by any chance?" Obama is ecstatic. "She's recognized my name. That had never happened before … not in Hawaii, not in Indonesia, not in L.A. or New York or Chicago. For the first time in my life, I felt the comfort, the firmness of identity that a name might provide.... No one here in Kenya would ask how to spell my name, or mangle it with an unfamiliar tongue. My name belonged and so I belonged." In the market, a vendor takes him to be an American and he beats his chest and responds, "I'm a Luo." Later he reflects, "I feel my father's presence as Auma and I walk through the busy street.... I hear him in the laughter of the pair of university students.... I smell him in the cigarette smoke of the businessman.... The Old Man's here ... although he doesn't say anything to me. He's here, asking me to understand." On his way to his family homestead, Obama falls asleep and dreams that he is running through a village when his father appears to him, "a giant figure looming as tall as the trees, wearing only a loincloth and a ghostly mask. The lifeless eyes bored into me, and I heard a thunderous voice saying only that it was time, and my entire body began to shake violently with the sound, as if I were breaking apart."[17] One thing Obama is clear about—whatever the truth about his father, he cannot let go of the man.

Thus finally we come to the grave scene, Obama weeping at his father's grave. There Obama found a solution that was both creative and, in a way, frightening. Forced to confront the knowledge that his father was a deeply flawed individual, Obama split his father into two: bad Obama and good Obama. He rejected bad Obama, the drunk, the wife-beater, and the deadbeat dad. But he embraced what he took to be good Obama, namely, the stylish dresser, the charismatic speaker, and most of all the intrepid anti-colonialist. Obama changed that day, and emerged as a very different person. It is this Obama, remade in his father's image, that we see today in the White House.

CHAPTER FOUR

MOMMIE DEAREST

It wasn't a race thing. Barry's biggest struggles
were his feelings of abandonment.[1]
—Keith Kakugawa, *Chicago Tribune*

I t is a terrible thing to be abandoned by your mom, especially when you have already been abandoned by your dad. Those were my thoughts about young Barack Obama as I got off the plane at Jakarta Airport. I was there to see the place where Obama spent four years, from 1967 to 1971, between the ages of six and ten. But all I could think about upon first landing was the scene that had occurred there more than forty years ago. In 1971, Ann Obama sent her 10-year-old son, by himself, back to America. As Obama described it in *Dreams from My Father*, an Indonesian copilot led him to the plane as his mother, step-father, and step-sister Maya all stood by at the gate.[2] Ann wasn't going with him. And while she would return periodically to visit, she basically stayed in Indonesia for the rest of her life. During that period she was quite the globetrotter, making trips to China, Thailand, Nepal, India, Bangladesh, Pakistan, Morocco, and Ghana.

"My father left my family when I was two years old," Obama told a group of young people in September 2009. "I was raised by a single mother." This is what he consistently said on the campaign trail. But it is actually a half-truth. His father left the family before he was born. Moreover, from the age of ten until he left for college, Obama was raised by neither his father nor his mother. That responsibility fell to his maternal grandparents. Keith Kakugawa was a close friend of young Obama at the Punahou School in Hawaii. Kakugawa is profiled in *Dreams from My Father*, where Obama portrays him as obsessed with race, and most of their conversations as revolving around racial issues. Kakugawa, however, said that they almost never talked about race. Obama, he said, faced a different crisis. "Everybody said they always saw him smiling and happy. I didn't. I got to see the turmoil. I got to see how he really felt. He felt abandoned. He felt his father abandoned him and his mother was always pursuing her career." In another interview, Kakugawa recalled of Obama, "What was upsetting him—that his mother took off again. Seems like she never has time for him anymore."[3] It was only in 1995, when she was dying of cancer, that Ann Obama finally returned to Hawaii. Her daughter, Maya, was there at her deathbed, but her son, Barack Obama, didn't bother to show up. She had abandoned him when he was young, and he returned the favor toward the end of her life. My cameraman shook his head as I told him what happened. "It's a very sad story," he observed. "Yes," I said, "and we are now paying for it."

Ann Obama is very important to Obama's story, in a way I did not fully realize when I wrote *The Roots of Obama's Rage*. While researching that book I was taken in by Obama's innocuous descriptions of his mom. "She gathered friends from high and low, took

long walks, stared at the moon, and foraged through the local markets of Delhi or Marrakesh for some trifle, a scarf or stone that
would make her laugh or please the eye." Obama portrays his mom
as a kind of innocent abroad, a Midwestern girl on the road, "a
lonely witness for secular humanism, a soldier for New Deal, Peace
Corps, position-paper liberalism."[4] Naturally, I concluded, the father
was the dominant figure and the mother was peripheral.

But now I've modified my view. As a result of reading newly
published information, and interviewing people who knew Ann
Obama, I realized that Barack Sr. was indeed the dominant figure
in Obama's life, but that Ann Obama was Barack Sr.'s greatest dis-
ciple. As one who shared his anti-American, anti-colonial views, she
was the main vehicle for communicating those views to her son and
building his lifelong obsession with the absentee father.[5]

What do we know about Ann Obama? She was a white-bread
girl from Kansas who became a bohemian, a sixties girl before the
sixties. She rebelled against her parents, against Christianity, and
against her country. "She was not a standard-issue girl of her times,"
her school friend Chip Wall told the *Chicago Tribune*. "She wasn't
part of the matched-sweater set." Classmate Susan Blake said that
Ann at a young age considered herself superior to her parents. "It
seemed like every time her father opened his mouth, she would roll
her eyes." Ann liked to stress to her friends how boring her mother
was: "My mother's favorite color is beige." Ann's best friend, Maxine
Box, added that "she touted herself as an atheist, and it was something that she'd read about and could argue. She was already thinking about things that the rest of us hadn't." Later, Ann's Indonesian
friend Felina Pramono said that as a Christian she avoided the topic
of religion with Ann because of her mocking attitude. "She would
just smile and laugh, you know? And a sneer. I could feel it." For
Ann, religion was uncool but anything foreign or radical was cool.

One of Ann's teachers, Jim Wichterman, described her as an aficio-
nado of foreign films, jazz, and Karl Marx. "As much as a high-
school student can, she'd question anything: what's so good about
democracy? What's so good about capitalism? What's wrong with
communism?"[6]

Ann never dated "the crew-cut white boys," her classmates said.
In fact, as far as I can determine, Ann had no serious boyfriends
who were white and American. Nor was she initially interested in
marriage. Her friend and associate Nina Nayar commented that
"she always felt that marriage as an institution was not particularly
essential or important." Yet Ann didn't write off marriage completely.
Her close friend, the Dutch anthropologist Renske Heringa, said of
Ann, "She was completely not out to 'do the right thing' or behave
in the way people expected."[7] If Ann was ever going to marry, she
knew that it would likely be a foreigner, preferably non-white, ideally
anti-Western and anti-American. In Hawaii, when her family moved
there, she found the one: Barack Obama Sr. They met in a Russian
class. She called him "the African." A few months later she sent a
postcard to her friend Susan Blake. "I'm in love with the African."
And then, a bit later, "Big news! I married the African." Blake comments, "She was excited about her future with this man, who was
the rising hope of Africa, which was just about to emerge from under
British rule. It was all so romantic." Ann was swept up by all this,
and so perhaps understandably, when the marriage soon dissolved,
she kept the news to herself. "People said she went to Africa and
married a black king," classmate Kathy Sullivan recalled. "We all
thought that for years and years."[8]

Many observers emphasize how Ann was seduced by Barack's
confidence and charisma, and surely that was part of the story. But
Alice Dewey, Ann's thesis adviser in Hawaii who knew both Ann and
Barack, told me that there was a deeper bond between them that

was ideological; they shared core values, despite their cultural differences. Even though the differences ultimately proved insurmountable, Dewey said what brought the two together was their Third World affinity and anti-capitalist sentiments. "Senior and Anne would not have married unless they had things in common," Dewey said. "At some fundamental level they had a lot in common." And Dewey adds that eventually their son "Barry picked it up."

The union between Ann and Barack Sr. did not even last until their baby, Barack Obama Jr., was born. By August 1961, the two had already separated. Ann moved to Seattle and enrolled at the University of Washington, but returned to Hawaii in 1962. Barack Sr. left for Harvard that fall, when his son was one year old.

Even after Barack dumped her, Ann still thought of him as the noble embodiment of their shared ideological values. During this period, Janny Scott writes, "she dressed in dashikis, kept African artifacts on her desk, and gravitated in conversation toward international topics." Ann praised her former husband as "principled" and "uncompromising." She would defend him against her son's demands to know why he wasn't there. At one point she told her son, "It wasn't your father's fault that he left, you know. I hope you don't feel resentful toward him."[9] She implied he was away on some grand crusade, fighting to liberate his people from oppression. Actually, he was philandering at Harvard or getting drunk back in Nairobi, but this was Ann's continuing romance with her former husband. He was her perfect Third World, anti-American guy, and she looked for and found a second husband who was another Third World, anti-American guy.

His name was Lolo Soetoro, a student from Indonesia. Ann met him at "Indonesian Night" at the East West Center at the University of Hawaii. What appealed to Ann was that Lolo's family had been engaged in the anti-colonial struggle—his family home had been burned by the

Dutch during Indonesia's war for independence after World War II. Indonesia was now ruled by a left-wing dictator named Sukarno who refused to count himself in the Western camp. Sukarno called himself "non-aligned," but in practice he was anti-American and anti-Western, and effectively pro-Soviet. Sukarno had infuriated Western investors by nationalizing major industries, including oil. Ann adored Sukarno, and she planned to accompany her new husband Lolo to Indonesia so that the two of them could together support this Third World, anti-American dictatorship. In 1967, Ann took young Barack Obama Jr. to live in Indonesia.

But things went wrong for Ann right from the start. The year before she arrived, the Indonesian military launched a coup against Sukarno. Taking over was anti-Communist General Suharto, who ordered a purge of Communists inside and outside his government. In *Dreams from My Father*, Obama implies that Ann's romance was just as much with Sukarno as it was with Lolo. "In later years," Obama writes, "my mother would insist that had she known (about the coup and the purge), we never would have made the trip."[10] Even worse, Lolo was drafted into the Indonesian army to fight the Communists, the very people that Ann viewed as the true liberation forces in Indonesia.

Ann tried to make the best of it. She began doing anthropological research, and placed her son in the care of a different sort of nanny. This nanny was an openly gay man named Turdi, who enjoyed dressing in women's clothing and who carried on a public affair with a local butcher. The nanny later changed his name to Evi and joined a transvestite group called Fantastic Dolls, which collected money by playing street games and dancing.[11] Lolo added to the multicultural atmosphere by giving Obama a pet ape from New Guinea named Tata. Obama's backyard was a swamp that was said to contain crocodiles. For the first time he ate dog, snake, and grasshopper. He attended schools with Muslim students and learned about Islam, which was no surprise, since Indonesia is the largest Muslim country in the world. Jakarta in those days was not the megacity that it is now; rather, it was a tapestry of towns and villages. Obama recalls rickshaws, animals crossing the road, beggars asking for money. It reminds me a lot of my own upbringing in a suburb of Mumbai, although my exposure to transvestites was considerably less than Obama's.

Obama spent four years in Indonesia, and during that period he became very close to Lolo. Indonesia was, at least at first, an elusive and strange place, and Obama recalls that "it was to Lolo that I turned for guidance and instruction." After all, "his knowledge of the world seemed inexhaustible." He offered the young boy "a manly trust." Mostly Lolo taught Obama that the world was a tough place and that men must learn self-reliance. At one point Obama asked Lolo, "How many beggars are there on the street?" Lolo replied, "Better to save your money and make sure you don't end up on the street yourself." Lolo taught Obama to box and frequently gave his step-son lessons in the importance of strength. "Better to be strong," he said. "If you can't be strong, be clever and make peace with someone who's strong. But always better to be strong yourself."[12]

While Obama relished having a step-father, Ann was dismayed to see her husband becoming more pro-American and pro-capitalist. After leaving the army, he took a job with the Jakarta branch of the Union Oil Company of California. He moved his family into a bigger house with three bedrooms, a library, and a terrace; he employed domestic staff, including a cook, a houseboy, and two other female servants. He joined the Indonesian Petroleum Club, where he socialized with Europeans and Americans. He began to listen to American music; his favorite song was "Moon River." While many other women might appreciate these trappings of success, Ann couldn't stand any of it and got into fierce arguments with Lolo. As Obama writes, "I would overhear him and my mother arguing in their bedroom, usually about her refusal to attend his company dinner parties, where American businessmen from Texas and Louisiana would slap Lolo's back and boast about the palms they had greased to obtain the new offshore drilling rights, while their wives complained to my mother about the quality of Indonesian help. He would ask how it would look for him to go alone, and remind her that these were her own people, and my mother's voice would rise to almost a shout. 'They are *not* my people.'"[13]

Ann made new friends, mostly left-wing academics from the West and an assortment of Indonesians: newspaper editors, artists, academics, foundation program officers, and local activists. To this group, she scorned Lolo. She told her friend Yang Suwan that Lolo seemed indifferent to corruption and he might even be involved, at least indirectly, with it. "She was upset," Suwan recalled. "She said, Suwan, after he did that, my whole respect for him was gone." She told another pal, Kay Ikranagara, that Lolo was a crass materialist. As Ikranagara puts it, "She felt that he had grown up without material things, and now he put so much importance on material things." Lolo, Ann told her friend Bill Collier, "was becoming more American all the time." Ann thought of herself as becoming more Indonesian, more Javanese. Yet she refused to play the role of the dutiful Indonesian wife. "By the time I knew Ann," says the Dutch anthropologist Renske Heringa, "she was a hefty woman. She didn't care about getting dressed, wearing jewelry, the way Indonesian women do. That was not her style. He expected her to do it. She absolutely refused."[14] Soon Ann and Lolo were living in different worlds, and a divorce between them seemed imminent.

Ann recognized, of course, that Lolo was just trying to survive in a Third World country where corruption was a way of life. Lolo found Ann's leftist and anti-American sympathies impractical; he thought in terms of power rather than ideals. "Guilt," he once told her, "is a luxury only foreigners can afford." Ann understood this, but she understood it in terms of Lolo being an ideological sellout. Obama puts the point very well. "Power. The word fixed in my mother's mind like a curse.... Here power was undisguised, indiscriminate, naked, always fresh in the memory. Power had taken Lolo and yanked him back into line just when he thought he'd escaped, making him feel its weight, letting him know that his life wasn't his own.... And so Lolo had made his peace with power." This fact, Obama writes, created an "unbreachable barrier between them." Yet she had an option. "She could always leave if things got too messy." But then it struck Ann with the force of a revelation that her son admired Lolo, and might pattern his life after him. "She looked out the window now and saw that Lolo and I had moved on, the grass flattened where the two of us had been. The sight made her shudder slightly, and she rose to her feet, filled with a sudden panic. Power was taking her son."[15]

Right here we see why Ann Obama packed up her son, age ten, and sent him back on his own to America. She didn't want his values to be shaped by Lolo. She viewed Lolo as a sellout, a power-seeker who had made his peace with capitalism and with America. She wanted her son to be a principled anti-capitalist, anti-American, like her and like someone else she used to know: Barack Obama Sr. Obama writes that his mother "had taught me to disdain the blend of ignorance and arrogance that too often characterized Americans abroad." Lolo, from Ann's point of view, was undermining these lessons, and in her conflicts with him, Obama writes, "She had only one ally ... and that was the distant authority of my father.... His life had been hard, as hard as anything that Lolo might have known. He hadn't cut corners, though, or played all the angles. He was diligent and honest, no matter what it cost him. He had led his life according to principles that demanded a different kind of power, principles that promised a higher form of power. I would follow in his example, my mother decided. I had no choice. It was in the genes."[16]

In my previous book, *The Roots of Obama's Rage*, I noted Ann's desire to transport her son away from Lolo's influence, but I missed her secondary motives for sending him back to Hawaii in 1971 and not going with him. Ann wanted an independent career and she wanted to be single without having to look after young Obama. Though she did not formally divorce Lolo until 1980, Ann lived the life of a Western swinging single in a Third World milieu. At first she went through an identity crisis reflected in the way she constantly changed her name: she was Ann Soetoro, then Ann Sutoro, then Ann Dunham Sutoro, then S. Ann Dunham. In short order, however, she hit her stride. Her best friend during the 1970s and 1980s was Julia Suryakusuma, the "feminist and femme fatale," in the description of Ann's biographer Janny Scott. Suryakusuma says of Ann, "We were both very sexual. We talked a lot about sex and our sex lives." Renske Heringa says that Ann's taste in men was strictly Third World and dark-skinned. "She never was really interested in white guys." Suryakusuma, however, was married to a white man. Suryakusuma adds of Ann, "She used to say that she liked brown bums and I liked white bums."[17] While I was in Indonesia, I tried contacting Suryakusuma to find out more about Ann's romantic tastes. Suryakusuma, however, refused to talk to me, possibly because I don't possess a white bum.

Ann's sexual adventuring may seem a little surprising in view of the fact that she was a large woman who kept getting larger. Her friends, however, said that Ann cut a very distinctive figure with her flowing batik skirts, Indonesian fabric shawls, locally made sandals, and large hoop earrings. Moreover, Ann was a confident woman who did not hesitate to approach Indonesian men. She was a woman of power because she was American and had money and knew influential people at the Ford Foundation, the American embassy, and in Indonesia itself. Thus Indonesian men found her alluring as well as powerful, and over the years she had a succession of romantic relationships. One of them was with Indonesian journalist I. Made Suarjana, a reporter for the Yogyakarta newsweekly *Tempo*. Ann was forty-five when she met Suarjana; he was twenty-eight, just one year older than Ann's son Barack. Suarjana describes his relationship with Ann as "a romantic-intellectual friendship." They traveled around the country together, and Suarjana is thanked in the acknowledgements that accompany Ann's published thesis. Ann was clearly the senior partner in their relationship. She assigned herself the task of teaching Suarjana English grammar. She gave him a four-volume set of books on the topic, and was not above asking him "how far did you study?" and administering surprise pop quizzes. Suarjana, however, is coy about the physical element in their relationship and it is not hard to see why; he was already married at the time. When Janny Scott asked Suarjana whether Ann would have liked to have married him, he replied that she knew from the outset that he was already married.[18] Learning about Ann's sexual adventuring in Indonesia, I realized how wrong I had been to consider Barack Obama Sr. the playboy. True, he was a polygamist, but polygamy is traditional in Kenyan Luo culture. Ann, by contrast, was the real playgirl, and despite all her reservations about power, she was using her American background and economic and social power to purchase the romantic attention of Third World men.

Although Ann typically dated younger Indonesian men, it would be wrong to say that she sent young Barack back to Hawaii so that she could pursue the life of a Western "cougar." Clearly Ann's bigger motive was her career. She fell in love with Indonesian peasant culture—specifically the culture of peasant blacksmithing. She once informed fellow anthropologist Don Johnston that if she could be reincarnated, she would come back as a blacksmith. What appealed to Ann most about the traditional blacksmithing industry in Indonesia was that it preceded colonialism. This was the world before the white man came. Ann saw it as her mission to preserve and affirm that culture, and show its viability even in modern Indonesia. She dedicated her life work to this, and chose it over the task of raising her son. In fact, studying the blacksmiths and writing and publishing her thesis about them took Ann most of her adult life.

Ann's thesis is a lengthy response to and rebuttal of the work of a Dutch economist named J. H. Boeke, whose work dates to the early twentieth century. Ann refers to him simply as "a colonial officer named Boeke." Boeke argued that traditional Indonesian culture is pre-modern while the West brought modern capitalism to Indonesia. Thus Indonesian culture is dualistic, reflecting pre-modern elements and modern Western elements. Ann disputed this portrayal of traditional Indonesian culture as pre-modern. She accused Boeke of perpetuating "the myth of the lazy native." She even faulted current anthropologists for espousing similar ideas, what she termed "neocolonialism in bad disguise." She sought to demonstrate the durability of traditional art and handicrafts in modern, postcolonial Indonesia. Her thesis ended up being more than a thousand pages, and it was published two decades after she first entered graduate school. In the course of writing it, Ann got to do the multicultural thing that she enjoyed. She traipsed around the world to New Delhi, Mumbai, Bangkok, Nairobi, Cairo, Dhaka, and Kuala Lumpur, not to mention all over Indonesia.[19]

In 1995, diagnosed with third-stage uterine and ovarian cancer, Ann Obama left Indonesia and returned to America. She was admitted to the Straub Clinic in Honolulu. Ann was in treatment for most of that year, but Obama never visited her in Hawaii. He was busy with his book tour, and running for the Illinois State Senate. Later Obama tried to make an issue of how his mother couldn't get approval for her health insurance, even though the insurance papers were not properly filed, and ultimately the insurance company accepted the policy and paid her claim. Obama has also insisted that he tried and tried to get to his mother but, to his lifelong regret, he didn't arrive "in time." Actually there was plenty of time. He seems to have had no intention of getting there. Ann died on November 17, 1995, with her daughter, Maya, by her side. Ann didn't do very well by her son; in fact, mother and son seem to have rejected each other. Even so, she had an enduring impact on Barack Obama, and it is a pity, in a way, that she did not live to see that impact carry him to the White House. For us, however, there is a different kind of pathos in seeing Obama thrust on the world stage, where his actions are shaped by years of neglect, abandonment, and trauma, with consequences for America and for the rest of the world.

OBAMA'S FOUNDING FATHERS

The American empire is in decline—economically,
politically, and in some ways culturally.
The empire is declining and the game is over.[1]
—Bill Ayers, May 2012 speech at the University of Oregon

This chapter is about Obama's founding fathers, the ones who, after his parents, shaped him the most. We all have founding fathers and they help make us who we are. In my case, there was a college mentor, the literary scholar Jeffrey Hart. I was also influenced by the conservative writer William F. Buckley Jr., and neoconservative pundit Irving Kristol, theologian Michael Novak, economist Thomas Sowell, and of course Ronald Reagan. Countries also have founding fathers, and America is no exception. Obama's founding fathers are very different from mine, but more important they are very different from America's founding fathers. In fact, it is harrowing to think what George Washington, Alexander Hamilton, James Madison, Thomas Jefferson, and Benjamin Franklin would make of Obama's founding fathers, if the two groups could somehow encounter each other across the barriers of time.

There are two good reasons, at this stage, to consider Obama's founding fathers. First, this group helps us to answer the question: Where did Obama learn chapter and verse of the anti-colonial ideology? Earlier we answered the objection that Obama could not have been influenced by his father because he hardly knew his father. We saw that Obama, like many abandoned sons, went in search of the missing father. Still, the objection is valid in one respect. Even if Obama got the general outlines of the anti-colonial ideology from his father, he still needed tutors and mentors to instruct him in the elaborate details of that ideology. This is where Obama's founding fathers come in. They reinforced and made concrete the dreams of the father. Still, Obama makes it clear that none of his mentors was as important to him as his real father. Writing of people who influenced him, Obama says he could "respect these men for the struggles they went through, recognizing them as my own," and yet he had to admit that they fell short of his father's "lofty standards."[2]

Second, some critics of *The Roots of Obama's Rage* fretted that I was painting Obama with too foreign a brush. As Tim Cavanaugh of *Reason* put it, "There is no need to go to Kenya" to locate anticolonial and socialist indoctrination because for Obama "it was widely available at Occidental and Columbia."[3] Writing more broadly, Shelby Steele observes that "Barack Obama is not an 'other' so much as he is a child of the 1960s.... Obama came of age in a bubble of post-sixties liberalism that conditioned him as an adversary of American exceptionalism," and as president Obama has sought "to recast our greatness as the product of racism, imperialism and unbridled capitalism." This is also right. Obama is not alone on the left in attempting to make what Steele terms "a virtue of decline ... as if we can redeem America only by making her indistinguishable from lesser nations."[4] So where did Obama learn this? He learned it in America as much as he did in Kenya, and this is hardly surprising, because he encountered all of his founding fathers in America. Their influence on Obama shows how anti-colonialism is not confined to the Third World. Rather, anti-colonialism came to America during the 1960s. We will see through Obama's mentors how anti-colonialism was imported into America. Mainly it came from three sources: the Vietnam War, the civil rights movement, and liberation theology.

Obama drank deeply from these anti-colonial springs not just in college, but from his early years in school and also in his later activist years in Chicago. While other Americans—Bill and Hillary Clinton come to mind—were influenced by anti-colonial ideas in the faculty lounge, these ideas were casually absorbed and could easily be moderated or even jettisoned in later life. For Obama, however, anti-colonialism was embedded in his mind from earliest childhood to adult life. That's what makes Barack so different from Bill: Barack can't shake off his convictions, even when political advantage would seem to dictate that he should, because they are too much part of his psyche.

So who were Obama's founding fathers? In Hawaii, he came under the influence of the former Communist Frank Marshall Davis; at Columbia, he encountered the Palestinian radical Edward Said; at Harvard, Obama's mentor was the Brazilian socialist Roberto Mangabeira Unger; in Chicago, Obama befriended the revolutionary preacher Jeremiah Wright and also the former Weather Underground terrorist Bill Ayers. Together Obama's mentors make up quite a group. Never before has America had a president tutored and mentored by a Communist and part-time pornographer; by a "professor of terror" who advocated armed resistance against America and her allies; by a socialist so radical that he was ejected by the foreign socialist government he served in; by an incendiary theologian whose philosophy can be summed up in the phrase "God damn

America"; and by a former terrorist who, like Osama Bin Laden, attempted to blow up the Pentagon and other symbols of American power.

How did Obama discover his founding fathers? With the exception of Frank Marshall Davis, Obama didn't accidentally encounter them; he sought them out, because he was looking for surrogate fathers who thought the way his father did. If Obama wanted to become a revolutionary like his dad, he needed to hang out with real revolutionaries. Yet Obama later recognized that he needed to erase some of these figures from his biography. Obama mentions two of his five founding fathers—Frank Marshall Davis and Jeremiah Wright—in his autobiography, but as we will see, he downplays and distorts them. Obama refers to Davis merely as "a poet named Frank." Obama certainly doesn't let on what Davis and Wright really believe. Obama tells us only what he wants us to know.

We can see this from the example of Frank Marshall Davis. Dawna Weatherly-Williams, his close friend and next door neighbor, says that in his radicalism Davis was "way ahead of his time." She was surprised at Obama's abbreviated description of his relationship with Davis: "I am sure he influenced Barack more than Barack is saying." This remark is quoted in David Remnick's biography of Obama, *The Bridge*, but Remnick ignores it and insistently downplays the ties between Davis and Obama, writing that their relationship was "neither constant nor lasting, certainly of no ideological importance."[5] Yet if Remnick is right, why would Obama recall Davis so vividly and affectionately two decades later? Remnick seems eager to downplay Obama's ties to Davis because of Davis's Communist and radical associations.

Obama first met Davis in 1971 when he was ten years old. Davis was then in his mid-sixties. The two of them, the old man and the young boy, remained close until Obama left for college. Obama was introduced to Davis by his grandfather, Stanley Dunham. Recall that Obama had just been sent back to Hawaii by his mother to be raised by his grandparents. Stanley Dunham, a bit of an oddball, decided that since Obama was black he needed a black role model. And so he found Davis, who lived in a cottage near the Waikiki beach. On a regular basis, Stanley Dunham would take Obama to see Davis. Dunham and Davis would drink whiskey or smoke dope and play Scrabble. This would go on for hours. And Obama would sit in the corner and listen to Davis deliver his anti-American diatribes. Sometimes Obama would privately seek out Davis for advice on racial matters on which he could not trust his grandparents. And this close rapport between Davis and Obama continued for eight years, until Obama left Hawaii for Occidental College in Los Angeles.

What precisely Davis taught Obama we cannot know, but we do know a lot about Davis and what he believed. Davis, who started out as a writer and civil rights activist in Chicago, was a one-time member of the Communist Party. He moved to Hawaii because he came to the conclusion that mainland America was too racist. In Hawaii he worked for a labor newspaper with Communist ties, the *Honolulu Record*. For years he wrote a column called "Frankly Speaking." On the side he wrote a pornographic novel, *Sex Rebel*, which was published in 1968, three years before he met Obama. The novel was written under the pseudonym Bob Greene, but Davis later acknowledged being the author. Billed as the "story of a fantastic Negro's four decades of bedroom adventures," *Sex Rebel* according to Davis was largely autobiographical: "all incidents I have described have been taken from actual experiences."

When I was filming in Hawaii, I went looking for the shack where Frank Marshall Davis lived. It's gone; the place has now been turned into a parking lot. But I did walk through the park where Davis solicited sex from women and young girls. From his account,

Davis's "actual experiences" were quite varied and harrowing. He describes wife-swapping, orgies, sadomasochism, urolagnia (I had to look it up), and even the statutory rape of a thirteen-year-old girl. Davis concludes that he did the girl a favor. "She learned the finer points of cunnilingus, fellatio, 69, and basic sex facts she was unlikely to get elsewhere." Obama says nothing about any of this, merely noting that in his late-night discussions with Davis, he and his grandfather would sometimes assist Davis in "composing dirty limericks."[6]

Much more important, for our purpose, is Davis's ideology. He was a race guy who became an anti-colonialist. The transformation occurred in Hawaii and was helped by Davis's recognition of Hawaii's extreme diversity of races and colors. "On the mainland I have never thought of myself as anything but black," Davis wrote. But in Hawaii "I have been mistaken frequently for Hawaiian, Tongan, and Samoan; once it was assumed I was a native of India." Davis was amazed to see that "the white-black confrontation doesn't exist here." Hawaii, in this respect, was unique. But Davis also found in Hawaii a way to broaden his ideological framework. Hawaii, Davis saw, suffered from the same malady as Africa and most of the non-Western world. Davis termed this "a disease known as colonialism."[7]

Race isn't a big issue in Hawaii; colonialism is. To see this you have to go beyond tourist Hawaii; you have to sample the local literature and hang out with the natives. On my recent trip to Honolulu, I picked up Haunani-Kay Trask's book, *From a Native Daughter*. "We are Hawaiians, not Americans," Trask declares. The book is one long rant against "the foreign, colonial country called the United States of America." Trask details how Hawaii was victimized by missionaries and planters, and how the ultimate colonization occurred when the United States first annexed Hawaii and then turned it into a state. If we think that all of this is ancient history, we are wrong; statehood came in 1959, just two years before Obama was born. And statehood, Trask writes, was nothing to celebrate. Rather, it was part of an "ugly and vicious history that visited genocide on American Indians, slavery on Africans, peonage on Asians, and dispossession of both lands and self-government on native Hawaiians."[8]

At the University of Hawaii I also interviewed Willy Kauai, a graduate student who recently gave a talk on "Why the Birthers Are Right for All the Wrong Reasons." Kauai's argument is very interesting. He says that of course Barack Obama was born in Hawaii, but he is still ineligible to be president. That's because the Constitution specifies not only that the president must be a U.S. citizen but also that the president must be "natural born." The president, in other words, must be born in the United States. But Kauai's argument is that Hawaii is not legally part of the United States because U.S. forces illegally annexed Hawaii in the late nineteenth century. So from Kauai's point of view the birthers are right not because Obama was born in Kenya, but because Hawaii, where Obama was born, is actually a foreign country. The only difference between Hawaii and Kenya is that Hawaii is under direct U.S. occupation. Kauai said he would like to see a restoration of the Hawaiian kingdom, what he calls "independence for Hawaii." I asked him if this would amount to Hawaii seceding from the United States. He said no. "Seceding would imply that Hawaii was ever part of the United States."

Frank Marshall Davis likewise saw the world from the special vantage point of Hawaii. What he saw was a great movement of non-white peoples, black, brown, and yellow, all fighting against Western colonialism and imperialism. The civil rights movement, Davis saw, was only a tiny part of that broader struggle. Davis wrote,

"I opposed any and all white imperialism and backed the nations seeking independence following World War II." Even during World War II, Davis worried that America and Western Europe would impose a new form of neocolonial rule over the rest of the planet. Davis, for instance, blasted Winston Churchill for seeking a postwar alliance between Britain and the United States. This, Davis said, was simply to continue the project of British colonialism now aided by the wealth and power of America. "The postwar world envisioned by Prime Minister Churchill is obviously Anglo-American imperialism and global control." Davis added that "big business of course would like to see it," and while President Franklin Roosevelt seemed undecided, "plenty of powerful interests back the dream of Anglo-American imperialism."[9] Davis despised Churchill as an imperialist. Years later, Davis's protégé Barack Obama baffled many Americans by removing a bust of Winston Churchill from the White House and ordering it returned to Britain. (The bust now sits in the home of the British ambassador.) Davis also hated President Harry Truman and was vehemently opposed to the Marshall Plan to rebuild Europe after World War II. Most historians regard the Marshall Plan as a remarkable gesture of far-sighted magnanimity. For Davis, however, the Marshall Plan was a "device" to maintain "white imperialism." Truman and Marshall were using "billions of U.S. dollars," Davis wrote, "to bolster the tottering empires of England, France, Belgium, Holland and the other western exploiters of teeming millions of humans." Davis noted that "I have watched with growing shame … as our leaders have used our riches to re-enslave the yellow and brown and black peoples of the world."

While Davis reviled Churchill, Truman, and Marshall, he praised Communist China and the Soviet Union. He credited the Soviet Union for "its determination to stamp out discrimination…. Knowing also that Russia had no colonies and was strongly opposed to the imperialism under which my black kinsmen lived in Africa.... I considered Red Russia [my] friend."[10] Davis's Communist sympathies were driven largely by his anti-colonialism, and young Obama recognized this anti-colonialism as the ideological tie between Davis and Obama's father Barack Sr.

Another influence on Obama—one who might help explain Obama's thinking on Israel—was the Palestinian scholar Edward Said. Said had been a member of the Palestine National Council and supported armed resistance against Israel, causing one Jewish magazine to call him the "Professor of Terror." Said's actual field was literary studies, and his best-known books include *Orientalism* and *Culture and Imperialism*. "Orientalism," as Said defines it, is "a Western style for dominating, restructuring, and having authority over the Orient."[11] Prior to his death in 2003, Said was the leading anti-colonial thinker in the United States. Obama studied with Said at Columbia University, and the two maintained a relationship over the next two decades. Obama attended a Palestinian fundraiser in Chicago in 1998 in which Said was the featured speaker, and Obama also befriended Said's protégé Rashid Khalidi, who currently occupies the Edward Said chair of Arab Studies at Columbia.

We can see Said's influence on Obama in their literary interests. Said's *Culture and Imperialism* has a detailed critique of Joseph Conrad's *Heart of Darkness*. Said condemns Conrad for being insufficiently anti-colonial. "Conrad does not give us the sense," Said writes, "that he could imagine a fully realized alternative to imperialism: the natives he wrote about in Africa, Asia or America were incapable of independence, and because he seemed to imagine that European tutelage was a given, he could not foresee what would take place when it came to an end.... As a creature of his time, Conrad could not grant the natives their freedom." True to form, Obama describes a scene in college where he lays into Conrad.

"It's a racist book," Obama says of *Heart of Darkness*. "The way Conrad sees it, Africa's the cesspool of the world, black people are savages, and any contact with them breeds infection." Obama goes on to say that "the book's not really about Africa. Or black people. It's about the man who wrote it. The European. A particular way of looking at the world."[12] In fairness, I'm not convinced that Obama is merely reflecting Said here, but it's worth noting that Said's sophisticated, unconventional reading of Conrad is echoed in Obama's cruder but similar-minded rant.

While Said's field was literary studies, however, his main interests were always political. He was a vehement critic of the United States and an even more vehement critic of Israel. America, Said argued, is a genocidal power with a "history of reducing whole peoples, countries, and even continents to ruin by nothing short of holocaust." Israel had been a victim, Said conceded, yet "the classic victims of years of anti-Semitic persecution and the Holocaust have in their new nation become the victimizers of another people." Said argued that Zionism was an expression of European imperialism. "In 1948, Israel was created ... as an integral aspect of the great age of expanding colonialism. European Jews ... sought to create a Western colony in the East." Moreover, "True to its roots in the culture of European imperialism, Zionism divided reality into a superior 'us' and an inferior 'them.'" The Palestinians, according to Said, are the victims of "a continuing process of dispossession, displacement and colonial de facto apartheid." Theirs is the last anti-colonial struggle, part of what Said terms "the universal struggle against colonialism and imperialism." Since 1967, the West Bank and Gaza have been "occupied territories, militarily under the control of Israeli soldiers, settlers and colonial officials." And now Israel has a new sponsor: in recent decades it is America, not Europe, that has most actively sustained this latest form of colonialism. "The United States," Said alleged, "virtually underwrites the occupation of the West Bank and Gaza and in effect pays for the bullets that kill Palestinians." The Palestinians have every right to resist the Israelis, and such resistance cannot be dismissed as terrorism. Rather, Said insisted that the Palestinian resistance is "one of the great anticolonial insurrections of the modern period." The use of force against Israel is entirely legitimate "to repossess a land and a history that have been wrested from us."[13]

My goal here is not to assess the merits of Said's argument; it is merely to suggest that whatever Said taught Obama, we can safely assume it wasn't positive sentiments toward America or the state of Israel. Said is dead, but his protégé is now in the White House at a time when Israel is gravely imperiled and Obama can put Said's radical ideas into effect.

Obama's third founding father is the Brazilian socialist and leftist Roberto Mangabeira Unger, whom Obama first encountered at Harvard Law School when he enrolled there in 1988. There were other professors at Harvard whose courses Obama took and who subsequently claimed to be Obama mentors: Lawrence Tribe, Charles Ogletree, and so on. But these were run-of-the mill liberals of a type that Obama was wearily familiar with; he didn't have much interest in them. Obama went looking for a man like Unger. As Obama wrote, "The study of law can be disappointing at times, a matter of applying narrow rules and arcane procedure to an uncooperative reality, a sort of glorified accounting that serves to regulate the affairs of those who have power—and that all too often seeks to explain, to those who do not, the ultimate wisdom and justness of their condition." Obama said in an interview that Harvard Law School was "the perfect place to examine how the power structure works." He went there, he wrote, to "learn power's currency in all its intricate detail" so that this knowledge would "help me bring about real change."[14]

Bringing about real change has been Unger's life work, gaining him the reputation of being the leading anti-colonial scholar in the field of legal studies. Obama took two courses from Unger: Jurisprudence and Reinventing Democracy. The two maintained a relationship that persisted long after law school. Unger says that they were intellectual partners rather than friends. Mostly, he says, they communicated by email and Blackberry. In fact, Unger skipped town and declined all interviews during the 2008 presidential campaign, fearing that his radical views might hurt Obama. "I am a leftist," he later told an Obama biographer, "and by conviction as well as by temperament, a revolutionary. Any association of mine with Barack Obama in the course of the campaign could only do harm."[15] Unger's leftism was apparent when he left Harvard a few years ago to join the socialist government of Brazil. He was appointed to head a government-sponsored think tank called the Institute for Applied Economic Research. Yet the Brazilian Senate refused to approve his nomination, fearing that he would destroy the group's reputation for reliable, independent analysis. President Lula da Silva gave Unger the job in a recess appointment, and Unger proceeded to do precisely what the Senate feared. He began to replace all the senior economists who had been critical of socialist policies. The uproar in the Senate and the media was so great that the president fired Unger. At this point Unger accused Lula of being a compromiser and a sellout. Unger proved too radical for the socialist government of Brazil, and he returned to Harvard, where he seems to fit right in.

Reading through Unger's corpus of work, as I have, is no easy task. He is a serious, passionate, and frequently abstruse writer. He began as a Critical Legal Scholar—a radical within the world of legal studies—but his work is now massively interdisciplinary, drawing on the fields of economics, political science, and international relations. I must say I admire the broad sweep of his vision, and the intensity of conviction and analysis that he brings to it. He is truly a global thinker. Even his obscurity has a kind of charm. I told myself, this is the type of figure who would be comical anywhere except in academia. Reading his works, I asked myself: How can you change the world, as this man seeks to, when you write in such an abstract and arcane academic dialect? What Unger needs, I realized, is a "translator," someone to take his revolutionary ideas and figure out how to apply them. In Obama, Unger may have found such a man.

Unger's basic complaint is that the world is grossly unequal in its distribution of power and resources. For this reason, he says, democracy has failed. Democracy for Unger doesn't mean voting rights; it means a basically equal distribution of global resources and opportunity. So how do we solve this problem? For Unger, the key is to realize that the whole structure of global institutions, from globalization to free trade to property rights, is the main obstacle to achieving greater universal equity. We should not, he says, regard these social arrangements as part of "the natural order of things." They are man-made institutions, and thus they are subject to change. Unger argues that to achieve true global democracy, these institutions have to be transformed or, in Unger's favorite word, "remade." But before we can remake something, we have to re-imagine it. Once we can envision the alternative, we can set about realizing it. Unger's work is focused on achieving this re-imagining. This should not, however, be thought of as a benign academic exercise. "The advancement of alternatives like these," Unger writes, "would amount to world revolution."

Unger thinks that legal decisions should not take the language of the U.S. Constitution too seriously. "The cult of the Constitution is the supreme example of American institution worship." Basically, he argues, the Constitution means what we want it to mean. Nor is Unger a fan of traditional property rights. He calls for "the dismemberment of the traditional property right" in favor of what he calls "social endowments." Basically, all citizens are entitled to certain things, such as health care and jobs and a stable retirement, and if other people's property gets in the way, that property has to be seized in order to meet the social entitlement. Unger insists, however, that he is not merely talking about the United States or the Western countries. These social entitlements must be globally recognized. Consequently, we have to redesign and remake the institutions of globalization and free trade. "The doctrine of free trade, as it has been understood, is fundamentally defective." Unger calls for an end to immigration laws in the West that prevent a free traffic of people across national borders. Why should goods, he writes, be free to move across national frontiers but not people? Everyone, he insists, is socially entitled to seek opportunity where it can be found. Finally, Unger calls for a global coalition to reduce the influence of the United States. He calls this a "ganging up of lesser powers against the United States." He specifically calls for China, India, Russia, and Brazil to lead this anti-American coalition. Unger says global democracy is impossible when a single superpower dominates. He wants a "containment of American hegemony" and its replacement by a plurality of centers of power. "Better American hegemony than any other that is now thinkable," he writes. "But much better yet no hegemony at all."[16]

We can see in later chapters how these ideas may have shaped Obama's policies. But recently a strange video surfaced on the web in which Unger called for Obama's defeat. At first I thought it was a "cover," an arrangement by which Unger would safely distance himself from Obama by denouncing him. As I listened to Unger's remarks, however, I realized he was attacking Obama for not being radical enough.[17] Perhaps Obama should remind Unger that he hasn't been re-elected yet. Some founding fathers just don't understand the virtue of patience.

Next we turn to the Reverend Jeremiah Wright, Obama's longtime pastor and friend. I was, in retrospect, unduly harsh on Wright in my previous book, *The Roots of Obama's Rage*. Knowing more about him and his relationship with Obama, I now feel sorry for him. Wright is a genuine intellectual. He has a fully developed political theology. He was up-front about that in his pulpit, and it resonated deeply with Obama. Yet when Wright became an issue during the campaign, Obama betrayed him and got rid of him, making it seem that Wright had become some sort of a crank. Wright's reputation was ruined, and Obama moved on to gather praise for his famous race speech in Philadelphia; in fact, the speech did deserve a prize—a prize for skillful political deception.

In the speech, "A More Perfect Union," delivered at Philadelphia's National Constitution Center, Obama pretended that the controversy over Jeremiah Wright was typical of the confusions and contradictions that color race relations in the United States. Obama implied that he stood above such confusions and contradictions. He proceeded to lecture us about how America has never come to terms with our racial heritage, how we need to acknowledge the complexities of race in this country, and blah, blah, blah. Americans were so taken with Obama's rhetoric that they forgot the main issue involving Wright had very little to do with race. Rather, it had to do with American foreign policy. In his sermon "The Day of Jerusalem's Fall," delivered after 9/11, Wright portrayed America as the source of evil and terrorism in the world. The evil of American hegemony was Wright's central theme, leading to his resounding conclusion, "God damn America!" Yet Obama deftly shifted the topic from whether America is the bad guy in the world to a completely irrelevant discussion of the unfinished work of race relations in this country. And we bought it; we let him get away with it.

Now we need to understand Wright better to see what suckers we were, and how there always was, and is, a close resemblance between Wright's political theology and Obama's. Wright is not fundamentally a race guy, although he started out that way. In the 1960s, he read Stokely Carmichael and Afrocentric literature, and he was highly influenced by James Cone, the founder of Black Liberation Theology. Cone, however, expanded Black Liberation Theology to include the non-white people of the Third World.[18] Essentially he became a Third World liberation theologian. And Wright also broadened his theology to encompass a global, Third World perspective. Sure, there were plenty of blacks in Wright's Trinity church, and for them he supplied a steady diet of blackness: the so-called Black Value System, "black learning styles," the suggestion of government conspiracies involving blacks and AIDS, and a whole bunch of Afrocentric propaganda, basically adding up to the idea that blacks invented civilization and whites stole all their ideas. We can see from Obama's writings that he was never attracted to any of this nonsense. What interested him was Wright's global theology which identified the West, and specifically the United States, as a global occupier and oppressor, and the rest of the world as a global victim seeking equality and justice.

Remarkably, we all know about "God damn America," but hardly anyone has bothered to analyze Wright's sermon to determine the context of those remarks. The sermon was called "Confusing God and Government," and it was delivered at Trinity on April 13, 2003. Wright began by talking about how there is no peace in the world, just division and conflict and war. And he traced the problem to America and colonialism. "Regime change, substituting one tyrant for another tyrant with the biggest tyrant pulling the puppet strings, that does not make for peace. Colonizing a country does not make for peace. If you don't believe me, look at Haiti, look at Puerto Rico, look at Angola, look at Zimbabwe, look at Kenya, look at South Africa. Occupation does not make for peace, and subjugation only makes for temporary silence." Wright says the problem is one of tyranny and colonialism. "The Roman government failed. The British government used to rule from east to west. The British government had a Union Jack. She colonized Kenya, Nigeria, Jamaica, Barbados, Trinidad and Hong Kong. Her navies ruled the seven seas all the way down to the tip of Argentina in the Falklands, but the British failed." Then Wright moves to the failures of the current instrument of tyranny and occupation, which is America.

> We cannot see how what we are doing is the same thing al-Qaeda is doing under a different color flag, calling on the name of a different God to sanction and approve our murder and our mayhem…. We believe in this country, and we teach our children that God sent us to this Promised Land. He sent us to take this country from the Arawak, the Susquehanna, the Apache, the Comanche, the Cherokee, the Seminole, the Choctaw, the Hopi, and the Arapaho…. We confuse God and Government…. We believe God sanctioned the rape and robbery of an entire continent. We believe God ordained African slavery. We believe God makes Europeans superior to Africans and superior to everybody else too…. We believe God approved Apartheid…. We believe that God approves of six percent of the people on the face of the earth controlling all of the

resources on the face of this earth while the other 94 percent live in poverty and squalor, while we give trillions of
dollars of tax breaks to the white rich.... We believe we
have a right to Iraqi oil. We believe we have a right to
Venezuelan oil. We believe we got a right to all the oil on
the face of the Earth, and we've got the military to take it
if necessary.... We believe it's all right to decimate the
Afro-Colombian community by arming the paramilitary
with United States tax dollars—our dollars—by hiring
military whose real job is to protect the oil line owned by
United States companies.... The government lied about
Pearl Harbor.... The government lied about the Gulf of
Tonkin.... The government lied about Nelson Mandela,
and our CIA helped put him in prison and keep him there
for 27 years.

This prelude leads to the final consummation: God damn
America.[19]

When Wright became the focus of campaign controversy, he
vainly attempted to clarify his true position. In an interview with
TV host Bill Moyers, Wright stressed that his argument with America was not limited to race. "We have members from Cuba. We have
members from Puerto Rico. We have members from Belize. We have
members from all of the Caribbean islands. We have members from
South Africa, from West Africa, and we have white members."
Wright insisted that his church made up a coalition of the oppressed,
all united in a theological understanding of the distinction between
colonizer and colonized. Third World liberation theology means
looking at history and at the world from the point of view of the
victims of empire. Throughout biblical history, Wright pointed out,
the people of God suffered "under Egyptian oppression, Syrian

oppression, Babylonian oppression, Persian oppression, Greek oppression, Roman oppression. So that their understanding of what God is saying is very different from the Greeks, the Romans, the Egyptians."[20]

Wright developed these same themes in his speech to the National Press Club. He emphasized that his theology was no longer confined to James Cone's Black Liberation Theology; rather, "I take it back past the problem of western ideology and white supremacy." Wright introduced the concept of Third World liberation theology. "Now in the 1960s the term liberation theology began to gain currency with the writings and teachings of preachers, pastors, priests and professors from Latin America. Their theology was done from the underside—their viewpoint was not from the top down or from a set of teachings which undergirded imperialism.... Liberation theology started in and from a different place. It started from the vantage point of the oppressed." Wright said that his congregation maintained a global outlook. "Our congregation ... took a stand against apartheid when the government of our country was supporting the racist regime of the Afrikaner government of South Africa. Our congregation stood up in solidarity with the peasants in El Salvador and Nicaragua." For Wright, the basic enemy was and always has been imperialism. Specifically, he compared Roman imperialism and American imperialism. "The Roman oppression is the period in which Jesus was born. Imperialism was going on when Caesar Augustus sent out a decree that the whole world should be taxed—they were in charge of the world, sounds like some other governments I know. We have troops stationed all over the world, just like Rome.... because we run the world. The notion of imperialism is not the message of the Gospel of the Prince of Peace nor of the God who loves the world." No one present could miss Wright's logic: just as the people of Israel called on God to damn Rome, so

Wright was, in effect saying, that we the people of God today should call on God to damn America.[21]

Wright today seems a broken, bitter man. The Obama people have tried everything to shut him up. Wright said in a recent interview that in 2008 "one of Barack's closest friends" offered him $150,000 in exchange for his agreement "not to preach at all until the November presidential election." Wright has left Trinity, and maintains an office at the Kwame Nkrumah Academy, a school named after the first president of Ghana. Wright now wonders whether the Obamas ever had a real interest in Christianity. "Church is not their thing," he says. "It never was their thing." Instead, he says, "the church was an integral part of Barack's politics." So Wright feels used, and I suspect it's because he was used. One day, he continues to hope, Obama will come back and make amends. "He'll talk to me in five years when he's a lame duck," he told journalist David Remnick. "Or in eight years when he's out of office."[22] I doubt Obama will bother. Wright has served his purpose, and he is disposable. But we should understand what Wright and Obama had in common: a set of beliefs, grounded in anti-colonialism. This is why Obama embraced Wright as a mentor and enthusiastically participated in his church for two decades.

Finally, we turn to Bill Ayers, Obama's terrorist pal. With Ayers we don't have an Obama mentor; rather, we have a case of two fellow travelers, a generation apart, who view the world in similar ways, although their strategies for dealing with the world differ considerably. Basically it was the press that covered for Obama when the Ayers connection surfaced. The Obama team said, to quote campaign manager David Axelrod, "Bill Ayers lived in his neighborhood. Their kids attend the same school. They're certainly friendly, they know each other, as anyone whose kids go to schools together." Obama himself said, "The notion that somehow as a consequence of me knowing somebody who engaged in detestable acts 40 years ago, when I was eight years old, somehow reflects on me and my values doesn't make much sense."[23] But in fact Ayers and his wife, Bernardine Dohrn—another Weather Underground terrorist—had held a fundraiser for Obama in their apartment as early as 1995, so their relationship with Obama was at least a decade old. Moreover, Obama and Ayers served together on the Woods Foundation board for three years, beginning in 1999. In 1995, Ayers founded the Chicago Annenberg Challenge with a $50 million grant, and he chose Obama to be the first chairman of the board, a position Obama held for eight years. Bottom line: Obama knew Ayers quite well; the two worked closely together for years; Axelrod was lying and hardly anyone called him on it.

In distancing himself from Ayers's history as a terrorist, Obama neglected to mention that Ayers has never regretted committing those "detestable" acts. When Ayers published his memoir, *Fugitive Days*, in 2001, *Chicago* magazine ran a cover story with a color photo of Ayers standing atop an American flag. The headline was, "No Regrets." Ayers told *New York Times* reporter Dinitia Smith, "I don't regret setting bombs. I feel we didn't do enough." Smith's article, eerily enough, was published on September 11, 2001, the same date that Osama Bin Laden attempted what Ayers had tried to do earlier, the bombing of the Pentagon. Not only is Ayers unrepentant; he can even envision the chance of an encore performance. Ayers writes in his memoir, "I can't quite imagine putting a bomb in a building today ... but I can't imagine entirely dismissing the possibility either."[24] So Obama turns out to be friends with a man who even now has no compunction about being a terrorist.

Anti-colonial themes leap from Bill Ayers's commentaries, which makes it all the more remarkable they have been totally ignored. Why did Ayers and his co-conspirators bomb the Pentagon? "The

Pentagon was ground zero for war and conquest, organizing head-
quarters of a gang of murdering thieves, a colossal stain on the
planet, a hated symbol everywhere around the world." Why did they
attack the Capitol? "We have attacked the Capitol because it is, along
with the White House, the worldwide symbol of the government
which is now attacking Indochina. To millions of people here and
in Latin America, Africa, and Asia, it is a monument to U.S. domination over the planet."

What single issue convinced Ayers of the evils of America? "The
basic story line for us—a story I accepted instinctively and intuitively
without knowing a lot—was that Vietnam was fundamentally united
fighting an aggressive invader from the West." What sources did
Ayers read to develop his broader understanding? "We read Castro
and Che Guevara, Lenin and Mao, Cabral and Nkrumah, but on any
point of ideology we turned most often to Ho Chi Minh." And what
did Ayers learn from them? "Seen through one lens, the madness
was the war in Vietnam, and the monster was the politics and policy
of that war. Through another, the madness was an aggressive and
acquisitive foreign policy, and the monster the military-industrial
complex. And through a third lens, our lens, the madness was the
export of war and fascism into the third world, racism and white
supremacy at home, the inert, impoverished culture of greed and
alienation: the monster would be capitalism itself, the system of
imperialism." In a volume he edited with his wife and fellow terrorist Bernardine Dohrn, Ayers writes, "U.S. imperialism is the greatest
destroyer of human life on earth. It is a whole: an economic, political, and cultural system. It feeds on the piracy of the Third World....
Because of imperialism people live in shanty towns in Saigon and
Rio de Janeiro.... Imperialism has its origin in the necessity for
capitalism to expand or face stagnation. Imperialism is therefore
the defining characteristic of modern capitalism as a whole."

So what was Ayers's solution?

> The world was on fire; masses of people throughout
> Africa and Asia and Latin America were standing up
> everywhere to demand independence and democracy and
> national liberation ... the worldwide anti-imperialist
> struggle had a counterpart inside the borders of the
> U.S.—the black liberation movement; and the responsibil-
> ity of mother country radicals here in the heartland of
> imperialism was to aid and abet the world struggle.... I
> threw my lot in with the rebels and resistors.... Our job
> is to drive a stake into the heart of the monster, we
> insisted, opening up a front behind enemy lines and fight-
> ing, then, side by side with black people and with the
> people of the world.

To what end? The way Ayers saw it, "I'm not so much against the
war as I am for a Vietnamese victory. I'm not so much for peace as
for a U.S. defeat." But not just in Vietnam. "We meant to learn to
fight through fighting, moving from small to large, developing skill
and experience, growing in strength and power through the practice
of revolution. We set about to found an American Red Army."[25] So
that's why Ayers became a terrorist, to fight the monster of U.S.
imperialism.

It says something about our media that none of this information,
although widely available and easy to find, was even reported during
the Obama-Ayers controversy. It also says something about academia and the education establishment in Chicago that Ayers is
currently the Distinguished Professor of Education and Senior
University Scholar at the University of Chicago in Illinois. But what
is most troubling, even chilling, is that we have a man in the White

House who has had longstanding associations with men like Frank Marshall Davis, Edward Said, Roberto Mangabeira Unger, Jeremiah Wright, and Bill Ayers. This is a dangerous and radical group, and in at least one case the radicalism has led to terrorism against the United States. Obama has distanced himself from his founding fathers, but we cannot say they are gone, because their influence lives on in the mind of the president of the United States.

CHAPTER SIX

SELLOUTS

What Granny had told me scrambled that image completely, causing ugly words to flash across my mind. Uncle Tom. Collaborator. House nigger.[1]
—Barack Obama on his grandfather, *Dreams from My Father*

We were all set to interview "granny" Sarah Obama at the Obama Homestead in Kogelo, Kenya. But then granny decided that before she granted the interview, she had to make a phone call. She called Auma Obama, Obama's half-sister, who lives in Nairobi. And Auma directed granny Sarah not to do the interview, not to allow us to film at the family grave, not even to accept our three goats! Granny was visibly distressed—she wanted the goats. Ultimately, however, she acceded to Auma's wishes. No goats, no filming, and no interview. We packed up our gear. We packed up the goats. But before we left, we had to ask why. After all, granny Sarah seemed amenable to meeting us, and we had come well-introduced through a local tribal chief. One of our group got Auma on the phone. And Auma said that they would not grant the interview for a single reason: we had previously interviewed George

Obama. Auma said the Obama family was following George; they had an informer who told them what George did and with whom he met. George, we learned, is the black sheep of the Obama family. "He even takes money for giving interviews," Auma fumed. The family considers him a sellout.

But what is wrong with George giving interviews? Why is he forbidden from taking money? If he needs money, why doesn't the Obama family help him; why instead do they go to the trouble of following him and spying on him? How has George Obama become the enemy?

This chapter is about sellouts. According to the anti-colonial guerilla fighter Amilcar Cabral, it is imperative for the cause that "in the face of destructive action by imperialist domination, the masses retain their identity, separate and distinct from that of the colonial power."[2] Cabral's point is that the world must be clearly divided between oppressor and oppressed, the bad guys and the good guys. Moreover, the good guys must stick together and never do anything that helps the cause of the bad guys. Cabral knows, of course, that there are many people in colonized countries who support the colonizers, who cooperate with the police, and so on. In anti-colonial revolutions these people were known as sellouts, and they were routinely targeted and killed. During the Mau Mau rebellion in Kenya, for instance, the rebels killed far more black sellouts than they killed British settlers. And ultimately it was the so-called sellouts who worked closely with the British to defeat the Mau Mau.[3]

In Obama's world, too, there are role models and there are sellouts. The sellouts are ideological betrayers of Obama's father and his anti-colonial cause. Most of the sellouts come from Obama's own family. By seeing what their offenses were, and how Obama turned on them, we can better understand how he thinks. The original sellout, in a sense, was Lolo Soetoro. Obama was too young to recognize Lolo's apostasy—his anti-Communism, his pro-Western sentiments—but his mother certainly did, and she conveyed her sentiments to young Obama. As Obama grew older, however, he developed his own capacity to identify ideological traitors and treat them with appropriate scorn and neglect.

For Obama, the first traitor was, oddly enough, his own grandfather, Onyango Obama. As we see from the quotation at the beginning of this chapter, Obama goes so far as to entertain the thought that his grandfather was a "house nigger." We have a striking phenomenon here: the first African-American president using the word "nigger," and to refer to his own grandfather! Ordinarily this would be occasion for extensive comment and analysis, but if there has been any, I am not aware of it. Once again, I find myself in the peculiar position of breaking new ground in asking: What could possibly cause the president to describe his own grandfather in this appalling way?

Onyango is an odd candidate for such abuse, because he was himself a victim of colonialism. In fact, he suffered far more under colonialism than did Barack Obama Sr. Onyango Obama was born around 1895, the very year the British established Kenya as a "protectorate." By the time Onyango was twenty-five, Kenya was an official British colony. Onyango was a house servant in Nairobi. He had to carry around identity papers that included evaluations of his previous domestic work. During World War I Onyango enlisted to help the British who were fighting the Germans in East Africa. He worked for several years with road crews in the former German protectorate of Tanganyika, which was taken over by the British. Onyango also served during World War II in a British regiment called the King's African Rifles; in this capacity he traveled to Europe and Asia. During the Mau Mau rebellion in the 1950s, he was detained in an internment camp, along with tens of thousands of other Kenyan males. He was there for approximately six months and, according to his wife Sarah, endured torture at the hands of British soldiers. Eventually he was released, lice-ridden and looking aged. Obama biographer David Maraniss questions Sarah Obama's reliability here; he doesn't think Onyango was detained and tortured. Maraniss notes that "there are no remaining records of any detention, imprisonment or trial," but that is hardly surprising, since many of the Mau Mau records were destroyed. Maraniss also quotes a handful of local Kenyans, including a local police chief, saying if Onyango was in prison, they would have known it.[4] I cannot settle this dispute between Maraniss and Sarah Obama, but I don't have to. What we are concerned about here is Barack Obama's state of mind. Sarah Obama told him about Onyango's harsh treatment at the hands of the British, and Obama believed her. Clearly we would expect Obama to react with sympathy for his grandfather, and indeed he did.

It is what followed in Onyango's life that got Barack Obama thinking very differently about him. His grandfather, Obama learned, was an Anglophile. No, he did not consider the British to be inherently superior to the Africans, and he did not approve of British mistreatment of Africans. But at the same time, he performed admirable service for the British, as the evaluations on his identity card showed. One employer said Onyango "performed his duties as personal boy with admirable diligence." Another commented, "He can read and write English and follows any recipes.... Apart from other things his pastries are excellent."[5]

Throughout his life, Onyango identified the British with civilization and progress. He had grown up in an Iron Age society. He saw what British rule meant in Kenya and around the world. Onyango had the good fortune to study English at an English mission school, and consequently was one of the first in his tribe to learn to read and write in a Western language, something in which he took great pride. He grew skeptical of shamans and witch doctors at a time when such figures were highly revered in his village. He took regular baths and became obsessed with cleanliness, not permitting cows to come near his hut because they brought insects with them. Obama's brother Roy told him that their grandfather "would make you sit at the table for dinner, and served the food on china, like an Englishman." Onyango was considered the first Luo tribesman to discard traditional garb and wear Western clothing, not just pants and a shirt but, more controversially, shoes. One of Onyango's prize possessions was an RCA gramophone. Onyango permitted only his closest friends to come and listen, but they had to sit outside the gate of his compound, and no one was permitted to touch the gramophone.[6]

None of this is to suggest that Onyango was a modern man. He had five wives and was known to beat them even in front of visitors if they disobeyed him. He carried around a cane, and occasionally struck women who failed to keep their children quiet or even women who did not immediately respond to his call. Onyango's daughter, Hawa Auma, said that if Onyango was caning one of his children and an onlooker asked him why he was doing it, he would swing around and cane them too. I found this caning business a bit much, so I asked African journalist Philip Ochieng, a drinking buddy of Barack Obama Sr., about it. To my surprise, Ochieng informed me that Luo women like to be caned! Caning is just one way, Ochieng said, that Luo women preserve their femininity! So let's just say that Onyango had his "multicultural" side. He was "diverse" in other respects also: in keeping with Luo custom, his front six teeth had been removed. Yet in this case, Onyango decided to break with tradition. He grew dissatisfied with the large gap between his teeth; eventually he adopted the Western solution of getting dentures.[7]

From Obama's point of view, Onyango's unforgivable heresy came after he returned from his confinement, returned to his farm, and contemplated the differences between Western and African ways. The question he was trying to resolve was how the British, from their tiny island, were able to conquer so much of the globe. Here I must quote Sarah Obama on her husband: "He respected the white man for his power, for his machines and weapons and the way he organized his life. He would say that the white man was always improving himself, whereas the African was suspicious of anything new." Sarah quoted one of Onyango's periodic sayings, "The African is thick. For him to do anything, he needs to be beaten." According to Sarah Obama, Onyango admired three things about the British. The first was their level of knowledge. "To him knowledge was the source of all the white man's power," she said. Onyango also considered the British to be generally fair-minded. "If you do a good job for the white man," he liked to say, "then he will always pay you well." Finally, Onyango unfavorably contrasted African organization with Western organization. "How can the African defeat the white man," Onyango would ask his son Barack Sr., "when he cannot even make his own bicycle." Sarah Obama continued, "And he would say that the African could never win against the white man because the black man only wanted to work with his own family or clan, while all white men worked to increase their power." In Onyango's words, as recalled by his wife, "The white man alone is like an ant. He can be easily crushed. But like an ant, the white man works together. His nation, his business—these things are more important to him than himself.... Black men are not like this. Even the most foolish black man thinks he knows better than the white man. That is why the black man will always lose."[8]

Obama reports that as he heard this, "I ... felt betrayed." Of Onyango he says, "I had imagined him an independent man, a man of his people, opposed to white rule.... What Granny had told us scrambled that image completely." Onyango's contempt for the abilities of Africans, combined with his favorable disposition toward the West, provoked in Obama a visceral reaction. And thus it came to be that Obama began to consider his grandfather an "Uncle Tom," a "Collaborator," and a "House Nigger."[9]

Another sellout, in Obama's thinking, is his half-brother Mark. Mark Obama is the son of Barack Sr. and Ruth Nidesand. When Obama met Mark in Kenya in 1987, Mark disavowed the name Obama. He called himself Mark Ndesandjo, taking the name of Ruth Nidesand's second husband. Mark even relinquished his first name "Okoth" and switched to his middle name. Here was a young man severing himself from his past. Mark seems to have had very good reason for eschewing his biological father's name. He vividly remembers how Barack Sr. used to come home drunk and threaten and beat his mother. Mark has written an autobiographical novel in which the main character writes of his father, "Some men are born wolves." Mark's character also says that "although he racked his mind for memories of love and compassion, he found none." All he could recall is his father shouting, "This place is filthy. Do something about it. Give me food and stop tending to that brat." And then "in a Dionysian rage" the father would "thrash his white wife and terrify his coffee-colored child."[10] Barack Jr., most likely, didn't know any of this. All he knew about Mark was that he had rejected the name of their father, the Great One. That is where the problem started.

When Obama showed up at Mark's door, Ruth Nidesand met him and said, "Your name is Obama, isn't it? But your mother remarried. I wonder why she had you keep your name." Obama writes, "I smiled as if I hadn't understood the question." But he is obviously already irritated at the Great One's claims being cast into doubt. "So Mark," Obama says to his young half-brother. "I hear you're at Berkeley." Mark replies, "Stanford. I'm in the last year of the physics program there." At this point, Mark's mother praises his academic accomplishments, saying of his father, "You must have gotten some of his brains. Hopefully not the rest of him though." She turns to Barack Jr. "You know Obama was quite crazy, don't you? The drinking made it worse." Young Obama is furious, and it gets worse over dinner when Ruth contrasts Mark's achievements with Barack Sr.'s failures. Obama finds this excruciating. He writes, "I wanted to leave as soon as the meal was over."[11]

The next week, young Obama and Mark had lunch. Here is a sample of the conversation, as recounted by Obama himself. Obama asks Mark how it felt to be back in Kenya for the summer.

> **Mark:** Fine. It's nice to see my mom and dad of course.... As for the rest of Kenya, I don't feel much of an attachment. Just another poor African country.
>
> **Obama:** You don't ever think about settling here?
>
> **Mark:** No. I mean, there's not much work for a physicist, is there, in a country where the average person doesn't have a telephone.
>
> **Obama:** Don't you ever feel like you might be losing something?
>
> **Mark:** I understand what you're getting at. You think that somehow I'm cut off from my roots, that sort of thing. Well, you're right. At a certain point I made a decision not to think who my real father was. He was dead to me even when he was still alive. I knew that he was a drunk and showed no concern for his wife or children. That was enough.
>
> **Obama:** It made you mad.

Mark: Not mad. Just numb.

Obama: And that doesn't bother you? Being numb, I mean?

Mark: Toward him, no. Other things move me. Beethoven's symphonies. Shakespeare's sonnets. I know— it's not what an African is supposed to care about. But who's to tell me what I should and shouldn't care about?

At this point Obama is crushed. "We stood up to leave," he writes, "and I insisted on paying the bill. Outside we exchanged addresses and promised to write, with a dishonesty that made my heart ache." Basically Obama never intends to see the guy again. Their sister Auma, who was present, describes the event as "The Reluctant Meeting of Two Brothers."[12] Mark is guilty of two heresies: he doesn't pay obeisance to the Great One, and he seems to prefer Western culture and the Western way of life to living in Kenya. In some ways I cannot help but admire Mark. He managed to exorcise his father's ghost. He moved to China and became a business consultant in Shenzhen. He married a Chinese woman and started a new life. But there is an ironic conclusion to the story. Obama recently visited China, and he dropped in on Mark. Mark's Chinese wife, it turns out, is a big Obama fan. And so Mark responded warmly to Obama. Mark has even started using the name Obama, perhaps to help with sales of his novel.[13] This sellout may be trying to rejoin the fold.

Finally we come to George Obama, who is, like Mark Obama, the president's half-brother. I mentioned earlier how George has been living in a hut in the slums of Nairobi. When I first heard about George in 2008, he expressed the hope that he could one day become an auto mechanic. I found it extremely odd that Barack Obama, multimillionaire and presidential candidate, would not lift a finger to help George. Obama, after all, had met George twice and knew his circumstances. The first time was in 1987, when George was just a young boy. He was playing soccer when Obama showed up. The meeting was, from both their points of view, awkward. George said that his half-brother Barack "was light skinned, and to me he looked more like a *mzungu*, a white person, than he did a black African.... He spoke with an odd, foreign-sounding accent, so I could barely understand him." Obama for his part described the encounter as "painful" and possibly "a mistake." Even so, he concluded the meeting with this observation: "Perhaps one day, when he was older, George too, might want to know who his father had been, and who his brothers and sisters were, and that if he ever came to me I would be there for him, to tell him the story I knew."[14]

George met Barack Jr. a second time, in 2006, when Obama visited Kenya as a U.S. senator from Illinois. George took public transportation from the slum to the Serena hotel, which George describes as "the best hotel in the entire city ... popular with aid workers, UN officials, diplomats and businessmen." George saw Obama in the lobby, but he was just leaving. "George," Obama said, shaking his brother's hand. "It's good to see you again. But listen, I got to rush to a meeting. I've got two days in Nairobi, and I'll call you. We'll arrange a time so we can meet." George waited two days for the call that never came. "I got the strong sense that the failure to fetch me was less by forgetfulness and more by design."[15]

Okay, so Obama didn't have time to hang out with George. I didn't find this surprising. Much more surprising was Obama's complete refusal to help George. What made this particularly strange was that Obama was going around the world talking about our responsibility to the less fortunate. Obama was particularly fond of quoting from the Bible: "We are our brother's keeper." Recently at the National Prayer Breakfast, he repeated that phrase, noting it meant "treating others as you want to be treated," "requiring much from those who have been given so much," and "caring for the poor and those in need."[16] Yet here was his actual brother, very much in need, and for some reason Obama made no effort to "keep" him. What was going on?

In 2008, I was doing a daily blog for AOL and there I announced I was starting the George Obama Compassion Fund. My blog entry read, "Help George Obama Move Out of His Hut." I put up $1,000, and I asked people to send me small amounts—a dollar, two dollars—to help Obama's brother get some training and become self-reliant. I didn't want big sums because it doesn't take big sums to overcome poverty in Kenya. George was living on a few dollars a day. A couple thousand dollars would be sufficient. And in a couple weeks I had the money. I found a Christian missionary working in Kenya who offered to deliver it to George. But then I heard from a Kenyan journalist that George had disappeared. Even the missionary could not locate him. I was told that the Obama family got to George. They convinced him that I was doing this in part to embarrass Barack Obama—which of course was true. They convinced George that he should not take help from me, because the Obama family would be there for him. So George went into hiding, and that, I thought, was that.

But when planning my Kenya trip, I got the idea of contacting George and seeing if he would be willing to do an interview. I approached George through a British journalist, Damien Lewis, who knew George and had co-authored a book with him, telling George's story. Damien contacted George and, to my surprise, George said yes. Later I learned that George had been given assurances by the Obama family that turned out to be lies. They made him give up the money that I had for him, and then they didn't help him at all. George felt betrayed, because he had been. And so George decided that maybe I wasn't such a bad guy after all. Perhaps it even crossed his mind that if he granted the interview, I might have a present for him.

I met George in the lobby of the Hyatt Hotel. He came with an entourage—an adviser, a security guy, and an affable woman with her teenage son. The son, I learned, was a soccer player, and George is now a coach for a soccer league in the slums. I paid for brunch for the whole group, and we got acquainted. Then we moved to an outdoor location for the interview. But George wanted to talk first. Where, he asked, is my money? I had brought $2,000 to give him, but I said it was a present, not only from me but from a number of hard-working Americans who wanted to help him. I asked if I could film my presenting the check to him. George said no. Then he said, "How do I know you only raised $2,000 using my name?" I said, "George, half of this money is mine. I didn't have to bring any of it to you." George responded, "So this is the money you raised to help me. But what is my payment for doing the interview?" He insisted on an additional $1,000 to do the interview, and somewhat reluctantly I agreed.

I now realized something about George that I didn't know before. He was not an innocent—he had been hardened by the slums. I knew from Damien Lewis, whom I'd met in London, that George was not a bad guy. He used to be a teenage delinquent, but he had reformed his life. Now he was, as Lewis put it, "on the side of the angels." But it's not easy to live so close to the edge of survival. George, I saw, was sly and cunning; he was a survivor. And yet I wanted to interview George because I wanted to find out why his rich brother didn't help him get out of the ghetto. I had read George's book, and I had some theories. But I wanted to ask him directly.

George's book is called *Homeland: An Extraordinary Story of Hope and Survival*. The book was published by Simon & Schuster, but Damien Lewis told me that before it came out in America the publisher without explanation decided to shred the entire print run. The book was published in Britain, however, and Damien Lewis sent me a copy. "George and I thought the book was a story of triumphing over difficult circumstances," Lewis said. "We expected President Obama to embrace the story, to embrace George. But that never happened. And I believe that Obama has powerful friends at Simon & Schuster who felt that what George has to say may make Obama look bad. They decided they would rather take a loss and take the book out of circulation. This is the effect that Obama has on some people. Even I used to feel it, but not anymore." Lewis also told me that George had been trying to come to the United States to visit his mother Jael Otieno for several years. "But he can't get a visa. The U.S. government won't let him in. Twice he tried to come, and twice he was rejected." I must say I found this incredible. Suppressing a book is one thing, but on what grounds could you deny a guy—who happens to be the president's half-brother—permission to come to America to visit his own mother?

I asked George about all this, and he expressed frustration that the American embassy denied him a visa; despite his earlier juvenile delinquency, he has no criminal record. He has a mother living in Atlanta and was given no explanation why he was turned down. George was also bitter about Simon & Schuster shredding his book so he couldn't tell his story in the United States. He refused, in each instance, to blame Obama. No, Obama wasn't responsible for the visa denial; it was those guys at the U.S. consulate. No, Obama wasn't the reason his book had been suppressed; the publishers had their own inexplicable, and uncommunicated, reasons. George even insisted that his wealthy and powerful brother doesn't owe him anything. George said he believes in self-reliance, in making it on your own. I told him I agreed, but pointed out that Obama claims we have a responsibility to help those who are less fortunate than we are. Obama is even willing to compel people to assist others who are unrelated to them. So why would Obama refuse to discharge his own moral duty to help George, especially considering it would cost him so little? At this point George became very defensive and ashamed. I felt it was to his credit that he made his best attempt to defend Barack Obama. Somehow George had no idea why he had become objectionable to his famous brother, and *persona non grata* in the Obama family.

The answer, I believe, can be found in George's book. First, George tells us things that make President Obama look bad, not because George is trying to be negative, but because the facts are damning by themselves. George describes a scene, for example, in which he is in a bar in Nairobi on America's election night. When Obama is elected, people cheer and express astonishment. George observes, "What would the drinkers think, I wondered, were they to realize that Barack Obama's half-brother sat in their very midst— George Obama, an unremarkable resident of the Huruma slum?"[17] This episode is poignant as narrative, but it's probably not what Obama wants the American people to hear.

Second, George expresses complete indifference to his biological father, Barack Obama Sr. He pays no obeisance to the Great One. Then George goes on to recount that after his father died, his mother moved in with a white man, a French aid worker named Christian. This man treated George as his own son, taking him to games, helping him with his homework, and doing all the things that Barack Obama Sr. never did for his own children. George makes the point that Christian, a white man, took the trouble to raise him while his own black father drank himself into oblivion. So that seems to be George's offense number two: when the African father fails, a white Westerner comes to the rescue.

Perhaps most telling, George through his experience develops a very independent set of opinions—toward colonialism, toward Africa, and toward the British. In school, George says, he had "been taught that all Kenya's problems were owing to the British colonial legacy." George, however, doesn't buy it. He says, "I didn't believe the myths people told about our country and the cause of its ills." George tells a friend that at the time of Kenya's independence in the early 1960s, "Kenya was on an economic par with Malaysia or Singapore. We were at the same level in terms of development. Look where we are now, and where they are. They're practically developed and industrialized, while Kenya is still a basket case." To drive the point home, George adds, "The British granted those countries independence about the same time as us, so what's the difference? What's our excuse for failure? We don't have one. We've only got ourselves to blame, or at least those at the top of our messed-up society."

George compounds his heresy by suggesting that American troops, having liberated Iraq in order to establish democracy there, consider the prospect of invading Zimbabwe and getting rid of the dictator Robert Mugabe. While some say Mugabe's anti-colonialism justifies his corruption, thuggery, and tyranny, George is skeptical. "If there was a crazed and autocratic dictator who needed removing from power," he writes, "Robert Mugabe was it. If there was one people who truly needed liberating, it was the Zimbabweans." George isn't finished. He next addresses the taboo subject of why South Africa is the most economically advanced country in Africa, suggesting that this seems related to the whites who until recently ruled the country. "Look at South Africa," George says. "They were under the whites until the 1990s, and look where they are now. They're practically a developed nation. The corruption there is nothing like what it is here. So who is better off? Us, who kicked out the British, or the South Africans? Maybe if we'd let the whites stay a bit longer, we'd be where South Africa is today."[18]

If Barack Obama read these words, he no doubt winced at them. George's sin, I concluded, isn't that he's sly or conniving, but that he is a standing rebuttal to everything that Barack Obama represents. George doesn't idolize Barack Sr., and he doesn't go along with his father's and brother's anti-colonial, anti-Western ideology. I can't think of any other reason why Obama won't help George, and is even willing to hurt him. Vindictively, the Obama administration refuses to let George come to the United States and visit his mother. Equally appalling, Obama continues his moral exhortations on the campaign trail, demanding that the rest of us pay higher taxes to help needy people who are unrelated to us; meanwhile, Obama refuses to give even a little help to his own half-brother who desperately needs it.

Obama's behavior toward George tells you something about the man, about his supreme hypocrisy. His behavior toward the sellouts also reveals his Manichean mindset, one that eagerly embraces those who share his anti-colonial sympathies and reviles those who reject them. Now we understand why Obama demonizes those who disagree with him, implying that they are not just wrong but unholy. He attributes to his Republican and conservative opponents evil motives that transcend the normal differences of policy debates. We can also see better why Obama refuses to compromise on issues like debt and health care. He will make strategic retreats, to fight another day, but he doesn't believe in searching for middle ground with his adversaries. He could have won some Republican votes on health care reform had he moved a little to accommodate some GOP ideas, but he refused and got the bill passed without a single Republican vote. For Obama, the GOP is the neocolonial party, and to compromise with it is a form of ideological sellout. We can expect more of the same from Obama if he is granted a second term. Freed from the demands of re-election, he may be even more polarizing, further fracturing the fragile bonds that have held this country together.

CHAPTER SEVEN

CERTIFICATES OF ABSOLUTION

*We must first see the world as it is
and not as we would like it to be.*[1]
—Saul Alinsky, *Rules for Radicals*

Now we are in a position to admire the political genius of Barack Obama. Actually "genius" is probably too strong a word. I don't think that Barack Obama is a genius. He is, however, a highly intelligent man, and he is possessed of a certain kind of low cunning that makes him politically formidable. Obama's skill—that is perhaps a more appropriate term—is to figure out what the American people want to *see* and *hear*, and then give it to them, while *doing* something entirely different. Obama has also injected fear on the right, and inspired giddy enthusiasm on the left, by playing the "race card" in a way never previously done in American politics. Such techniques not only enabled Obama's meteoric political rise, they also enabled him to win the presidency. Moreover, they have muted effective criticism and sustained for him a level of political loyalty that would be unthinkable in any other president with a comparable record. If Obama were white, he would have virtually no chance of being re-elected. Yet his success is not due to affirmative action; something else—something more interesting and strange—is going on here.

Let's review our theory about Obama to this point. We have seen that Obama was abandoned by both his parents, and underwent a profound search for roots, for who he is and where he is from. He found his roots in Africa, and in an epiphany at his father's grave he saw that he could eschew aspects of his father's personality while embracing his father's ideological dream. Obama's anti-colonialism, inspired by his father, was nevertheless developed and reinforced by a series of radical mentors, not in Kenya but right here in America. And where have we gotten this story? We got it from Obama himself and from everything that is known about Obama. It is supported by Obama's family members and by those who knew Obama during his formative years, and it is corroborated by Obama's actions toward those people. As we have seen, Obama was drawn to anti-colonial radicals and even terrorists, while he was repelled by people who turned away from his father and his ideology. All the biographical information we have about Obama, much of it from Obama himself, supports our theory, and there are no facts so far that contradict it.

Even so, anti-colonialism is a foreign ideology with its roots in Third World history. While it came to America in the 1960s, anti-colonialism is still an unfamiliar concept to most Americans. So here is Obama's problem. How does he sell this Third World, anti-American philosophy to American voters? How does he market it to mainstream liberals and independents who are not anti-American? Not only has Obama done this, but even today he continues to sustain a largely uncritical camp of followers in the media, in academia, among young people, and in the country at large. We have already

seen the way that biographers and journalists apologize for Obama
and cover for him. How has Obama managed to make ordinarily
diligent people behave so irresponsibly? Obama has also immobi-
lized some conservatives who know that Obama is not a traditional
Democrat, but they cannot find the language, or the resolve, to say
why. They seem nervous, even apprehensive, to trace Obama's roots
and connect them to his actions—actions that only make sense when
viewed against his background. How did Obama pull off this silenc-
ing trick, inhibiting even his determined adversaries?

For Obama, the story begins in Chicago, but I only understood
the story recently while walking the streets of New York. I am the
president of the King's College in New York. Ours is a Christian, free
market college, until recently located in the Empire State Building,
now right off Wall Street. For many months, Wall Street has been
swamped with protesters calling themselves Occupy Wall Street. A
group of our students recently visited the protest sites and engaged
the protesters in discussion about economic and religious issues. I
too decided to visit, although my goal was not to argue with the
protesters; rather, it was anthropological, to study them as members
of a distinct tribe. And this they surely were. I could not believe
media accounts that portrayed Occupy Wall Street as a mainstream,
all-American movement. Sure, the group was broad and diverse in
a sense. There were men and women, young and old, fat and thin.
But what united the group is that everyone was kind of unhappy,
angry, dirty, and disheveled.

Yet this was a particularly American kind of dirtiness. One of the
most shocking aspects of Occupy Wall Street, to observers, was the
tendency of the protesters to defecate and urinate on the street.
Actually, I find that sight quite familiar: I see it all the time in India.
But the people who do that in India are slum-dwellers who have
nowhere else to go. They go on the street because they have to. In

the case of the Occupy protesters, they were doing that to make an ideological statement. They wanted to show their contempt for cleanliness, for the middle class lifestyle, for the cops, and for the city. Yet while they railed against the establishment, they expected to be catered to by the city establishment and lionized by the establishment media. I was especially amused by their slogans about the 1 percent and the 99 percent: they wanted redistribution of income from the top 1 percent to the remaining 99 percent. Yet they sought this redistribution only in America; somehow global redistribution wasn't on their agenda.

These Occupy Wall Street types reminded me of the protesters that I saw on the Dartmouth campus in the 1980s; they were the most miserable, unclean, and poorly dressed segment of the student body. One of my professors, Jeffrey Hart, wrote a column in the campus newspaper calling them "The Ugly Protesters." In that column, Hart speculated on what would cause relatively affluent and well-fed students to be so angry all the time? He concluded that most likely they were protesting their own ugliness! I'm not sure I agreed with this analysis in the mid-eighties, but it did come back to me as I surveyed the Occupy Wall Street guys. Wow, I said to myself, it's been a quarter-century, and these are the same people!

Listening to the rants of the Occupy Wall Street group—its denunciations of the rich, of the big bad corporations, of American occupation of Iraq and Afghanistan, of America's support for Israel, of globalization and free trade, and so on—I heard many familiar Obama themes. So I asked: What makes Obama appear so different from these guys? If you review pictures of Obama from his student years, he too looks like a disheveled urban thug. There is one especially revealing picture, where Obama flashes a street-smart look, a cigarette dangling from his mouth. That Obama would fit right in with the Occupy gang. Yet Obama now seems quite different. He wears impeccable suits, he speaks in a measured and reassuring way, he eschews the obscenity that flows so copiously from the Occupy protesters, and of course he doesn't defecate or urinate in public. So what distinguishes Obama now from his Occupy counterparts? Or to put it differently, what distinguishes Obama now from Obama then?

In *The Roots of Obama's Rage*, I suggested an answer to this question, but it turns out to be an incomplete answer. In that book I attributed the change in Obama to the influence of Saul Alinsky. On my recent trip to Kenya, however, I learned that Alinsky's influence came only later. Obama began to change his appearance in 1987, when he learned more about his dad. Gradually, but self-consciously, Obama began to imitate his dad's stylish and classy dress and demeanor. This change of style and deportment in Obama was then reinforced by Saul Alinsky, who gave Obama a political reason to do it. Obama fully embraced Alinsky's program soon after he returned from Kenya.

A good deal has been made of Obama's connection with Saul Alinsky. Alinsky was a legendary labor and community organizer in Chicago. Even Hillary Clinton was inspired by him and studied his approaches. And here we find ourselves in a position to solve one of those small Obama mysteries. The mystery is why Obama kept going back to Chicago. Obama grew up in Hawaii, not Chicago. He went to college in New York and then Boston. After graduating from Columbia, and then Harvard Law School, and being the first black president of the *Harvard Law Review*, Obama surely could have gone anywhere. Yet he took a series of low-paying jobs as a community organizer in Chicago. He worked in Chicago before law school, and he went back to Chicago after law school. So why Chicago? The answer, I believe, is that Obama wanted to learn what Saul Alinsky and the Alinsky organization had to teach him. So he studied Alinsky's works. He collaborated with Alinsky's associates. He even taught Alinsky's techniques to other activists. And he applied Alinksy's counsel to himself, to his own career.

Alinsky's influence on Obama was not ideological; it was tactical. This was Alinsky's specialty: he was a master tactician. Born in 1909, Alinsky got his experience as an organizer by establishing "people's organizations" in industrial slums, mostly in immigrant communities in Chicago that had been the setting for Upton Sinclair's muckraking novel *The Jungle*.[2] By the late 1960s, Alinsky was a veteran organizer, well into middle age, and he was not impressed by the radicals and hippies who came to him for advice on how to change things. Alinsky wrote two books, *Reveille for Radicals* and *Rules for Radicals*, in which he attempted to instruct the activists of the sixties. From Alinsky's point of view, these people were going about their radicalism all wrong. "Activists and radicals, on and off our college campuses—people who are committed to change—must make a complete turnabout. With rare exceptions, our activists and radicals are products of and rebels against our middle-class society." So far Alinsky's description is true of the sixties activists, true of the Occupy Wall Street types, true of Obama.

"All rebels," Alinsky continues, "must attack the power states in their society. Our rebels have contemptuously rejected the values and way of life of the middle class. They have stigmatized it as materialistic, decadent, bourgeois, degenerate, imperialistic, warmongering, brutalized and corrupt." Alinsky says, "They are right. But we must begin from where we are if we are to build power for change." Alinsky writes:

The power and the people are in the big middle-class majority. Therefore, it is useless self-indulgence for an activist to put his past behind him.

Instead he should realize the priceless value of his middle-class experience.... Instead of the infantile dramatics of rejection, he will now begin to dissect and examine that way of life as he never has before. He will know that a "square" is no longer to be dismissed as such— instead, his own approach must be "square" enough to get the action started.... Instead of hostile rejection he is seeking bridges of communication and unity.... He will view with strategic sensitivity the nature of middle-class behavior with its hang-ups over rudeness or aggressive, insulting, profane actions. All this and more must be grasped and used to radicalize parts of the middle class.[3]

Alinsky recognized, of course, that he was advocating a strategy of deceit. This didn't bother him. Alinsky's *Rules for Radicals* is dedicated to a most unusual figure: the devil. Alinsky calls Lucifer "the first radical known to man who rebelled against the establishment and did it so effectively that he at least won his own kingdom." Given this, we should not be surprised at Alinsky's contention that "ethical standards must be elastic to stretch with the times." Alinsky wrote that morality and ethics were all very fine for those who didn't seek to improve the world for the better. But for those who do, the ends always justify the means. "In action," Alinsky wrote, "one does not always enjoy the luxury of a decision that is consistent both with one's individual conscience and the good of mankind. The choice must always be for the latter." This is not to say that Alinsky eschewed appeals to conscience and morality. He used them, but only when they proved strategically effective. Morality for Alinsky is a mere cloak that the activist puts on when it suits him or her. One of Alinsky's ethical rules was that "you do what you can with what you have and clothe it with moral arguments."[4] Here we get a glimpse of why Alinsky's disciples, including Obama, have shown a willingness on occasion to say anything, no matter how distant from the truth. What they learned from the master tactician is that even truth is a tactic; use it when it helps you, and lie when you have to. Of course Obama had a second instructor in the art of fabrication—his father, Barack Sr., who as we have seen was a notorious liar and fabulist.

If we consider the population of angry, dirtball activists, both in his day and ours, here's how we can summarize Alinsky's advice to them: You can be a freak, but you shouldn't come across like a freak. You can be a revolutionary, but you should not look or act or smell like a revolutionary. Take a bath. Use deodorant. Cut your hair. Put on a tie if you have to. Don't use obscenities. Don't call the police "pigs" and U.S. military personnel "fascists." Suppress your anger; go for cool anger which is camouflaged rather than hot anger which scares people. Feign an interest in middle class tastes; in other words, pretend to be like the people you hate. Speak their language, even to the extent of using local colloquialism and slang. Meanwhile, work creatively and even unscrupulously to build these people's resentment against the rich and the big corporations and the military and the power structure. In this way the radical can harness the power of the white middle class majority even to undermine the values and interests of the white middle class.

Few of the sixties radicals listened to Alinsky. And from what I saw, clearly no one at Occupy Wall Street follows his counsel.

Obama, however, recognized its strategic value. Already upon returning from Kenya he had improved his appearance. Now he stopped smoking in public and began to practice using a Midwestern accent. Obama says this himself. "The fact that I conjugate my verbs and speak in a typical Midwestern newscaster voice—there's no doubt that this helps ease communication between myself and white audiences." Yet with blacks Obama adopts a different tone. "And there's no doubt that when I'm with a black audience, I slip into a slightly different dialect."[5]

At first glance it may seem implausible that a man can actually change the way he talks. But Obama has a particular talent for accents. We can verify this by listening to the audio version of Obama's autobiography. There Obama uses a wide range of accents, African and American, young and old, even male and female. During the dialogue portions of the book, he switches back and forth effortlessly between characters.[6] Quite obviously, Obama could have been a successful actor. As a matter of fact, he is a successful actor. In politics, Obama found a profession that allowed him to play the role of a lifetime. Thus we see that Obama underwent a major transformation under the tutelage of Saul Alinsky. Again, it was a transformation not of ideas but of appearance, not of philosophy but of technique. Yet appearances and technique are very important. I call this the mainstreaming of Barack Obama, a process that proved crucial to his acceptance by the American middle class.

Yet mainstreaming by itself is not enough to solidify Obama's middle class appeal. After all, if you have policies that thwart and undermine the middle class, or diminish the country to which your middle class is attached, short hair, a calm demeanor, and comforting talk will only get you so far. Even lying and unscrupulous tactics can backfire if they are found out. This happened regularly in the life of Barack Sr., and even Barack Jr. has lost many middle class and independent voters who seem to have figured out that there is something deceptive and untrustworthy about him.

Even so, Obama continues to hold on to a surprising number of white middle class voters. Moreover, Obama exercises a formidable captivity over many liberals, especially in the media. We know all about MSNBC host Chris Matthews, who responds to Obama with thrills running down his leg, and who recently blurted out that "Everything he's done has been good for this country."[7] Another classic example is the *New York Times*, which has become, on its front page no less than on its editorial page, a publicity arm of the Obama administration. Now certainly the *New York Times* is a liberal newspaper, but its liberalism did not prevent it from being at least on occasion critical of previous Democratic administrations. The *Times*, for instance, showed that it could be tough on Jimmy Carter and Bill Clinton. But when it comes to Obama, the *New York Times* is a cheerleader. A great newspaper doesn't so easily give up its credibility and become a rag. We need to explain what has happened not just to this newspaper but to a substantial segment of American liberalism.

The answer, I believe, comes from an ingenious psychological theory advanced by the African-American scholar Shelby Steele in a series of books: *A Dream Deferred*, *White Guilt*, and most recently, *A Bound Man*. In his earlier books, Steele makes the point that the collapse of the ideology of white supremacy in America has created in whites a powerful sense of moral illegitimacy. Steele calls this the "great shaming of white Americans and American institutions."[8] Whites feel stigmatized by past racism and its continuing legacy, and whites also worry that they may harbor, perhaps even unknown to themselves, racist beliefs and sentiments. This may seem like a terrible thing to say about whites, but actually Steele means it as a compliment. The vast majority of whites, in his view, reject the ide-ology of white supremacy. Their moral code is anti-racist. They don't just want to avoid being perceived as racist; they don't like to think of themselves as racist. Again, this says something good about America—it is a measure of genuine racial progress. It also says something good about these white people—they want to bring their thoughts and actions into line with their anti-racist moral code.

But here the plot thickens, because blacks know this, and the white need for racial vindication provides blacks with a source of political and financial opportunity. White guilt, Steele writes, is the real source of black power. Consequently, in Steele's words, "White guilt made racism into a valuable currency for black Americans."[9] Blacks know that whites have given up their claim to moral author-ity on the issue of race, and that in this area they acknowledge blacks as their moral authorities and also, in a sense, moral superiors. How, therefore, can blacks cash in on this advantage? Steele takes his analysis to a new level in his most recent book, *A Bound Man*. In that book, Steele argues that throughout black history there have been two types of blacks who have risen to the occasion, and they have employed two quite different strategies for capitalizing on white guilt: the strategy of the challenger, and the strategy of the bargainer. In the real world, of course, there are blacks who fall somewhere in between these two poles; still, the distinction between the bargainer and the challenger helps us understand two very dif-ferent ways for blacks to get ahead in American life.

The challenger is the guy who, in Steele's words, "forages for opportunities to cry racism." And in fact he presumes that all whites are racist. The challenger even lets whites know this, to put them on the defensive. The challenger wants to embarrass and humiliate whites; he also wants whites to know that a reputation for racism could be lethal. "Once a person or an institution is stigmatized in this way," Steele writes, "they become radioactive, the worst kind of pariah."[10] Given the right opportunity, the challenger will even threaten to expose a particular white person or organization as racist. The point is to put enough pressure on the white person or group that payment is forthcoming. The challenger is a shakedown artist. In a way I'm reminded of the film *The Godfather*—the challenger always intends to make his white target an offer that can't be refused. The main difference is that the racial challenger doesn't have to use direct force. In a sense, the challenger trades on his target's own conscience and inbuilt sense of guilt and remorse. Moreover, while Don Corleone and Luca Brasi didn't claim to occupy the moral high ground, racial challengers do. They actually think their shakedowns are a demonstration of high moral principle. They believe they are doing good for society at the same time that they are doing well for themselves.

Steele notes that challengers do pretty well, and this is obviously true. Jesse Jackson, the prototypical challenger, often travels around by private jet even though the guy hasn't had a real job in decades! Steele adds, however, that challengers produce resentment in the people whose wallets they pick. People, after all, don't like to be shaken down, and they become even more indignant when they are being taken by someone who pretends to be a moral exemplar. Consequently, challengers are controversial figures who may be popular in black America, but they rarely win a big following in white America. Jesse Jackson ran for the presidency, but he never had a serious chance.[11]

A contrasting approach, and potentially a much more effective one, is that of the bargainer. According to Steele, bargainers make a deal with whites. They make it clear at the outset that they are not going to presume whites are racist. In fact, they are going to presume the opposite. Bargainers begin by giving whites the benefit of the doubt. What they ask in return is that whites appreciate this generosity and show it. Steele remarks that when black bargainers treat whites in this way, whites are inwardly thrilled. The bargainer affirms their desire to have an anti-racist reputation and confirms what they wish to believe about themselves. Consequently, whites are incredibly excited to have their own self-image ratified and confirmed by blacks through the subtle transaction of bargaining. And when blacks behave this way in public, Steele writes, they have a chance to become national heroes not only to blacks but also to whites. They become, in Steele's term, Iconic Negroes. Steele writes that Iconic Negroes are so popular because they offer "absolution for whites and redemption for blacks."[12]

A perfect example of an Iconic Negro in popular culture is Oprah Winfrey. Steele writes that "she gives Americans their decency." What does he mean by this? For years, Oprah had millions of fans, most of them white and female. And Oprah in a sense had a tacit bargain with those fans. Her bargain was that she would never point the finger at them and accuse them of being racist. On the contrary, she would take them to be fair and decent human beings with whom she could even share her inner conflicts and struggles. This grant of trust across the racial divide, Steele writes, was a gift that no white talk show host could offer an audience. Consequently, Oprah became the queen of the talk shows, and legions of white women developed a powerful rapport with her, rushing to buy the books she endorsed and recommended. She flattered them with her trust, and they returned it in the form of loyalty and affection. Other examples Steele gives of Iconic Negroes are Tiger Woods, Bill Cosby (as seen in the 1980s on *The Cosby Show*), and even O. J. Simpson in the years before he was accused of murdering his wife.[13]

Barack Obama, according to Steele, demonstrated the remark-able power of the bargaining strategy in American politics. Steele calls him "an artist at bargaining." From a scene that Obama recounts in his autobiography, we see why. While Obama was a senior in high school, a friend of his was arrested for drug possession. Ann Obama confronted her son, demanding to know if he was involved. Obama says he gave her "a reassuring smile and patted her hand and told her not to worry." Obama knew exactly what he was doing. "It was usually an effective tactic," he writes, "another one of those tricks I had learned: People were satisfied so long as you were courteous and smiled and made no sudden moves. They were more than satisfied; they were relieved—such a pleasant surprise to find a well-mannered young black man who didn't seem angry all the time."[14] So now we know that Obama knows. He has from an early age learned the value of forgoing angry black man routines and using the bargainer's technique to get what he wants.

As Steele points out, Obama is not the first bargainer to prove effective in the political arena. That was Colin Powell. And Powell had a very good chance to become president, but for whatever reason, he chose not to run. Consequently Obama must be ranked as the most successful bargainer in American politics. His success is largely due to the fact that he offers whites a certificate of racial absolution, and in return he gets an avalanche of white loyalty and enthusiasm. Steele's psychological diagnosis, clinically accurate in my view, helps to explain why Obama retains a following among moderates and independents. It also explains, in quite an amusing way, the phenomenon of the Obama worshipper and sycophant. It suggests that when choirboys like Chris Matthews, Joe Klein, Jonathan Alter, or Andrew Sullivan sing their hymns to Obama, they aren't in a sense praising or even excited about Obama. They are excited about their discovery about what morally wonderful people they are. They are actually praising themselves for their spectacular virtue. This isn't Obama worship; it's self-worship. And so immersed are these fellows in their political glossolalia that they are completely unaware of how absurd they make themselves.

Once we see what motivates the Obama devotees in the media, we can understand their daily devotions as well as their wounded rage against critics of Obama. Recall the fury that attended my last book; we can expect even more blowback against this one. And throughout this year's election campaign we are going to have to endure shameless hymns to Obama and vile vitriol directed against those who refuse to attend Obama worship services. The Obama cult is largely devoid of substance; its orisons and denunciations both have the same source: these are people who are trying to protect their own self-image as much as Obama's. They are not real analysts; they are penitents looking for absolution. By diagnosing their malady, we can see through them and safely ignore them.

So that's Obama's secret weapon, namely, his continuing ability to offer white America a certificate of racial absolution. As Steele puts it, "His presidency flatters America to a degree that no white Republican can hope to compete with." Moreover, "He is an opportunity to vote for American redemption."[15] This weapon isn't as strong today as it was in 2008, but it still wields power. I believe it accounts for conservative anxieties about Obama's background and even his ideology: conservatives also bask in the approval that racial bargainers confer on the whole nation, and they have a stake in protecting the racial credibility of the bargaining community. I also believe that Obama's absolving power is the main reason that so many people say in polls that they "like" Obama even when they disagree strongly with his policies. Actually, Obama isn't that likeable; even his admiring biographers like David Mendell acknowledge that Obama can be "imperious, mercurial, self-righteous and sometimes prickly," even toward people who are on his side.[16] So why claim that Obama is so likeable? It's a way for people to say that even when they don't approve of what he does, they still appreciate the fact that Obama isn't Jesse Jackson or Al Sharpton. White Americans will always take a bargainer over a challenger. Consequently, there is an unspoken force drawing Obama forward, and this makes him much harder to beat at the ballot box than a white Democrat who might be identical to him in all other respects. This is something Obama's opponents must always keep in mind. They must figure out how to give people permission to vote against Obama; if they cannot do this, they will never beat him.

CHAPTER EIGHT

THE WEALTH
THEY DIDN'T EARN

Theoretically there is nothing that could stop the government from taxing 100 percent of income so long as the people get benefits commensurate with their income which is taxed.[1]

—Barack Obama Sr., "Problems Facing Our Socialism," *East Africa Journal*

A
t this point in the book we are familiar with Obama's anti-colonial ideology, but how do we know that this ideology drives Obama's actions in the White House? Actually, there is one way to know. We have to match the anti-colonial ideology with Obama's actions. Or, to put it differently, we have to compare the ideology of the father with the behavior of the son. That is what we are going to do in the next few chapters. In each case we test our theory by laying out what, on that basis, we would expect Obama to do. Then we see if he does it. Of course there could be other explanations for why he is acting in a particular way. So we examine competing theories, liberal and conservative, to see if they give a

better account of his motivations. Our goal is to understand Obama more clearly than he has been previously understood.

A president's actions must be viewed both from the prism of domestic policy and of foreign policy, but sometimes there is a single goal that unifies them both. Reagan, for instance, built his whole career in opposition to the idea of collectivism. For Reagan, collectivism could be seen in the expansion of the welfare state at home, and the expansion of the Soviet empire abroad. Reagan's presidency was dedicated to stopping collectivism on both fronts. He did so by fostering free market policies like tax cuts, deregulation, and privatization here in America. And he sought to roll back and bring down the Soviets by building up America's defenses and by supporting anti-Communist resistance movements in countries like Afghanistan and Nicaragua.

Obama, in a way, is the anti-Reagan. Yet he too has the Reaganite goal of reshaping America and at the same time reshaping the world. Only Obama wants to do this in a radically different way. With the perspective of four years, let's see what he has so far been doing. Domestically, he is increasing the power of the state over the private sector. Internationally, he is reducing America's power and influence in the world. We will see overwhelming evidence of this in the coming chapters. So Obama's policies operate seemingly in opposite directions: in one area he seeks to expand state power, and in another area he seeks to diminish the power of the United States.

The interesting question is why he is doing it. We are going to test the anti-colonial theory by asking if it can explain both Obama's domestic policy and his foreign policy. That would make the theory very powerful. Other theories simply don't have this kind of reach. Consider the theory that Obama is a socialist. As I suggested in an earlier chapter, even if this is true, it can explain only Obama's economic policy, but not his foreign policy. Conversely, if Obama is a secret Muslim, this might explain his foreign policy—or his Mideast policy—but it can't account for his domestic or social policies. Muslims, for instance, aren't particularly known as advocates of socialized health care or oil drilling moratoriums or gay marriage. The beauty of the anti-colonial theory is that it makes predictions: Obama will view free market capitalism as a selfish and exploitative ideology. He will relentlessly attack its champions—whether they be rich guys or big bad corporations. He will diminish America's standard of living and burden future generations of Americans, narrowing the gap in living standards between America and the rest of the world. He will view America as the Rogue Nation and global plunderer. He will reduce America's footprint in the world, in order to prevent America from stepping on the world. He will weaken America and strengthen her enemies, so that Amercia can no longer impose its will as a neocolonial superpower.

Therefore we have to watch carefully to see if Obama is actually doing these things. Of course, those who have no clue about his ideology will always seek to explain his actions another way. Liberals in general view Obama as toeing the liberal line, or compromising away from it, even when many of Obama's actions fit neither characterization. Conservatives in general view Obama as a bungler: he doesn't understand that tax hikes don't promote economic growth; he misses the fact that government control over banking, health care, energy, and other industries makes them less efficient; he is blind to the reality that Syria and Iran are not our friends; he cannot see how his actions are isolating Israel in the world; he is dangerously naive in reducing our nuclear weapons in the expectation that this will inspire Iran and North Korea to reduce theirs; and so on. When I hear such arguments, I find my sympathies moving toward Obama; we should at least credit him with being smarter than this. I think his critics sometimes forget how much of his domestic and foreign agenda he has realized in a single term.

The anti-colonial theory gives Obama the benefit of presuming him to be at least modestly intelligent. Of course Obama understands the consequences of his actions—that's why he is doing them. He's doing what he does because he has objectives quite different than fostering economic growth; he intends to use the rod of government control to tame exploitative capitalists and severely regulate the private sector; he wants to strengthen Iran and Syria's roles in the Middle East while diminishing that of the United States; and he cares more about reducing America's nuclear arsenal than about preventing Iran from getting a nuclear bomb. I admit it is scary that a president might actually be seeking these objectives. But if my contentions are right, then we should be scared.

Let's begin the process of comparing anti-colonial ideas and presidential actions by considering domestic policy. Here, as it turns out, we have a valuable document that was produced by Barack Obama Sr. himself. In 1965, Obama Sr. published an article in the *East Africa Journal* which considered what a country should do when a large portion of its wealth is controlled by a small number of people at the top. Obama Sr. states his objective: "We need ... to eliminate power structures that have been built through excessive accumulation so that not only a few individuals shall control a vast magnitude of resources as is the case now." But how to achieve this? Obama Sr. proposes the use of state power to take over large parts of the private, or as he puts it "commercial," sector. Obama Sr. says there is no reason to worry about economic freedom or individual rights; what matters is the good of society as a whole. "We have to look at priorities in terms of what is good for society and on this basis we may find it necessary to force people to do things they would not do otherwise." Obama Sr. recommends that the state compel private firms to become what he calls "clan cooperatives." These are basically government-regulated or government-managed companies that produce goods less with a view to profit than with a view to meeting the government's own social and political objectives. Obama Sr. also proposes that the rich be dealt with through very high rates of taxation. Again, he's not worried about how much the government is confiscating. "Certainly there is no limit to taxation if the benefits derived from public services by society measure up to the cost in taxation."[2] As cited in the quotation at the beginning of this chapter, Obama Sr. is even willing to consider tax rates up to 100 percent!

It's remarkable that this paper by Obama Sr. has gotten so little media coverage. One would expect it to be on the front page of every newspaper and a lead item on the evening news, especially during public debates in America over taxes and massive government intervention in the health care and financial sectors. Notice the two-part economic strategy proposed by Obama Sr.: forced state control over private enterprise, and confiscatory tax rates with no upper limit. We will find it instructive to compare this to President Obama's economic policies. For example, President Obama frequently talks about people being forced to pay their "fair share" in taxes, but he never specifies what that share is. Here, we have a document that explicitly states his father's thoughts on the subject and may provide some guidance to the son's own thinking. Yet for many in the media, these father-son comparisons are completely taboo. For them, it seems, the ghost of Barack Obama Sr. must be quietly ignored, so it cannot be seen haunting the corridors of 1600 Pennsylvania Avenue.

Clearly the shocker of the paper is the suggestion of a 100 percent tax rate. We may think: How can a man in his right mind propose something so ridiculous? We can imagine the income tax form, a mere postcard with just two line items: a) List what you earn, and b) Send it in. Yes, by conventional economic considerations Obama Sr. is a crank. The law of incentives holds that it makes no sense to impose taxes that eliminate the motivation to work. But when we insert the anti-colonial premise, we can see why confiscatory tax rates—even 100 percent rates—do make a kind of sense. Recall that the central anti-colonial idea is theft. In this view, countries get rich through invasion and plunder, and people and corporations acquire wealth through their greedy exploitation of others. Now imagine if you came to my house and stole all my furniture. In terms of those goods, what's the appropriate tax rate for you? The answer is: 100 percent, because it's not your furniture. Thus when you assume that income is not the result of effort or work; when you assume that it is not "earned"; when you consider income and wealth to be the product of greed, exploitation, and theft; then you have no qualms about taking as much of that income and wealth as you can get away with. After all, the rich people and the corporations are a bunch of thieves; the money doesn't really belong to them! The government shouldn't seek to motivate thieves, but rather to punish them and seize their ill-gotten wealth.

The centerpiece of Obama's re-election campaign is an attack on the rich, the millionaires and billionaires, the top 1 percent of income-earners in this country. From Obama's point of view, these are greedy, selfish people who are not paying their appropriate share. Obama champions the Buffett Rule, which calls for capital gains and dividends to be taxed at a minimum rate of 30 percent. The rule is named after investment guru Warren Buffett, who declared that at 15 percent he pays a lower rate of taxation than his secretary. Buffett's observation seems to buttress Obama's point that the rich get unfair tax breaks. In fact, however, capital gains and dividends are taxed twice. They are taxed as corporate profits—and America has one of the highest corporate tax rates in the world—and then they are taxed again as payouts to individuals. The real capital gains tax rate is closer to 45 percent. Moreover, when rich people have money they can spend it or invest it; the purpose of a relatively low capital gains tax rate is to encourage them to invest it and help foster innovation and job growth. Finally, as an editorial in the *New York Times* noted, the Buffett Rule would generate an estimated $50 billion over ten years, a pittance compared to our annual trillion-dollar deficit. Even if Obama got his way, the *Times* conceded, his solution would "not make an appreciable dent in the deficit." In fact, I'd like to add, it would not pay for a single one of Obama's extravagant spending programs.[3]

Rich people already pay a lot of taxes; indeed, they shoulder most of the nation's income tax burden. Government data show that the top 1 percent of U.S. taxpayers currently pay around 40 percent of all federal taxes. The top 10 percent pay 70 percent of all taxes. About half of Americans pay no federal income tax, and nearly 25 percent pay no taxes whatsoever. Now these numbers reflect what the government takes in from various groups. But what percentage of their income do those groups actually pay? According to the Tax Foundation, the average federal income tax for the top 1 percent is 25 percent. The average for the middle-fifth of income earners is 14 percent. The average for the bottom half is 3 percent. Anomalies like Warren Buffett aside, it is simply false to say that the rich are paying less than the rest in taxes; they are actually paying a lot more.[4]

Never once has Obama made the case for why the rich ought to pay a higher percentage in taxes than they currently do. And there is a solid economic argument for avoiding confiscatory taxes on this group. During the Reagan years, economist Arthur Laffer

famously devised his "Laffer Curve." The curve posits that there are
two levels of taxation that produce an identical level of government
revenue. Imagine two scenarios: a tax rate of 0 percent and a tax
rate of 100 percent. In both cases, the amount of revenue the government can expect in tax receipts is zero. In the first case the
answer is obvious: the government doesn't tax people, and so it
doesn't take in any money. But Laffer's point is that a 100 percent
tax rate produces the same result; if the state takes away everything
that a group of citizens produces, then they have no incentive to
work and so will produce nothing. Once this principle is grasped,
the Laffer Curve becomes self-evident. Laffer's core contention is
that once the marginal tax rate—the rate on an additional dollar of
income—reaches a certain point, it has such a deleterious effect on
incentives that entrepreneurs will stop producing and the government will take in less money. Now no one knows exactly what this
tipping point is, but tax policy for three decades has been based on
keeping rates away from this tipping point. In recent years, some
liberal economists like Emmanuel Saez have insisted that we are
not at the tipping point yet; from Saez's point of view, higher tax
rates on the rich would not have a measurable impact on their
productivity.[5]

One might expect Obama to join this debate, but he hasn't. The
reason is evident from a 2008 interview that Obama did with Charlie Gibson of ABC News. The topic was raising the capital gains tax
rate on the rich.

> **Gibson:** George Bush has taken it down to 15 percent.
> And in each instance, when the rate dropped, revenues
> from the tax increased—the government took in more
> money. And in the 1980s, when the tax was increased to
> 28 percent, the revenues went down. So why raise it at

all, especially given the fact that 100 million people in this country own stock and would be affected?

Obama: Well, Charlie, what I've said is that I would look at raising the capital gains tax for purposes of fairness.

Gibson: But history shows that when you drop the capital gains tax, the revenues go up.

Obama: Well, that might happen, or it might not.[6]

It's worth pausing to ponder what Obama is saying. Basically, he is saying that it doesn't matter whether higher tax rates on the rich generate additional revenues for the government or not. This is not about government revenue. Rather, Obama's own basic notion of fairness demands that the rich pay more. Perhaps—to take a cue from his father's paper—if the highest income earners paid tax rates of "up to 100 percent," Obama would finally be satisfied that they were contributing their fair share.

Since we're back to Obama Sr.'s paper for the moment, it's worth recalling the second theme of that paper. Not only did Obama Sr. recommend limitless tax rates, but he also called for the state to use its power to control and dominate the institutions of the private sector. For Obama Sr. the private sector is the neocolonial sector. This sector is made up of the big bad corporations: banks, insurance companies, pharmaceutical companies, oil companies, and so on. Obama Sr. proposed that the government seize control of these industries and turn them from private profit-making entities into regulated arms of the state. In effect, he called for turning them into state utilities serving socialist conceptions of the public good.

How does the vision of Obama Sr. match up with the actions of Obama Jr.? After four years of Obama's presidency, we can see that there is a very good match. Obama used the banking crisis to establish the strong arm of government control over the banks. He backed the so-called Dodd-Frank legislation that basically empowers the government to take over any financial institution it considers to be imperiled; the government can then run that institution however it wants. The Dodd-Frank Bill is an 848-page encyclopedia containing 400 or so rules; moreover, nearly every page asks regulators to fill in the details by adding more rules. Already Dodd-Frank has dramatically raised the cost of doing business for the financial sector, and according to *Investor's Business Daily* it may force 1,000 small banks to close down.[7]

Next Obama pushed through his health care reform—commonly dubbed Obamacare—without a single Republican vote. Obamacare takes the reach of government regulation far beyond what it has been previously. While upholding Obamacare under the government's taxing power, the Supreme Court recognized this. Previously the government could tell you what you couldn't buy; Obamacare is a case of the government telling you what you must buy. Imagine if the government, in the name of protecting your health, told you that you must buy exercise equipment or two pounds of broccoli every week at the supermarket. Most of us would consider that a ridiculous overreach, an infringement of personal liberty. Well, Obamacare is the same, because it forces people who don't want to buy health insurance to buy health insurance. Moreover, Obamacare, like Dodd-Frank, institutionalizes a labyrinth of new rules, regulations, fines, costs, penalties, boards, and bureaucracies. The federal government can now specify who must have insurance, how much insurance companies can charge, what profit they can make, which medical ailments receive coverage, and what doctors are paid. Further, as *The Economist* noted, "the bill does almost nothing to control costs."[8] Obamacare, which takes effect in 2014, represents a government takeover of one-sixth of America's economy.

In keeping with the recommendations of his father, Obama has not opted for nationalization of private industries; rather, he has pursued what may be called decolonization. The government doesn't own the assets of the private sector, but it does essentially control them, at least when it decides it's time to step in. Obama has also increased regulation of the auto industry, the coal industry, and the oil industry. In each case the pretext is different—we have to protect the homeowner, we have to save Detroit, we have to widen the availability of health insurance, we have to protect the environment—but the effect is always the same. To a degree that seemed almost inconceivable four years ago, large domains of private industry are now under government control. If you had read Obama Sr.'s paper four years ago, you might have seen it coming.

So what's next? If Obama is re-elected, Americans can over the next four years expect to see a sharp increase in a whole host of taxes. The good news for Obama is that he doesn't have to do anything to achieve this increase. It occurs automatically, with the expiration of the Bush tax cuts. So the top tax rate is scheduled to rise in 2013 from 35 percent to 39.6 percent. The top rate on long-term capital gains will rise from 15 to 24 percent, and on dividends it will jump from 15 to 44 percent. The death tax, which is currently 35 percent and kicks in at $5 million, will go up to an astonishing 55 percent, and the tax kicks in at just $1 million.

Obama's re-election means that these increases are a done deal. But if we know anything about Obama, they are only a starting point. He will push for much higher rates, and if he has a Democratic Congress, he will probably prevail. Moreover, we can expect Obama to seek increased federal control over industries that are now not under the full control of the federal government. Education at the grade school level is already under government control—and largely for this reason, it is a mess. But higher education, although regulated, remains mostly private, and America has a higher education system that, for all its problems, remains the envy of the world. If the federal government largely takes over higher education, we can expect America's colleges and universities to go the way of our public schools.

Doesn't all this point to a poorer, less efficient America? Isn't the American standard of living, which has been stagnant at best over the past four years, likely to decline over the next four? Yes, and I believe this is what Obama wants; it is part of his anti-colonial objective. The objective is not to stimulate American business or boost productivity, but to make the rich and the big bad corporations pay for their misdeeds. It is to punish these greedy, selfish exploiters for what they have done to the rest of us, and to the rest of the world. If Obama has to bring down the economy in order to bring down the fat cats he loathes so much, if he has to sap America's economic vitality to end America's reign as a global superpower, I believe he will do it.

CHAPTER NINE

DRILLING THERE BUT NOT HERE

We can't drive our SUVs and eat as much as we want and keep our homes on 72 degrees at all times … and then just expect that other countries are going to say okay…. That's not going to happen.[1]

—Barack Obama, speech in Roseburg, Oregon, May 2008

Scarcity is a major theme with Barack Obama. In his inaugural address he issued a specific warning to rich countries like the United States: "And to nations like ours that enjoy relative plenty, we say we can no longer afford indifference to suffering outside our borders, nor can we consume the world's resources without regard to effect." One of Obama's constant refrains is that "we consume more than 20 percent of the world's oil but we have less than 2 percent of the world's oil reserves." Listening to Obama, we get the sense that the problem with energy is that there is just too little of it to go around. Americans have, as Obama puts it, become "addicted" to oil and this has made us dependent on oil from the Middle East. As Obama sees it, we have to break this addiction. Part of the solution, as Obama portrays it, is for America to shift to wind and solar energy, which are both harnessed from nature itself. But since wind and solar cannot for the foreseeable future solve our energy demands, the simple reality is that Americans must learn to consume less.[2]

The only problem with this "reality" is that it is not congruent with the facts. America has vast resources of oil that are not being tapped. Moreover, America has pioneered the new technology of hydraulic fracturing—fracking—which not only facilitates oil exploration, but also opens up a 100-year supply of cheap natural gas. Already fracking accounts for 20 percent of domestic natural gas production, and it is growing so fast it could soon account for half of it. Fracking, like oil exploration, is a labor-intensive industry that creates hundreds of thousands of well-paying jobs. This has already happened in places like Texas, Arkansas, Oklahoma, and North Dakota. While America is a large oil importer, the nation has the chance with natural gas to be a big exporter. Together, America's untapped oil and natural gas reserves offer an unprecedented opportunity for the country to reduce its reliance on foreign energy and also to boost its economy at a time when it could use a little boosting.

Oddly, however, the Obama administration has been blocking oil drilling in America, and it is already moving to restrict and control the use of fracking. Indeed, Obama actively promotes policies that reduce America's access to energy, raise energy prices, and cost jobs which often end up moving abroad. These policies seem not only ill-advised, but politically risky for Obama. So why would he do this? The obvious explanation is that Obama is a dedicated environmentalist, deeply worried about global warming and oil spills and wary of the environmental and safety risks involved in the relatively new technology of fracking.

Yet this environmental explanation of Obama's behavior is clearly wrong. Even as Obama blocks and restricts energy exploration in America, he has been helping other countries exploit their energy resources. Specifically, the Obama administration has bankrolled oil drilling in Brazil, Colombia, and Mexico. This oil is destined not for export to America, but for Brazil's, Colombia's, and Mexico's own use, which includes selling some of it to the Chinese. Obama also supports massive wealth transfers from the West to the developing world so that developing countries can grow and meet their increasing demands for energy.

So what explains Obama's double standard? Why is Obama generally opposed to drilling and increased energy use over here while he supports drilling and more energy use in other countries?

Here is where our anti-colonial theory pays big dividends. Our theory predicts that Obama should want to enrich the previously colonized countries at the expense of previous and current colonizers. Anti-colonialists insist that since the West grew rich by looting the resources and raw materials of the colonies, it is time for global payback. The West must have less and the rest must have more. Unlike in the colonial era, we are no longer concerned with cotton, corn, or groundnuts; today there is a global demand for oil and other forms of energy. So Obama is attempting a global redistribution of energy. Now if this anti-colonial way of thinking is deeply imprinted in Obama's mind, we might not be surprised to see Obama push this agenda despite the political risk.

From the time he assumed office, Obama began his ideological crusade against the American oil industry, cancelling dozens of oil and gas lease sales, even at the cost of thousands of new jobs and billions of dollars of economic activity. The oil spill in the Gulf of Mexico gave Obama a good pretext to impose a moratorium on oil-drilling; even when the moratorium was eventually lifted, the Obama administration issued only a small number of drilling permits. In the energy industry, this came to be known as Obama's "permitorium." The number of exploration and development permits issued by the Obama administration was at only about half the level of permits issued prior to the moratorium. Companies had equipment that went unused, and jobs were lost. Eventually much of that equipment and those jobs moved abroad, creating work someplace else and boosting economies other than that of the United States.

In the months leading up to the midterm election, Obama announced a plan to open parts of the Atlantic coastline, the eastern Gulf of Mexico, and the north coast of Alaska to oil and natural gas drilling. Even though the plan was a modest one—the coastline north of New Jersey, the entire Pacific Coast, and Alaska's Bristol Bay were all closed to drilling—some environmental groups like the Sierra Club protested, with one executive fretting about the effect on "marine life and coastal tourist economies." Still, the tone was muted. After all, as the *New York Times* reported, "drilling in much of the newly opened areas, if it takes place, would not begin for years" because the Obama Interior Department planned to "spend several years conducting geologic and environmental studies" to determine if each area was "deemed suitable for development." If not, no drilling could take place. So what Obama was "giving" through his announcement his administration could easily "take away" through delays and regulation. And with the exception of approving Royal Dutch Shell's proposal to drill four wells in the Beaufort Sea off Alaska's north coast, the Obama administration has imposed regulatory hurdles and allowed very little actual drilling in the new areas.[3]

In November 2011, the Obama State Department announced that it would delay indefinitely a final decision on the Keystone pipeline which would transport Canadian oil through American markets. Alberta, Canada, has some of the largest oil reserves in the world, and the Canadians wanted their pipeline—parts of which have already been built—to bring Alberta oil to Texas Gulf Coast refineries. The pipeline would also transport oil and natural gas drawn from shale formations around the Rocky Mountains. Canadian oil is so plentiful that experts say it could meet U.S. oil needs for two centuries. What American would not rather buy from the Canadians than from Hugo Chavez in Venezuela or from the Muslims of the Middle East? The Keystone pipeline, experts said, would quickly produce 20,000 new American jobs, with as many as 65,000 more by 2020.

Yet the Obama administration refused to approve the project, delaying a final decision for perhaps another two years, stunning the Canadians who assumed its merits were obvious. Congress attempted to pressure Obama to expedite the pipeline review and make a decision. But Obama refused, saying the congressional deadline was "arbitrary." Not surprisingly, the Canadians are furious. Canadian Prime Minister Stephen Harper said Canada would not allow its energy future to be held hostage to a process that could be "hijacked." Canada, he said, would "continue to work to diversify its energy exports." Natural Resource Minister Joe Oliver said that meant relying less on the United States and "expanding our markets, including the growing Asian market." Translation: If the Americans don't want to work with us, we can always sell to the Chinese.[4]

Many in America professed surprise and bafflement at Obama's Keystone decision. "Here's the single greatest shovel-ready project in America," said Senate Minority Leader Mitch McConnell, "and for some reason he's suddenly not interested." Critics said that Obama must be a fervent environmentalist or a victim of pressure from the environmental lobby. "To give the go-ahead before the election," wrote columnist Joe Nocera, "was to risk losing the support of environmentalists who make up an important part of his base." Yes, there was certainly environmentalist opposition to Keystone. But the State Department's detailed review showed that the project would cause no significant environmental impact, and Obama needs to be concerned about another constituency—workers— as much as he does about environmentalists. Nocera himself concluded that Obama was wrong to refuse Keystone, and he said he couldn't blame the Canadians for doing business with the Chinese. "At least one country in North America understands where its national interests lie. Too bad it's not us."[5]

If you're thinking along anti-colonial lines, you will immediately recognize that Obama understands perfectly well what our national interests are; it is precisely to undermine those interests that he opposes Keystone.

There are environmental interests involved as well, but not in the way that most might think. In his September 23, 2009, speech at the United Nations, Obama said, "We must … energize our efforts to put other developing nations … on a path to sustainable growth. Those nations do not have the same resources to combat climate change…. That is why we have a responsibility to provide the financial and technical assistance needed to help those nations…. We seek an agreement that will allow all nations to grow and raise living standards without endangering the planet."

So here is Obama's idea. The rich countries, specifically Europe and the United States, pay to reduce their own carbon emissions. Then the same rich countries make large transfers of wealth to the developing countries so that those countries can continue to grow in an environmentally responsible way. The amount the Obama administration has agreed to—a number derived from a United Nations scheme—is around $100 billion a year. This money would enable the developing countries to develop, but with a limited impact on the environment, because while developing countries use more energy, the West would use less. The developing countries will be happy because their economic growth will be subsidized by the rich countries, and the rich countries should agree because, as Obama put it, "the developed nations that caused much of the damage to our climate over the last century ... have a responsibility to lead." Call it global climate reparations. But for Obama this $100 billion is only a first step. Speaking at the Summit of the Americas in Trinidad in 2009, Obama said that America would join with other countries "to set aside over a trillion dollars for countries going through difficult times, recognizing that we have to provide assistance to those countries that are most vulnerable." For Obama, what it all comes down to is: we pay, and they develop.[6]

This may seem like a very peculiar sort of environmentalism, and it is, because it's not really about environmentalism at all. I noticed this a few years ago, when I saw a headline in the *Wall Street Journal*, "Obama Underwrites Offshore Oil Drilling." As the article explained, "The Obama administration is financing oil exploration off Brazil." I read that the U.S. Export-Import Bank had given an initial commitment letter for $2 billion in loans and loan guarantees to the Brazilian state-owned company Petrobras to drill for oil in the Santos Basin near Rio de Janeiro. The *Journal* expressed bafflement. "Americans are right to wonder why Obama is underwriting in Brazil what he won't allow at home."[7]

I reported this incident in *The Roots of Obama's Rage*, drawing a torrent of criticism from the left-wing watchdog group Media Matters. The group noted that several of the people who had approved the Export-Import transaction were Bush appointees. This, of course, might be true, but policy is set by the Obama administration. And as it turns out, billionaire George Soros, a major Obama supporter and funder of leftist causes in the United States, has a substantial investment in Petrobras, the Brazilian company receiving the American subsidy.

So was Obama repaying a big donor and political ally? I don't know, but Obama's defenders who claim he was not involved in the Brazil subsidy were recently confounded by Obama himself. Obama visited Brazil in March 2011 and praised America's financing of Brazilian oil exploration. "We want to help you with the technology and support to develop these oil reserves safely," Obama told the Brazilians. "The United States could not be happier with the potential for a new, stable source of energy. And when you're ready to start selling, we want to be one of your best customers." Back in America, Gulf Oil CEO Joe Petrowski said he found Obama's remarks "puzzling." Petrowski made the obvious point that "it would be a lot better if we had the drilling here." And Senator Mark Begich, Democrat of Alaska, said that "President Obama didn't have to go all the way to Brazil to find a new, safe and stable source of oil. Energy opportunities are right here in Alaska." As for the Brazilians, they welcomed Obama's subsidy, but they have decided to sell most of their surplus oil to the Chinese. Just a month after Obama's visit, Brazilian president Dilma Rousseff headed to Beijing to sign contracts to sell oil to two gigantic Chinese state-owned companies.[8]

If the Obama administration made a single loan to Brazil for oil drilling, that could perhaps be discounted as an isolated episode. But around the same time, the Export-Import Bank guaranteed a $1 billion loan to Mexico. And this money was for Mexico to drill in, you guessed it, the Gulf of Mexico. One news report said, "Despite President Obama's moratorium on U.S. deepwater drilling in the Gulf of Mexico, the U.S. Export-Import Bank intends to guarantee $1 billion in loans to PEMEX, the Mexican state oil company, to bolster the company's oil drilling in the region." Earlier, we learn, the Export-Import Bank "also guaranteed two loans totaling

$300 million made by a commercial lender." And in May 2011 the Export-Import Bank disclosed that it had just approved $2.84 billion in financing for an oil refinery project in Colombia. The bank's press release noted that the money was for direct loans and loan guarantees for Colombia's Refineria de Cartagena SA (Reficar), a majority owned and controlled subsidiary of Colombia's national oil company Ecopetrol. The release boasted that "the financing approved for Reficar amounts to the second largest transaction ever approved by the Bank." Just a few months earlier, the Export-Import Bank approved an additional $880 million in other loans and guarantees to Reficar's parent company Ecopetrol. So the total amount of financing provided by the U.S. government to the Colombian oil company and its subsidiaries amounted to $3.72 billion.[9] Clearly there is a pattern here—the Obama administration is doling out billions in U.S. taxpayer money to finance oil drilling in Brazil, Mexico, and Colombia.

How then can we sum up Obama's energy policy? When it comes to developing countries, Obama's philosophy seems to be: Drill, baby, drill. But when it comes to the United States, Obama takes the opposite tack. Oil drilling? Let's block it when we can, and delay it with regulations when we must. Nuclear energy? No way. Coal? The Obama administration has issued new regulations that make it virtually impossible to build new coal power plants, and a few years ago Obama candidly said he sought to make coal power generation so expensive that existing coal plants would have to close. And now, the Obama administration has targeted fracking. Even though burning natural gas emits half as much carbon dioxide as coal, the Obama administration has been waging, as Steve Forbes put it, "an undeclared war against hydraulic fracturing methods of extracting natural gas."[10]

I predict that if Obama is re-elected this will only get worse. He will heavily restrict, if not shut down, the fracking industry. His pretext will be environmental and safety concerns, although his real reason will be quite different: anti-colonial leveling. If Obama succeeds, it would be catastrophic for the U.S. economy, which is an energy-driven economy. America has been, in effect, a hostage to foreign energy for half a century; now, thanks to Obama, we could lose our chance to take the lead as a global energy producer. Such chances don't come often, and if they are missed they seldom return. But that is precisely what Obama wants. In the name of his global redistributionist agenda, which calls for an equalization of living standards around the world, he wants to choke off America's chance for energy independence.

CHAPTER TEN

DISARMING THE ROGUE NATION

We have met the enemy, and he is us.
—Pogo

Three decades ago, President Ronald Reagan mobilized America's defenses to combat what he termed the "evil empire." The term was controversial, but at the same time accurate. The Soviet Union, after all, had an empire that included Poland, the Baltic States, and the rest of Eastern Europe, and the Soviets had occupied Afghanistan and had satellites in Cuba, Nicaragua, and a dozen or so other countries. Meanwhile, since the end of the Vietnam War, America had been in retreat across the world. Reagan set out to reverse this trend. He led a massive military buildup to counter the Soviets. He authorized the building of MX missiles and deployed medium-range missiles in Europe. He initiated the Strategic Defense Initiative, a missile defense program, to shoot down missiles fired at America or our allies. Reagan's goal was not merely containment but rollback—to push the Soviet Union back behind its original borders. Ultimately Reagan got even more than he bargained for. The Communist regime itself disintegrated, and Russia ceased to be a global superpower.

Now, thirty years later, we have a very different kind of president. If our theory is right, he is a man who views the United States as the evil empire, or perhaps we could say, the rogue nation. While Reagan pursued "peace through strength," Obama has pursued what may be termed "peace through weakness." To this end he slashes America's defense spending, even while potential enemies like China are rapidly expanding their military capabilities; he blocks missile defenses, both here and for our allies; and he dramatically reduces our nuclear stockpile, possibly to only a few hundred missiles, and eventually to none. The anti-colonialist theory predicts that Obama would seek not just containment but also the rollback of imperial America. Obama's ultimate wish would be for America to lose its position of unparalleled military supremacy and become, like the Soviet Union, a former global superpower, or, to put it differently, a second Canada.

It may seem odd for Americans to hear others—let alone their president—think of their country as an evil empire. We don't consider our nation, for all its flaws, to be a rogue nation. That's a term we associate with Iran or North Korea. Those are, after all, the bad guys. In North Korea's case, the rogue regime already has around ten nuclear bombs and seeks to build more. Iran has made rapid and startling progress in building its own nuclear capability, which would make Iran the first Muslim government in the Middle East to possess nuclear weapons. Here in America we perceive these as troubling developments, and hold that they pose a serious threat to peace and global security. But there is a hidden assumption behind this way of thinking. We assume that we are the good guys.

It is this assumption that the anti-colonial ideology calls into question. The anti-colonial assumption is that we are the bad guys. Let's see how this changes the whole equation. Consider the nuclear map of the Middle East. How many Muslim bombs are there now in the Middle East? None. The Iranians are trying to go from zero to one. How many Jewish bombs? Quite a few—no one knows how many bombs the Israelis have. How many Western bombs? A whole, whole lot. America has the capacity to blow up the entire region using just a few of its nuclear weapons. Anti-colonialists insist that the nuclear problem in the Middle East isn't Iran, it's America. Who cares if the Iranians get a single bomb or even a dozen bombs? From the anti-colonial point of view, nuclear bombs would actually give Iran a way to counter Israeli and American aggression. Meanwhile, America has the most sophisticated nuclear arsenal in the world, and America is the only country that has actually used nuclear weapons. Therefore, the anti-colonial mission is not to worry about Iran building a single nuclear bomb but rather to slash the American nuclear arsenal.

Now let's see how this anti-colonial approach squares with Obama's behavior. Just fifteen months into his presidency, in April 2010, Obama held a Nuclear Security Summit in Washington, D.C. The objective was to enhance global security by reducing the threat posed by nuclear weapons. Obama called for a "new international effort" aimed at "stopping the spread of nuclear weapons."[1] Observers, however, noticed that neither Iran nor North Korea was represented at the summit. They weren't even invited.[2] So who was there? America and its allies, some forty nations in all. Apparently Obama's idea was to stop the spread of nuclear weapons by reducing the number of weapons possessed by America and its allies.

Liberals and conservatives weighed in on the summit, and somewhat predictably both groups missed what Obama was doing. For

Jonathan Alter, Obama cheerleader, America and its allies could, by slashing their nuclear arsenals "advance efforts to pressure Iran to curtail its own nuclear program." This is classic Alter: a ridiculous assertion unaccompanied by any evidence or argument. If I slash my nuclear arsenal, how does that "pressure" you to stop building yours? The absurdity of Alter's claim was effectively countered by conservative columnist Charles Krauthammer. Krauthammer said it was dangerously naive of Obama to assume that if America set a good example by reducing its nuclear stockpile, the Iranians would meekly forgo their aspiration to build nuclear bombs.[3] Krauthammer's logic was entirely sound, but his whole argument was based on the premise that Obama's actions were aimed at influencing Iranian behavior. In that case, Obama would not only be naive; he would be a complete fool. But Obama is not a complete fool, so we have to reconsider the argument. What if Obama had no intention of influencing Iran at all? What if his goal was to achieve the result he was actually achieving, namely, reducing the nuclear arsenals of America and the West? In that case, Obama would be the one guy who knew what he was doing, and his critics would be the ones who were being naive.

Obama's efforts—or perhaps we should say non-efforts—to stop Iran from getting a nuclear bomb are illustrative of his lackadaisical attitude. For the past several years, America has pushed for sanctions against Iran. Each time the sanctions get a bit tougher, but really tough sanctions are impossible to coordinate since Russia and China, which have extensive commercial and military dealings with Iran, won't go along. And clearly the sanctions aren't working; Iran continues to make steady progress. In November 2011 the International Atomic Energy Agency, a division of the United Nations, provided new evidence that makes a "credible" case that "Iran has carried out activities relevant to the development of a nuclear device." Experts estimate that Iran could be months, or at most a year or two, away from being able to build such a device. This gives Iran the option of sharing its nuclear secrets with terrorist groups or, even scarier, of developing a plan for removing Israel from the map, a kind of Second Holocaust. At the very least, one would expect a sense of urgency on the part of Obama to stop this. The *New York Times* reported that the Obama administration's response to the new report of Iran's atomic progress was "strikingly muted."[4] Indeed, Obama's efforts seem focused not on deterring Iran but rather on deterring Israel from acting to bomb the Iranian nuclear facilities. Consequently, most intelligence analysts in America have become reconciled to the fact that Iran is soon going to get a bomb, and at that point there is not a whole lot anyone can do—at least not without risking that bomb going off and causing massive devastation and global economic upheaval.

None of this is to suggest that Obama is indifferent to the dangers posed by nuclear weapons. He is acutely alert to those dangers—but for him the dangers seem to be posed mainly by the United States. Once again, Obama's actions speak much more clearly than his words. In 2009, when Obama took office, the United States had approximately 5,000 nuclear warheads in its arsenal. Obama resolutely set about slashing that number. In 2011, Obama negotiated an arms reduction treaty with Russia, the so-called START treaty, in which both countries agreed to reduce their warhead count to 1,550. America and Russia also limited their launchers to 700. In convincing the U.S. Senate to support the treaty, Obama promised to modernize America's existing nuclear assets—a promise he subsequently abandoned. Some of the provisions of the treaty were downright odd: the limit on 700 launchers imposed no restrictions on Russia, for example, since Russia already had fewer than 700 launchers. So that was a unilateral restraint on the United States.

Once START was ratified and became law, Obama went much further. According to recent reports, he has asked the Pentagon to study reducing America's nuclear deterrent by up to 80 percent, which would bring us down to around 300 strategic warheads.[5]

All of this is occurring at a time when other nuclear-armed nations like China are expanding and modernizing their arsenals. Undoubtedly the leaders of those nations view with surprise bordering on incomprehension America's decision to wipe out the bulk of its own defensive arsenal. At this rate, China will soon have nuclear parity with the United States; eventually other nations may also reach this point. It is worth noting that never before in history has a global superpower disarmed itself so rapidly and so thoroughly.

It may seem to the uninformed that even 300 nuclear warheads is plenty. Who needs more in this post-Cold War era? But consider the following scenario. America has 300 warheads; so do Russia and China. Russia and China make an alliance with each other, and each nation agrees to launch 150 warheads against America in a first strike. True, America's entire arsenal won't be wiped out; some of the Russian and Chinese warheads may miss, and some of our warheads are carried on submarines and bombers that are much harder to target. Let's assume America has enough warheads left to destroy a dozen Chinese cities and a dozen Russian cities. America can strike back, to be sure, but if it does, the Russians and the Chinese have an additional 150 warheads each with which they can level every major American city. The point is that America is now deterred from striking back, because it fears a completely devastating second strike that would basically end America as we know it. These are not wild speculations; they are precisely the "war games" that the Pentagon has played since the dawn of the nuclear age. The Cold War is over, but the logic of deterrence has not changed.

Nuclear weapons are dangerous, but when two countries have a lot of weapons they are less likely to attack each other, because there are plenty of warheads left over to strike back. The paradoxical conclusion is that when a nation like the United States draws down to just a few dozen, or a couple hundred, warheads, it is actually increasing the danger of being attacked. A world in which nations have just a few nuclear weapons is in some ways a more perilous world than one in which those same nations have a lot. And a world in which there are no nuclear weapons may be the most dangerous of all, because even when the weapons are gone, the knowledge of how to make them remains, and in this situation the country that goes ahead and builds them first is in a position to obliterate its adversaries.

It is against this backdrop that we should understand Obama's speech, delivered in April 2009 in Prague, in which he said, "I state clearly and with conviction America's commitment to seek the peace and security of a world without nuclear weapons." Obama insisted that the United States should lead the march to global nuclear disarmament. Why? Not because we are the world's leader. Rather, "As the only nuclear power to have used a nuclear weapon, the United States has a moral responsibility to act."[6] Thus we should go first as an act of repentance. And in Obama's case repentance means unilateral nuclear disarmament. Obama calls for the whole world to get rid of its nuclear weapons and then, while the rest of the world ignores him, he sets about slashing the nuclear arsenal of the one nation that he happens to be in charge of, namely, his own.

Now Ronald Reagan during the 1980s also spoke of a world free of nuclear weapons. But Reagan had no intention of America disarming while other nations built up. Moreover, Reagan had a solution to the problem of vulnerability. That solution was missile defense. Reagan believed that if America was in a position to shoot down incoming missiles, then it could secure itself against outside attack. What makes Obama different is that he is disarming America's nuclear arsenal while also curtailing our missile defense program. Early in his presidency, Obama cut back on missile defense systems in Alaska and California. More recently, Obama seems to have signaled to Russia's former president Dmitry Medvedev that, upon re-election, he will grant further concessions on America's missile defenses. Nor does Obama want America's allies to have such defenses. A couple years earlier, Obama canceled an anti-missile system planned for Poland, as well as a missile-detecting radar system planned for the Czech Republic.

Now admittedly nuclear arsenals and missile defenses are only one aspect, although an important aspect, of a nation's defense program. America also has a Defense Department that manages an army, a navy, an air force, and the Marines. In fact, the bulk of military spending goes toward conventional forces. America has these forces deployed around the world, but especially in trouble spots: in the Middle East, to maintain stability and secure access to oil supplies; in Europe, to protect our strongest allies; in Asia, to protect South Korea from North Korea and Taiwan from China. Recognizing that more than one war can break out at a time, America's defense strategy has long been to prepare to fight two wars simultaneously: this way, for example, we can deal with a Middle East conflict while also protecting Taiwan from a Chinese invasion. If Obama wanted to reduce America's nuclear dependency but maintain America's strong defenses, we would expect him to push for a substantial increase in conventional force readiness and also in overall defense spending.

Actually, Obama has moved in the opposite direction. In 2009, Obama ordered $330 billion in defense cuts. The next year, he convinced Defense Secretary Robert Gates to pare an additional $100 billion. In 2011, Obama chopped an additional $487 billion from the Pentagon, thus bringing his total cuts to nearly a trillion dollars. The cumulative effect, according to General Martin Dempsey, chairman of the Joint Chiefs of Staff, is that the United States can no longer expect to be a global power.[7]

Obama usually announces his defense cuts with a practiced long face, and he says the cuts are necessary to reduce deficit spending. We have to, says our frugal man in the White House, put "our fiscal house in order." And of course Obama is right that our fiscal house is not in order. I quite agree that in dire economic times, government programs that we now have may prove unaffordable, and defense is no exception. Obama's Benihana defense policy could perhaps be justified in terms of a tough economy and national belt-tightening. But that is not Obama's scenario. He has been cutting the military while pushing for huge increases in domestic spending. While the defense department is being cut to the bone, other programs like health care and "green" technologies are bloated with money. Obama shows no evident interest in reducing overall spending, only in reducing military spending.

The consequences are already being felt on America's role in the world. Even with his rhetorical legerdemain, Obama has to acknowledge this. Given all that has happened in the Middle East and across the Muslim world—the subject of the next two chapters—Obama cannot deny that American power has greatly waned in those regions. Consequently he has sought to deflect the public's attention with a much-publicized "pivot" to Asia. By itself this may seem far-sighted, a sound recognition of the growing power of China. But in Obama's case, things are rarely as they seem. Obama has not actually redeployed America's defense forces to the Pacific. He has not increased the targeting of Chinese military assets. In fact, his "pivot" seems to be mostly a rhetorical move, unaccompanied by any change in strategy or measurable increase in force levels.

So America's military is in a bad way in 2012; what can we expect in 2016? If Obama is re-elected, we can expect further weakening. In my view, Obama's goal is to introduce fear in the United States—fear of an Iranian bomb, fear of the rising strength of China, fear of a first strike, fear of cities being incinerated. Obama's hope, if our theory is correct, is that fear will keep America humble. Call it humility through vulnerability. And in this way Obama hopes that America will stop acting like the evil empire. We will stop throwing our weight around and invading and bullying the rest of the world. Rather, we will accept that we have become, like the old Soviet Union, an irrelevant power, or like Canada, a large and harmless country. Instead of using American power to make the world safe for liberty or for democracy, Obama intends to use his own power to make the world safe from America.

CHAPTER ELEVEN

THE JIHADI AS FREEDOM FIGHTER

As the American approach to countering the Soviet menace came to be known as the "doctrine of containment," the Obama Doctrine may come to be known as the "doctrine of self-containment."[1]

—Douglas Feith and Seth Cropsey, *Commentary*

In this chapter, I intend to resolve the conundrum of why many people assume Obama is a Muslim. Obama, as we have seen, is not a Muslim. Yet polls show that approximately one-fourth of Americans suspect him of being one.[2] This is odd and requires explanation. Because I was born in India, people often presume I am either a doctor or a software guy. They are wrong, but they make that assumption because there are lots of Indian doctors and software guys in the United States. By the same token, Obama is not a Muslim, so why do so many people believe he is?

The surveys don't tell us, but it's probably because Obama seems so weirdly solicitous of Muslims and Muslim causes. One of Obama's first actions as president was to retire the phrase "war on terror," which he thought was too easily conflated with a war on Muslims. Obama took the position that America was simply battling an international criminal outfit called al-Qaeda whose members happened to be Muslim. Obama supported the construction of the Ground Zero mosque despite strong opposition from New Yorkers, especially Jews. As I documented in *The Roots of Obama's Rage*, Obama tacitly approved the Scottish government's release of the Lockerbie bomber Abdelbaset al-Megrahi—a terrorist responsible for the deaths of hundreds of Americans—so long as the man remained in Scotland. Obama sought to move jihadis from the detention center at Guantanamo Bay to civilian prisons in the United States. His Justice Department opposed military trials that would treat jihadis captured in Iraq and Afghanistan as war criminals. Instead, the Obama administration sought to give them civilian trials and provide them with constitutional rights and free legal counsel. Several radical lawyers who had previously represented or advocated on behalf of Muslim terrorists were subsequently hired by the Obama Justice Department. Obama also opposed terrorist interrogation techniques like sleep deprivation and water-dunking ("water-boarding") even though those techniques would subsequently lead to information about the whereabouts of Osama Bin Laden.

True, Obama was thwarted on some of his goals. Even Democratic members of Congress protested moving Muslim terrorists to prisons in their districts. So the detention center at Guantanamo remains open. Under pressure from both parties, and some in his own administration, Obama agreed to try 9/11 mastermind Khalid Sheikh Mohammed and some of his co-conspirators in a military court, although the venue of other terrorist trials is undecided. Yet in other ways Obama has been successful. The military has abandoned the very same interrogation techniques that resulted in the tracking of Bin Laden to his Abbottabad compound. The Islamic

Center near Ground Zero has been built. The Lockerbie bomber was released, and Scotland went one better by sending him home to Libya, where he lived as a free man until his death recently from cancer.

Obama's behavior in all this seems downright baffling. Consider the idea of giving civilian trials and constitutional rights to captured war criminals. In World War II the idea would have been considered so outlandish that no one seriously proposed it. The Nuremberg trials were military tribunals, and they were held only after the war ended. The rights in the U.S. Constitution are reserved for U.S. citizens; they emerge out of a social compact among people who implicitly agree to live under the same laws, pay taxes, and share certain social obligations. These rights don't automatically extend to illegal aliens, and they certainly don't apply to Muslim jihadis apprehended in foreign wars against the United States. Even if we consider international law, the Geneva Convention applies only to states that have approved the rules of the Convention. The jihadis don't represent a state, and they aren't conventional soldiers in that they don't wear uniforms or operate in accordance with the rules of war. They extend to their captives no protections whatever. Consequently, they have placed themselves outside the orbit of Geneva Convention rules. All of this is well known, so why does Obama persist? His behavior on behalf of the Muslim jihadis seems so inexplicable that some people conclude that Obama must be a closet Muslim.

But actually there's an anti-colonial explanation for Obama's conduct that works much better. Obama views America as an imperial invader, occupier, and aggressor that has looted Iraq and Afghanistan, while America's ally and satellite Israel has occupied and oppressed Muslim Palestine. If America and Israel are the aggressors, the Muslims fighting against American and Israeli occupation are freedom fighters. Obama considers them anti-colonial heroes, like Mandela or Gandhi or his own father, fighting to free a colonized people. Once we put this framework into place, we will see very clearly what Obama is doing in Iraq and Afghanistan. We will also be able to predict what, in his second term, Obama has in mind for Israel.

Even before we get started, however, we need to confront a powerful objection to our thesis. This objection was succinctly put to me by Conor Friedersdorf, an associate editor of *The Atlantic Monthly*, in an email following the news that Bin Laden had been killed. "In light of President Obama's success bringing Osama Bin Laden to justice," Friedersdorf wrote, "do you remain convinced that his actions are motivated by a Kenyan anti-colonial ideology?"[3] I could just see Friedersdorf's smug expression as he composed the email. And I understood clearly what he was getting at. Obviously Obama can't be sympathetic to Muslim jihadis if he ordered the killing of the most notorious and infamous Muslim jihadi of all, Bin Laden. So where does that leave your thesis now, Mister Smarty Pants D'Souza?

Actually, it leaves it quite intact. But this requires some explanation. I'd like to begin by strengthening Friedersdorf's objection. Bin Laden frequently portrayed himself as an anti-colonialist fighting against American occupation of Saudi Arabia. This was the theme of Bin Laden's *Declaration of Jihad Against the Americans*, in which Bin Laden stated, "Ever since God made the Arabian peninsula … it has never suffered such a calamity as these Crusader hordes that have spread through it like locusts, consuming its wealth and destroying its fertility, and all at a time when nations have joined forces against the Muslims as if fighting over a bowl of food." In his 2002 *Open Letter to America*, Bin Laden broadened his indictment of U.S. actions in the Muslim world. "The American people are the ones who pay the taxes which fund the planes that bomb us in Afghanistan, the tanks that strike and destroy our homes in Palestine, the armies which occupy our lands in the Arabian Gulf, and the fleets which ensure the blockade of Iraq." In both documents, Bin Laden portrays himself as a resister against American occupation and exploitation.[4] So if Bin Laden sees himself as an anti-colonial resister, shouldn't he be a hero to Obama? Why would Obama order his killing?

The answer to this question is given by Obama himself in his 2006 book, *The Audacity of Hope*. There Obama writes, "It's useful to remind ourselves … that Osama Bin Laden is not Ho Chi Minh."[5] This is a very telling observation. The context is that Obama is chastising American liberals for failing to make distinctions. And here is the distinction that Obama insists upon making: Ho Chi Minh, in his analysis, was a good guy. He was a true nationalist who was fighting to free his country, Vietnam, first from French and subsequently from American occupation. So Obama concedes that Ho Chi Minh is an anti-colonial hero. But Obama has a different view of Osama Bin Laden. Certainly Bin Laden started out as a Saudi nationalist, fighting against his own government for its willing subordination to the United States. But subsequently Bin Laden decamped for Afghanistan, where he began to plot terrorist attacks in Europe and America. Rather than defend his homeland, Bin Laden sent people to the United States to knock down buildings and bomb government and civilian targets. This for Obama is not anti-colonialism; it is criminal behavior. Obama viewed Bin Laden not as a freedom fighter, but as a kind of international gangster. So the purpose of Obama's comparison is to say to Bin Laden: You're no Ho Chi Minh! You're not a real anti-colonialist! No wonder Obama had no qualms about dispatching Seal Team Six to, in Obama's own words, "bring him to justice."[6]

Having answered the objection regarding Bin Laden, we now turn to Obama's actions in Iraq and Afghanistan. Here we need to concentrate on what Obama does, not on what he says. For one, what he says is garbled and makes little sense. Second, this incoherence seems quite deliberate, because Obama's goals are not ones that he can openly disclose. So it is futile to argue against Obama solely on the basis of what he says. One gets the sense that for him language is usually a camouflage, a way of diverting attention from what is really going on.

Consider this statement from Obama's 2009 Cairo speech, a speech that we know was prepared with particular care. "No system of government," Obama declared "can or should be imposed by one nation on any other."[7] Now what sense can we make of this remark? Of course it borders on idiocy to say that no nation *can* impose its system of government on others: throughout history, nations have done just that. It is almost as foolish to say that no nation *should* impose its system on another: America imposed its democratic system of government on Germany and Japan following World War II, and the results have been excellent.

Let's go beyond this single remark and examine a central theme of Obama's 2008 campaign. Obama basically argued that Iraq was the bad war and Afghanistan the good war. As we will soon see, Obama was saying that only for tactical reasons. He wanted to seem pro-defense, and therefore he used his supposed support for the Afghanistan war to credibly oppose the Iraq war. In reality, Obama from the outset opposed both wars.

But even as an argument, Obama's claims made little sense. Obama's core claim was that Iraq had nothing to do with 9/11 while Afghanistan was the node center for al-Qaeda. This, however, is questionable. Al-Qaeda is largely a Middle Eastern operation. Its leadership is largely Saudi (like Bin Laden) and Egyptian (like the current leader, al-Zawahiri), with a substantial number of Yemenis and Pakistanis. Bin Laden took al-Qaeda to Afghanistan because the Taliban regime gave them free access to terrorist training on the monkey bars there. Yes, 9/11 was launched from Afghanistan, but al-Qaeda's roots are in the Middle East.

Obama's real view of Iraq was probably most clearly stated in his 2002 speech opposing the war. Subsequently Obama acted like that speech was prophetic in predicting the absence of weapons of mass destruction. Yet Obama wrote in *The Audacity of Hope* that "I assumed that Saddam had chemical and biological weapons and coveted nuclear arms." So Obama opposed the Iraq war despite his belief that Saddam had very dangerous weapons in his possession and was pursuing even more dangerous weapons. Why would Obama do that? In the 2002 speech, Obama gives the reason. The Iraq war, he says, had virtually nothing to do with terrorism or Saddam Hussein. Rather, the Bush administration launched the war to "distract us from a rise in the uninsured, a rise in the poverty rate, a drop in the median income, to distract us from corporate scandals and a stock market that has just gone through the worst month since the Great Depression." Obama contends that America went to war in Iraq to shift attention from this domestic crisis; in a way, America sought to export the crisis to some other country. Obama's argument tracks an anti-colonial thesis that was made famous by Lenin, who argued that imperialism avoids the contradictions of capitalism by shifting them from home territory to foreign countries through invasion and occupation.[8]

Obama's real view of Afghanistan seems to have emerged in a casual remark he made in 2007. Obama described America's actions in Afghanistan as "just air raiding villages and killing civilians which is causing enormous problems there." Think for a moment about this remark: never before has an American leader, not even during

Vietnam, described the actions of the U.S. military in such a savage way. Obama's portrayal of America as a merciless occupying power could easily have been uttered by Jeremiah Wright or Bill Ayers. Here in the context of American military action in Afghanistan, we see the full force of Obama's ideological assault on his own country.[9]

We can see from his actions that Obama has been working assiduously from the beginning to get America out of both Iraq and Afghanistan. Now that alone is not enough to prove Obama's anti-colonial motivations. After all, Bush also planned to get America out of Iraq and Afghanistan. What matters is the way we are doing it. Obama inherited a situation in Iraq that was generally positive. The Bush "surge" had weakened the insurgency and helped to stabilize the country. National elections had given the Iraqi government a sense of legitimacy and popular support, at least among the Shia majority. What any president needed to do was to orchestrate a gradual draw-down of American forces and an orderly transfer or military authority to the Iraqis. America stands to benefit immeasurably from the existence, in the Middle East, of a democracy that is pro-American. Obama, however, went against the advice of his generals and ordered a rapid withdrawal of 30,000 American troops. Then Obama went further and announced a complete military exit by the end of 2011. Obama's defense secretary asked that 14,000 to 18,000 troops remain, to continue intelligence operations and train Iraqi security forces. Obama said no. Secretary of State Hillary Clinton pleaded for at least 10,000 troops to stay. Obama refused. In the end, he said, America would leave behind only 3,000 to 4,000 troops in Iraq.[10] Obama's actions seemed calculated to destabilize an already fragile government. Moreover, Obama opted out of negotiations for a long-term military alliance with Iraq and blamed Iraqi intransigence. As a result of Obama's actions, much of America's investment of blood and treasure in Iraq is now jeopardized.[11]

Instead of Iraq being an object lesson in how the U.S. can effectively intervene in and transform another country for the better, Iraq may turn out to be an object lesson in why the U.S. should not even try.

In Afghanistan, Obama and the American military faced two different problems. For the military, the problem was that the Karzai government controlled only the areas around Kabul, with the Taliban threatening large parts of the country. Obama's quite different problem was that he was being pressured by his top general, Stanley McChrystal, to do an Iraq-style "surge." As Bob Woodward documents in *Obama's Wars*, the president had no intention of increasing the level of U.S. troops in Afghanistan. But his defense secretary, secretary of state, CIA director, and senior military command in Afghanistan all insisted that he do so. In the words of CIA Director Leon Panetta, "No Democratic president can go against military advice, especially if he asked for it. So just do it. Do what they say."[12] Moreover, Obama had campaigned as if Afghanistan were the good war, the "war of necessity." So Obama relented and granted a troop surge; but at the same time he announced that those troops would be withdrawn in a year. The *New York Times* headline was revealing: "Obama Adds Troops, but Maps Exit Plan." Thus Obama effectively undercut the surge, because he was in effect telling the Taliban that if they held out for another twelve months, the new troops would be gone. The Taliban was quite willing to do this, the "surge" troops are now gone, and Obama has scheduled a full American withdrawal from Afghanistan. In a speech announcing the pullback, Obama honestly gave his reason: "We stand not for empire but for self-determination."[13]

But of course Afghanistan held free elections, and the Karzai government was in power as a result of self-determination. Obama, however, seems from the outset to have viewed Karzai as a pawn of American empire. Over four years, the Obama administration has gone out of its way to antagonize the Karzai government. Karzai has been a reliable U.S. ally, and his relationship with President Bush was excellent. The two men regularly talked about the Afghan situation. A recent article in *Foreign Policy* describes Karzai as "intensely loyal" to America because of Bush. That same article is titled, "How Obama Lost Karzai." First, Obama discontinued conversations with the Afghan leader. Then the Obama administration annoyed Karzai with a series of diplomatic insults. In 2010, for instance, Obama revoked an invitation to Karzai to visit the White House; Karzai retaliated by inviting Iranian president Mahmoud Ahmadinejad, who delivered a fiery anti-American speech in Afghanistan's presidential palace. Obama officials finalized the break with Karzai by publicly accusing his government of political and financial corruption. Corruption has been going on in Afghanistan since ancient times, and none of it is very surprising in the context of a tribal, warlord culture. What was surprising is for the United States to undermine the very government that it was supposedly working with to defeat the Taliban. Eventually Karzai became so frustrated with his treatment at the hands of the Obama administration that he said he was considering joining the Taliban! What a statement from a man whose own father had been gunned down by the Taliban only a few years earlier![14]

Had Karzai joined the Taliban, Obama probably would have treated him better. If our anti-colonial theory is right, then we know why Obama hates Karzai—he views him as a colonial puppet. By contrast, Obama views the Taliban as a group of intrepid Muslims who are, for all their religious fanaticism and antiquated social views, nevertheless fighting to free their country from American occupation. This anti-colonial perspective is consistent with Obama's actions. The Obama administration began secret negotiations with the Taliban in early 2011, shortly after Obama approved the troop surge. The negotiations became public a year later, when the U.S. agreed in principle to release several high-ranking Taliban officials from Guantanamo Bay. Karzai was apparently excluded from these negotiations, so he hit back by beginning talks with Hezb-e-Islami, a militant group with ties to al-Qaeda. Karzai's position toward America seems to have devolved to: If you can talk to the enemy, I can talk to the enemy.[15]

Yet from Obama's perspective, it's not even clear that the Taliban is necessarily the enemy. When these negotiations became public, Obama officials said that the Taliban was not al-Qaeda, and that there were "good" Taliban and "bad" Taliban. Obama himself said he wanted to "open the door to those Taliban who abandon violence and respect the human rights of their fellow citizens."[16] The U.S. has been fighting this radical Muslim group since 9/11, and until Obama's speech, the existence of non-violent Taliban who respect human rights was a closely guarded secret. Even now, Americans have yet to encounter these "good" Taliban guerillas that Obama keeps talking about. Obama wants to cut an Afghan power-sharing deal with the Taliban, and has removed as a precondition for these negotiations that the Taliban must renounce terrorism and accept democracy and the legitimacy of the Afghan constitution.

Afghanistan, it seems clear, is becoming a lost cause. America is getting out, and our European allies are trying to get out even faster. It may seem strange, therefore, to see Obama go to Afghanistan in May 2012 and declare victory. "We broke the Taliban's momentum," Obama asserted. "The tide has turned." None of this was even remotely true. As if to disrupt Obama's absurd declaration, the Taliban that very day launched a grenade attack in Kabul.[17] But in some ways Obama wasn't lying. For him, the outcome in Afghanistan is a success. As Ryan Lizza recently noted in *The New Yorker*, "Obama spent his first years fighting his generals, who sought to maneuver him into sending more troops and prolonging the nation's commitment there. He eventually gained the upper hand and won the policy he wanted: withdrawal." As he did, the departing defense secretary Robert Gates drew the obvious lesson: "Any future defense secretary who advises the president to again send a big American land army into Asia or into the Middle East or Africa should have his head examined."[18] It's hard to think of sweeter music to Obama's ears. He always wanted America to get out in a way that would reduce future American influence in the region. He worked to produce an outcome that would discourage future U.S. interventions of any kind. Obama seems to view defeat in Afghanistan as a victory for the anti-colonial cause, just as Bill Ayers and other radical leftists had cheered for Ho Chi Minh, in Obama's view a "nationalist," in the Vietnam War.

Finally, Israel. As I show in *The Roots of Obama's Rage*, Obama has a history of siding with the Palestinians over Israel. In his Cairo speech Obama said it was "undeniable that the Palestinian people … have suffered in pursuit of a homeland. For more than sixty years they've endured the pain of dislocation…. They endure the daily humiliations, large and small, that come with occupation." Pondering why Obama showed so much sympathy for the Palestinians, and so little for Israel, the writer Ian Buruma offered a telling comment: "Israel reminds people of the sins of Western imperialism. Israel is regarded in the Middle East, as well as by many people in the West, as a colony led by white people. The Palestinians are seen as colonial subjects." And here we would do well to recall Obama's mentor Edward Said, who said that Zionism was the last form of colonialism. "In joining the general Western enthusiasm for overseas territorial acquisition, Zionism never spoke of itself unambiguously as a Jewish liberation movement, but rather as a Jewish movement for colonial settlement in the Orient."[19]

From the time he became president, Obama demanded that Israel stop building new settlements, even within the city limits of Jerusalem. He made no reciprocal demands on the Palestinians. In fact, Obama has strong-armed Israel so much that the Israeli ambassador to the United States, Michael Oren, stated that U.S.-Israel relations were at their worst point since the 1970s. Partly as a reflection of this, Israeli prime minister Benjamin Netanyahu and Obama have a barely concealed dislike for each other: the antagonism was evident on both men's faces when Netanyahu visited in 2011. During that visit, Obama surprised Netanyahu by declaring publicly that the Arab-Israeli conflict should be resolved along the lines of the 1967 borders "with mutually agreed swaps."[20] So in Obama's view Israel must adopt as its starting point that all of the land acquired since 1967 actually belongs to the Palestinians. What would we think if someone recommended that the framework for future negotiations between America and Mexico should be that America give up all the land it acquired in the Mexican-American war? Of course the two situations aren't precisely the same, but still the analogy is illuminating. Even if the Israelis are ultimately willing to relinquish the land, the fact that Israel's critics think that the land doesn't belong to Israel in the first place means that the land can't be exchanged for peace or recognition of Israel's right to exist; the land simply has to be given up, period.

Obama's willingness to antagonize Israel may seem surprising given the strong Jewish support for the Democratic Party. Neither Bill Clinton nor John Kerry would have contemplated risking this support in the way that Obama has. Even when leading Jewish Democrats urged Obama to reconsider his position, he refused. True, Obama has changed his rhetoric in this election year. Now he sounds like a longtime friend of Israel. Very few people in Israel are fooled, but Thomas Friedman of the *New York Times* evidently is.

Friedman recently called Obama "Israel's best friend." Why? Because, in Friedman's words, Obama "redefined the Iran issue." Friedman quotes Obama: "Preventing Iran from getting a nuclear weapon isn't just in the interest of Israel, it is profoundly in the security interest of the United States," in part because "this would run completely contrary to my policies of nonproliferation." So Friedman is excited that Israel alone doesn't have to bear the responsibility of blocking an Iranian bomb; Obama has committed the United States to that task as well.[21]

But most Israelis from the prime minister on down realize that they cannot count on Obama to save them. Against Friedman's unrealistic hopes they have to consider a much more realistic set of fears. Let's consider a different interpretation of Obama's behavior that is more consistent with the man's anti-colonial sensibility. Obama wants to prevent Israel from acting by itself until he can definitely stop it from acting at all. Obama must prevent Israel from launching its own attack against the Iranian nuclear sites before the November election. If Israel attacks, then Obama may be forced, to protect his re-election prospects, to suppress his outrage and publicly back Israel. Obama wants to avoid this predicament, which for him would be an ideological sellout. So Obama has to find a way to delay any Israeli action. Obama seeks to achieve this by publicly assuring Israel, "I've got your back." Obama knows that Netanyahu won't believe him. Netanyahu probably knows that if Obama has his back, he is just as likely to be shot from the back as from the front. Still, Netanyahu cannot say this, because his nation is so reliant on America. Obama seeks to put Netanyahu in a position where, whatever his private opinions, he is diplomatically forced to place Israel's public trust in America. In this way, Obama buys time, and a little time is all he needs. Once Obama is re-elected, he can then bluntly say to Israel: if you now use military force, America will not support you. In fact, America will join the rest of the world in condemning you. Israel then faces a horrible choice: either refuse to act and live with an Iranian nuclear bomb, or act and face international condemnation and isolation, which is to say, global pariah status.

I believe this is what Obama wants: he wants Israel to be delegitimized in the way that South Africa was over apartheid. Eventually the South African system simply collapsed. In his first term, Obama has been content to back the Palestinians over the West Bank and Gaza. But I believe his longer-term goal is much more ambitious. Like any good anti-colonialist freedom fighter, he seeks to get rid of the occupying power itself. Let's remember that from the anti-colonialist view, Israel is the "little Satan" occupying Muslim land, and America is the "great Satan" backing Israel. Ultimately no true anti-colonialist can be content until all of occupied Palestine, which is to say all of Israel, is returned to the Muslims. I don't think Obama expects the Jews to go elsewhere. But he can delegitimize the Jewish state and perhaps he can force Israel to grant a right of return with full voting rights to Palestinian refugees. If that happens, then in relatively short order, the Muslims would outnumber the Jews, with obvious political consequences. An Obama second term could be fatal for the future of Israel.

CHAPTER TWELVE

OUR ARAB WINTER

Human history has often been a record of nations and tribes—and yes, religions—subjugating one another in pursuit of their own interests. Yet in this new age, such attitudes are self-defeating.[1]
—Barack Obama, speech at Cairo University, June 4, 2009

In the last couple years, we have seen protests and rebellions break out all over the Arab and Muslim world. It started in December 2010 when a 26-year-old Tunisian set himself on fire to protest unemployment and corruption. Pretty soon there were uprisings in Tunisia which spread over subsequent months to Egypt, Yemen, Bahrain, Libya, Morocco, Oman, Iran, and Syria. When the dust had settled a year and a half later, four governments had been toppled—the governments of Tunisia, Libya, Yemen, and Egypt. As of this writing, Syria continues to battle resisters in several cities. The overall impact of the so-called Arab Spring is two-fold: it has advanced the cause of democracy in the Muslim world, and it has undermined the strength and influence of the United States. As Fawaz Gerges put it in his recent book, *Obama and the Middle East*,

"U. S. influence … is at its lowest point since the beginning of the Cold War in the late 1940s. America's ability to dictate policy in the Middle East has diminished considerably, and it no longer determines the course of events in the region. America's moment is coming to an end."[2]

How did this rapid decline occur? The United States clearly didn't cause the Arab Spring. This was an indigenous revolution, a response to repression and corruption which are unfortunately widespread in the Muslim regimes of North Africa and the Middle East. Yet America's actions in responding to the Arab Spring have been wildly contradictory. In Libya, President Obama used military force to oust the dictator Muammar Gaddafi. Obama's stated reason was to prevent the Gaddafi regime from committing genocide against the Libyan people, even though at the time America launched its attack, fewer than 250 people had been killed. Meanwhile, Obama initially refused to take any action in Syria; finally, under pressure, he reluctantly provided modest non-military aid to the Syrian resistance. Obama's conduct is especially odd given that Syria's dictator Bashar Assad had, over a period of several months, killed more than 10,000 people. Evidently, genocide is more acceptable in Syria than in Libya.

Obama also played an active role in removing the Egyptian ruler, Hosni Mubarak, from power. Mubarak was replaced first by an interim government established by the military, and then by a new government led by the Muslim Brotherhood and other radical Islamic groups. These groups prevailed in the Egyptian elections. The Obama administration's role was, first, to use U.S. diplomatic pressure to back the military in pressuring Mubarak to leave; then, to turn on the military and back the street protesters' demands for elections. Obama did not bring the radical Muslims to power in Egypt—Egyptians voted them in—but he cleared the way for their ascent. Yet if this could be considered an exercise of American support for democracy, Obama responded in precisely the opposite manner in 2009, when there were equally massive demonstrations in favor of democracy in Iran. Then Obama urged patience and restraint, and the consequence was that the mullahs and the police were successful in subduing the rebels. So Mubarak was ejected in Egypt while the mullahs continue to rule Iran.

To date, no one has convincingly explained why Obama used force in Libya while eschewing it in Syria; or why Obama aided in the ouster of the Mubarak regime while acquiescing in the crackdown of the Iranian regime. Why intervene here rather than there? What is Obama's principle of selectivity that accounts for the seeming inconsistency in his foreign policy? There has been a good deal of head-scratching on this. The best we have is Walter Russell Mead's theory that Obama is "the least competent manager of America's Middle East diplomatic portfolio in a very long time. He has committed our forces in the strategically irrelevant backwater of Libya.... He has strained our ties with the established regimes without winning new friends on the Arab Street.... He has infuriated and frustrated long term friends, but made no headway in reconciling enemies."[3] But surely Obama knows that Libya is strategically irrelevant; surely he can see that he is antagonizing America's friends and strengthening America's enemies. So Mead's analysis only begs the question: Why would Obama continue to act in this way when the results are as obvious to him as to Mead and the rest of us?

Here I offer a coherent explanation that better accounts for Obama's conduct. There is in fact no inconsistency. Behind Obama's apparent "double standard" there is a single standard that is glaringly obvious. Obama is getting precisely the results he wants. He is attempting to get rid of American allies in Egypt and several other countries, and he has done that. He is trying to conserve anti-American regimes in Syria and Iran, and he has done that. Obama's goal is to reduce America's footprint in the Middle East, and in four years Obama has been wildly successful in doing that too. We can confidently project that if Obama is re-elected, American influence in the region, and in the world, will decline further.

Four rulers are gone: Ben Ali in Tunisia, Ali Saleh in Yemen, Hosni Mubarak in Egypt, and Muammar Gaddafi in Libya. What did they have in common? Sure, they were thugs, in a region of thugs. Sure, they were corrupt, in an area of the world where corruption is the norm. But here is the significant point: they were all also, to a lesser or greater degree, allies of the United States. Mubarak was our strongest ally in the region, not counting Israel. Ben Ali and Ali Saleh were both helping us fight al-Qaeda. Once called "the mad dog of the Middle East," Gaddafi had renounced his past support for terrorism. Since 2002 he had suspended his nuclear weapons program and given up his quest for weapons of mass destruction. He paid reparations for his role in the Lockerbie bombing. He turned over terrorist suspects and normalized Libya's relations with the West. He also banned radical groups such as the Muslim Brotherhood in Libya. Now all these men are gone, and in every case the United States helped push them out.

We're going to look more closely at Libya and Egypt later. But here for instance is the April 3, 2011, headline in the *New York Times*: "U.S. Shifts to Seek Removal of Yemen's Leader, an Ally." We read that "the United States, which long supported Yemen's president" because "he was considered a critical ally in fighting the Yemeni branch of al-Qaeda" had, under the Obama administration, "now quietly shifted positions" and was pushing to get him "eased out of office."[4] The article expresses very little curiosity about why Obama would want to push out a ruler who is pro-American and helping in the fight against al-Qaeda.

In two of the four cases, Libya and Yemen, the devil we know has been replaced by the devil we don't. In other words, America is quite possibly going to get new governments that are more anti-American and more sympathetic to radical Islam. In Tunisia and Egypt, we know this is the case. In Tunisia, the secular political parties were easily defeated by Nahda, a long-banned Islamist party led by the radical activist Rachid Ghannouchi. Tunisia's new prime minister, Hamadi Jebali, has been quoted saying that his goal is to establish a "sixth caliphate" under Muslim holy law in Tunisia.[5] The Egyptian elections brought to power the Muslim Brotherhood, in coalition with an even-more-radical Islamist party called the Party of Light.

The regimes in Syria and Iran have also been run by corrupt dictators, so there is nothing new there. What, then, distinguishes them from the regimes in Libya, Tunisia, Egypt, and Yemen? The distinguishing feature is that Syria and Iran are ferociously opposed to the United States. In fact, they have long been allied with each other in that opposition. If these regimes fall, we can't be sure what sort of regimes would replace them, but in Iran at least we can be confident that the new regime would be less anti-American and less anti-Israel. Yet it is the Iranian opposition that Obama has refused to assist at all. Obama apparently believes in helping to oust pro-American dictators and leaving anti-American dictators alone.

It may seem shocking to suggest that these are actually Obama's goals, as opposed to the unintentional consequences of his foreign policy. Yet if Obama didn't intend these results, you would expect him to regret what has happened or start pursuing a different policy. On the contrary, Obama forges ahead, offering aid and protection to the Islamic radicals who are now in power. Obama's actions suggest a man who knows exactly what he is doing, even as naive pundits continue to lecture him on how he can more wisely advance American interests and American influence in the Middle East. Obama coolly ignores these people because advancing American interests and influence in the region is the last thing he wants. Obama's actions are totally consistent with those of an anti-colonialist who considers America to be the global oppressor that needs to be cut down to size.

To understand the Arab Spring, we have to recognize a shift in strategy on the part of the Islamic radicals. Actually, it is a shift back to an old strategy. Consider what Osama Bin Laden and Ayman al-Zawahiri were doing before they launched al-Qaeda. Bin Laden was fighting to overthrow the pro-American government of Saudi Arabia, and Zawahiri was fighting to overthrow the pro-American government of Egypt. In their own understanding, they were fighting the "near enemy." The Islamic radicals in those days didn't bother with attacking America directly, and they weren't even that concerned with Israel. Both were regarded as the "far enemy." One of Zawahiri's famous slogans from that period was, "The road to Jerusalem runs through Cairo." This meant that Muslims had first to take over their own countries; then they would be strong enough to tackle Israel and eventually the United States.[6]

Al-Qaeda's formation represented a radical shift from fighting the "near enemy" to fighting the "far enemy." Zawahiri's rationale for the shift was that "it is clear that the Jewish-Crusader alliance, led by the United States, will not allow any Islamic force to reach power in any of the Muslim countries."[7] And on 9/11, the new strategy electrified the Muslim world by successfully striking at the symbols of American military and financial power. But now the radical Muslims have realized there is a strategy that works much better. This strategy is called: democracy! And it is the current strategy of the Muslim Brotherhood, the largest radical Muslim group in the world, with followings in dozens of Muslim countries. The Muslim Brotherhood never believed that attacking the far enemy was the right strategy, but its own strategy of domestic terrorism against the near enemy had failed because of effective government reprisals. The Muslim Brotherhood needed to find a better way, and in democracy it has found one.

True, historically the radical Muslims, including the Muslim Brotherhood and al-Qaeda, have been enemies of democracy. Their general view has been that it is wrong to subordinate the voice of God to the voice of the people. But while al-Qaeda still reviles democracy, the Muslim Brotherhood switched its position in 2005, when Brotherhood-affiliated candidates ran in Egypt's parliamentary elections. Mohammed Mahdi Akef, head of the Muslim Brotherhood, surprised many by saying, "The ballot box has the final say. We don't believe in any other means of taking power."[8] Since then, the Muslim Brotherhood's enthusiasm for democracy has only grown stronger, and the Brotherhood is now the most powerful voice in Islamic countries demanding a transition from dictatorship to democracy. They have realized that if there are free elections, they have a good chance to win. They first saw this in 1991, when a radical Muslim group called the Islamic Salvation Front won a free election in Algeria. The Muslim Brotherhood saw that its candidates won 20 percent of the seats in the 2005 Egyptian election, which was held under harshly restrictive conditions. And democracy paid off for the radical Muslims again with the 2006 election victory of Hamas in Gaza. This is why much of the Arab Spring's push for democracy has been promoted by radical Islamic organizations like the Muslim Brotherhood.

In assessing Obama's strategy for North Africa and the Middle East, let's begin with Libya, the one country where Obama was willing to use military force. At first he hesitated, but eventually he backed the efforts of the Libyan resistance with attack aircraft, refueling tankers, surveillance equipment, and other military aid, as part of a United Nations-authorized NATO military action. The campaign was billed as an effort to save lives, yet it was also clearly aimed at getting rid of Gaddafi, whose 41-year-old rule came to a violent end. Why did Obama hesitate, and why did he act? On *Hardball*, Chris Matthews said this was "a war without explanation" and added, "The Obama doctrine—can you define it? We can't." Actually, I believe we can. So let's take the two elements separately. The most reasonable explanation for Obama's hesitation is that he was reluctant to get America involved in another war; he would prefer America play a backseat role, which one Obama adviser described as "leading from behind."[9] I believe this explanation is correct, although I would interpret it in an anti-colonial way. For Obama, American intervention is generally the problem, as in Iraq and Afghanistan. So naturally Obama wanted to keep Imperial America out of Libya. But then why did he get America involved? My argument is that he got involved in order to get rid of the longtime anti-American ruler who switched sides and became, at least to a degree, pro-American. Gaddafi was once a hero of the anti-colonialists and the anti-Americans; now he had become an embarrassment. Obama's initial hesitation and then his "leading from behind" were the result of a clash of anti-colonial goals. He hesitated because he didn't want to lead Imperial America against a North African ruler, and he acted because ultimately he had the more important goal of toppling an anti-colonial sellout.

But this is not the standard explanation, so we have to weigh my theory against plausible rivals. The standard justification was given by Obama and then dutifully taken up by his allies in the media. "Some nations may be able to turn a blind eye to atrocities in other countries," Obama said. "The United States of America is different."

This of course is pure humbug. We can test Obama's professed unwillingness to turn a blind eye to atrocities by considering the case of Syria, where Human Rights Watch and other human rights groups have detailed the torture and execution-style killings that the government's thugs have meted out to protesters, especially in towns like Deraa and Homs, where the civilian death toll exceeds 10,000 people, more than forty times the number of deaths that were considered a sign of incipient "genocide" in Libya.[10] A United Nations peace plan had little or no effect in stopping the sieges, arrests, and street killings.

Typical of the Obama administration's response to the violence in Syria was a statement issued on April 22, 2011: "We regret the loss of life" in Syria and "our thoughts are with the families and loved ones of the victims." In mid-August, as the killings continued and pressure for action mounted, Obama called on Assad to step down. But he didn't actually do anything that would cause Assad to do this. Instead, the United States froze Syrian assets in America, barred U.S. citizens from having business dealings with the Syrian government, and made a few other symbolic gestures. None of this was likely to change Assad's mind, and none of it did. In February 2012, Obama agreed to shut down the U.S. embassy in Damascus, another symbolic move. Finally, Obama agreed to supply the rebels with non-lethal aid, including medical supplies and some communications equipment. Whenever he is asked about military intervention in Syria, Obama always says it would be "premature" and could actually lead to more deaths—a thought that seems to have eluded him when it came to Libya.[11]

This is not to say that the case for military intervention in Syria is obvious. But Assad's brutality has been far worse than Gaddafi's, Syria is openly allied with America's enemy Iran, and Syria shelters a raft of terrorist groups. Obama, of course, knows all this, so I can only smile when pundits lecture Obama about it. Here it would be difficult to top the neoconservative magazine the *Weekly Standard*. Max Boot informs Obama that he has an "historic opportunity" to "take Syria out of the Iranian camp and deny Hezbollah its main source of supply." Boot urges Obama to "put away any lingering illusions about the desirability of maintaining Assad in power and do whatever is needed to topple him swiftly." A few months later, Lee Smith in that magazine faults Obama with being "sadly oblivious" to the situation and therefore "dithering on Syria," thus making him "a hapless spectator" of events there.[12] It never occurs to these pundits and their ilk that maybe Obama refuses to use force because he wants Assad to remain in power. It's not that he misunderstands the situation; he understands the situation all too well. It is the pundits who presume that Obama shares their goals; they are the ones who misunderstand what Obama seeks to achieve. If Assad falls, it will be despite Obama, not because of him.

Now let's compare the situation in two countries that far surpass Libya and Syria in importance: namely, Egypt and Iran. Egypt and Iran are, along with Saudi Arabia, the most important countries in the region. We are all familiar with the mass protests that erupted in Egypt's Tahrir Square starting in January 2011. Soon the protests spread to other cities. The protesters appeared to be a coalition of disparate groups: liberals, leftists, secularists, religious traditionalists, as well as Islamists and radical Muslims. Their target was the tough but aged ruler Hosni Mubarak, who had ruled for thirty years. Mubarak was determined to defeat the protesters or at least outlast them. But to do this he needed the support of his military and also his most valuable ally, the United States of America.

Obama's response to the Egyptian uprising must be understood as a two-step maneuver. Stage one: Obama backed the Egyptian military high command against Mubarak. America gives $1.3 billion each year to the Egyptian military, which is estimated to cover three-fourths of the cost of its arms procurements. So Obama has tremendous leverage with the Egyptian military, and he used this leverage to pressure the generals to get Mubarak out. Defense Secretary Gates and Secretary of State Clinton reminded Obama of America's interests in the region and of Mubarak's reliability as an ally, but that did not deter Obama.[13] He called Mubarak and told him it was time to leave. At this point, Mubarak had no choice. His most powerful ally, America, and his own generals were now against him. So Mubarak gave up.

Following Mubarak's exit, a struggle began between the military and the protesters on the street. The military was willing to have elections, but wanted to protect its traditional prerogatives and control defense and foreign policy. "The position of the armed forces will remain as it is," insisted Hussein Tantawi, the chief military commander. He was opposed by the street protesters who demanded full democracy, including civilian control of the military. Stage two of Obama's approach was to turn on the Egyptian military and back the street calls for democracy. As the *New York Times* put it, "The Obama administration threw its weight behind the Egyptians who flooded into Tahrir Square to demand that the generals relinquish power."[14] Obama did this in the name of supporting full self-government in Egypt. Reluctantly, the military gave in, succumbing to pressure from the Egyptian people at home and from the American aid provider abroad. Elections were held, and that's how the radical Muslims came to power in Egypt.

The new government in Egypt is certainly more hostile to Israel and the United States than its predecessor. For decades Egypt had no diplomatic relations with Iran; one of the first acts of the new government was to resume them. Egypt also weakened Israel's position in the West Bank and Gaza by brokering a peace deal between the two rival Palestinian groups, Hamas and Fatah. Egypt's foreign minister said he would open the Rafah border crossing between Gaza and Egypt, frustrating the Israeli blockade of Hamas. The Egyptian government also cancelled a natural gas deal with Israel, which Israeli Finance Minister Yuval Steinitz said was a "dangerous precedent that clouds the peace agreement between Israel and Egypt." There are widespread fears in Israel that the peace agreement itself is in jeopardy, and that Egypt may join the ranks of Muslim nations who would like to see Israel cease to exist.[15]

So why did Obama support a process that produced an outcome hostile to the United States and its ally Israel? For anyone with even a basic knowledge of Egypt, it was apparent from the outset that the Muslim Brotherhood was by far the best organized group in the country, and could spread its message through Egypt's mosques. It had demonstrated its popularity in the 2005 parliamentary elections. So it was hardly surprising when the radical Muslims swept the Egyptian parliamentary elections with over 70 percent of the popular vote. The largest vote getters were the candidates of the Muslim Brotherhood. The Brotherhood's creed is, "Allah is our objective. The Prophet is our leader. The Quran is our law. Jihad is our way. Dying in the way of Allah is our highest hope." The al-Nour party, dominated by even more radical Salafi Muslims, was the second highest vote getter. As for the liberal and secular parties, they collectively managed a paltry 10 percent.

Obama has shown no regret whatever over the election outcome in Egypt. In fact, when the Egyptian courts and military made a last-ditch effort to thwart the rise of the radical Islamists, issuing rules that severely limited the power of the president and the parliament, the Obama administration moved quickly to block those rules. The Associated Press reported, "The Obama administration warned Egypt's military leaders … to speedily hand over power or risk losing billions of dollars in U.S. military and economic aid." The article quoted State Department spokeswoman Victoria Nuland saying, "We are particularly concerned by decisions that appear to prolong the military's hold on power."[16] Essentially the Obama administration demanded that the Egyptian military submit to civilian control—in practice, to control by the Muslim Brotherhood. This became even more clear when, a few days after Obama's threat, the Muslim Brotherhood's candidate, Mohamed Morsi, won the Egyptian presidential election.

Some say Obama could not oppose a popular democratic movement, even though it threatened to undermine U.S. interests. Fortunately there is a way to test this claim. In Iran, Obama had the opportunity to support a popular democratic movement just as large as the one in Egypt, and the success of this movement would unquestionably advance U.S. interests. Obama clarified what he really thinks about democracy in the Muslim world by how he reacted to the pro-reform movement in Iran.

Massive demonstrations broke out in Iran in mid-2009. At first glance this seemed to be a quarrel among the mullahs. The demonstrators supported the candidacy of Mir Hossein Mousavi over that of Mahmoud Ahmadinejad. Ahmadinejad was a proven demagogue, but since Mousavi was the former prime minister under Ayatollah Khomeini, he didn't seem like a big improvement. Yet Mousavi had become a fierce critic of the Iranian government. His candidacy symbolized a protest against rigged elections and an illegitimate Iranian political system. For the first time in three decades, there were widespread calls for the mullahs to relinquish power. This was a stunning development, comparable to Boris Yeltsin's call for the Communist Party in Russia to abolish itself.

Never before had the United States had the chance to back a popular democratic movement of this magnitude in a country that was unremittingly hostile to America and its allies. Yet Obama refused to support the protesters. He called for patience. He said he did not want to violate the sovereignty of Iran. He said that there was "an extraordinary debate taking place in Iran." He expressed respectful solicitousness in noting "some reaction from the Supreme Leader that indicates he understands the Iranian people have deep concerns about the election." He said that "the difference between Ahmadinejad and Mousavi in terms of their actual policies may not be as great as has been advertised." He said that the best course of action was to wait and see. The U.S. government would "monitor and see how this plays out before we make any judgments about how we proceed." And Americans waited and saw on television as the mullahs and their thugs beat the protesters into submission. Eventually the protests dissipated and the "debate" concluded. Obama's counsel of patience proved to be a counsel of inaction. The window of opportunity closed.[17]

Even many Obama supporters will not defend Obama's conduct during the Iranian revolt. Yet one Obama cheerleader, Jonathan Alter, insists that Obama was right. "It made sense.... He avoided full-throated support for the dissidents," Alter explains, "which would give the regime the excuse to say the revolt was inspired by the United States."[18] Perhaps it would, but at least there was a chance in Iran to turn things around. Obama's decision to leave the protesters on their own in 2009 ensured their defeat. Two years later, demonstrations in solidarity with the Arab Spring were crushed by the mullahs, arresting 1,500 people. Once again, Obama was silent and offered the protesters no support whatever.

From the contrasting situations of Egypt and Iran, we can conclude that Obama does in fact support democracy, but only a particular kind of democracy. He opposes popular Muslim movements that advance American interests while backing popular Muslim movements that oppose American interests. He rejects calls for democracy when they undermine radical Islam while affirming those same calls when they affirm the prospects of radical Islam. None of this is to suggest that Obama is himself a Muslim, but rather, that Obama seeks a diminution of American power and influence in the Muslim world. He has acted decisively and consistently to achieve that goal. And today America is far weaker in the region than it was four years ago.

So what's next? In my view, Saudi Arabia. Saudi Arabia is not only a crucial American ally, but also America's largest foreign source for oil. If Saudi Arabia falls, this would be a devastating blow to America's economy and foreign policy, and if the Islamists gained Mecca and Medina it would be the greatest victory of radical Islam since the Khomeini revolution in Iran. So here is my prediction. In a second term, Obama will work with Islamists in Saudi Arabia and in neighboring countries to support a rebellion against the Saudi royal family. When it occurs, he will say it is time for the Saudi royals to move aside in favor of democracy. If the Saudi royals refuse to abdicate, Obama will cut off American aid. Absent American assistance, the House of Saud could fall just as Mubarak did. Then there would be elections, which would bring the radical Muslims to power.

While a transition of power in Saudi Arabia would be a very big deal, I believe that Obama has an even bigger objective in the Middle East. There are three major countries in the region: Iran, Egypt, and Saudi Arabia. Since 1979, Iran has been in the hands of the radical Muslims. Now, with Obama's help, Egypt is moving into the radical Muslim camp. Saudi Arabia is the only one left. So once Saudi Arabia falls, the radical Muslims have a chance to achieve what they have long dreamed about: a complete unification of the Middle East under a single Muslim caliphate. If Iran, Egypt, and

Saudi Arabia unite, the smaller countries, from Jordan to the Gulf Kingdoms, would quickly succumb or be overrun. And what can we call this new nation? Let's call it the United States of Islam. The term is not mine. It was coined by Kamal al-Helbawy, a former spokesman for the Muslim Brotherhood, who is calling on Arabs to eliminate the borders "drawn up by imperialist nations" and over the next few years "have a country called the United States of Islam."[19]

What is necessary for this to occur? Just one thing: the Sunnis and the Shia have to work out their differences. The theological differences are minor, but the historical enmities are real. There may be clashes between the two, or even a war, as between the American North and South, but eventually America came together, and so could the Muslims of the Middle East. I predict that if they have the chance, they will come together in the name of Islam as a global power. This way the Muslims can put up a single front against the United States and Israel. So while history will credit Ronald Reagan with producing the dissolution of the Soviet empire, history might credit Obama with producing the unification of Islam.

CHAPTER THIRTEEN

DEBT AS A WEAPON OF MASS DESTRUCTION

The poorest Americans are better off than more than
two-thirds of the world population.[1]
—Branko Milanovic, *The Haves and the Have-Nots*

Thus far we have been examining various ways in which Obama has pursued his anti-colonial ideology by undermining and shrinking America's economic, political, and military influence. Still, America could, even in this shrunken state, dominate the world for a couple more decades. If Obama wants to change that, how can he do so in just four more years? Actually, there is a way. To do this Obama must go beyond promoting decline and work to create collapse. Yes, collapse would really change the global equation. In this chapter we explore an intriguing and somewhat frightening idea. I call it debt as a weapon of mass destruction. That's because at a certain level of debt, America is ruined as an economic power. Not only does that change life for Americans, causing a sharp fall in our standard of living, but it also changes America's place in the world. America ceases to be a superpower; perhaps America ceases to be a first world country.

From an anti-colonial perspective, debt is a beautiful weapon to deploy. Consider a revealing statement by one of Obama's former students. He said that when Obama taught law at the University of Chicago, the topic arose whether America and the West should pay reparations for slavery and other historical injustices. The student said of Obama, "He told us what he thought about reparations. He agreed entirely with the theory of reparations. But in practice he didn't think it was really workable." In order to have racial reparations you would have to settle such questions as "who is black, how far back do you go, what about recent immigrants," and so on. Considering such complexities, Obama told his class, "That is why it's unworkable."[2] But I believe Obama has found a way to achieve global reparations. This has nothing to do with race. It has to do with using debt to bring down the colonial oppressor and level the standard of living between America and the developing countries. Through debt we become beholden to the rest of the world. Debt will make them richer and us poorer; thus debt evens the scales. Debt is especially useful for Obama: he can use the accumulation of financial debt to settle the historical debts that America owes other nations on account of imperial aggression and exploitation.

Obama well knows how debt can paralyze a country. We know that he knows, because he wrote about it. In *The Audacity of Hope*, Obama attacked the Bush deficit. "We now have an annual budget deficit of almost $300 billion," Obama said. He called this "the most precarious situation that we've seen in years." Obama then considered how deficits add up to pile on debt upon debt. "So far," he added, "we've been able to get away with this mountain of debt because foreign central banks, particularly China's, want us to keep buying their exports. But this easy credit won't continue forever. At some point, foreigners will stop lending us money, interest rates will go up, and we will spend most of our nation's output paying them back."[3] When Obama published those words in 2006, the national debt was $8.5 trillion.

While $8.5 trillion is a huge amount of money—around 60 percent of America's annual GDP—that level of debt is still manageable for a rich country. Rich countries can do irresponsible things, like run up the national credit card, and still recover. Under Reagan, for example, deficits ran around $200 billion and America added $1.5 trillion in debt in eight years. Bush was even more profligate, and debt rose nearly $5 trillion during his two terms. Obama, however, has taken things to a new level. He has added $5 trillion in debt in less than four years. So Obama is adding to the debt at twice the pace of his predecessor Bush. While Bush's deficits never topped $500 billion, Obama's have averaged more than $1 trillion. In fact, between 1789 and 2000, America accumulated a national debt of less than $5 trillion. Incredibly, Obama will in four years have added more to the national debt than all U.S. presidents from George Washington through Bill Clinton combined.[4]

America is currently $15 trillion in debt. That's a gargantuan number, a number that seems more suited to astronomy than to economics. And it may be considerably understated. *USA Today* reports that the U.S. government uses all kinds of accounting legerdemain to hide its true level of indebtedness. The article concluded that "if the government used standard accounting rules to compute the deficit ... the government ran red ink last year equal to $42,054 per household—nearly four times the official number reported." So what was Obama's real deficit for 2011? Not $1.3 trillion as the Obama administration declared, but $5 trillion! Essentially the government avoids this frightening number by refusing to count promised retirement benefits. In theory, these aren't legal obligations since Congress can pass laws that scale back or get rid of these retirement obligations before they are due.[5]

But let's not haggle over accounting practices; let's go with current U.S. government accounting and set the debt at $15 trillion. That's still more than 100 percent of GDP; we are reaching the point where debt is unmanageable. If Obama is re-elected, he's likely to add another $5 trillion in debt—more, perhaps, if he can get away with it. At this point America would be over $20 trillion in debt. That point could be reached by 2016, and it's the tipping point, the point where America's economy faces total and irreversible collapse. At that point America is like Greece, except there is no one in the world to bail us out. There will, however, be countries that would like to take us over, or at least to prey on the spoils of our ruined nation.

We can understand the problem better by comparing the national situation to one faced by a typical American family. Imagine that you have an annual after-tax income of $100,000. So you are pretty well off, compared to most people. Yet you have been spending above your means, each year adding $15,000 to $20,000 to your family's debt. Now that total debt is $110,000, so it is higher than your annual income. You would have to work for a whole year and turn over all your earnings, just to pay it back. This would already be a bad situation. It would call for a serious reexamination of the family budget. Yet let's imagine that, instead of a doing this, you actually increased your spending. While previously you spent $20,000 above your income, now you spend $40,000. You are already in real trouble, yet one year you buy a new Lexus, the next you go on a $50,000 vacation, and so on. You show no sign of changing these habits; if permitted by the rest of the family, you would actually spend more. When confronted by others, you speak of "promises" you have made that you somehow feel obliged to keep, even though you don't have the money. Such behavior would not merely be irresponsible; it would risk financial disaster. You would be setting up for the day when people come to repossess the family house and take away the family cars. Now there are only two reasons why someone would actually do this. The first is that the person was insane. The second is that for some reason he wanted the family to be bankrupt.

One might be interested in Obama's take on all this. Unfortunately, Obama's statements on the subject offer little illumination. Recently Obama responded to allegations that he has, as a big spender, been running up the debt by saying that he is not a big spender and he has not been running up the debt. Rather, he said, he is like Bill Clinton, a Democrat who has "actually reduced the pace of the growth in government spending." Moreover, Obama laid the blame for America's debt squarely on the Republicans. "What happens," he said, "is the Republicans run up the tab, and then we're sitting there and they've left the restaurant, and then they point and say: why did you order all those steaks and martinis?"[6] Now anyone can easily verify that Obama's levels of spending are dramatically higher than Bush's. The deficit in 2008, Bush's last year, was $458 billion. And here are the Obama deficits:

2009: $1.41 trillion
2010: $1.29 trillion
2011: $1.30 trillion
2012: $1.33 trillion

Obama is the biggest spender in world history, so why won't he admit it? Charitably we may say that he is engaging in election-year obfuscation. But Obama's ability to flat-out fabricate suggests to me a deeper problem. He is displaying here the same fabulism that his dad was known for. He thinks that if he spins his fables often enough, and says them convincingly enough, then people will fall for them. And some do.

We shouldn't, however, join the camp of the deluded. So let's set aside Obama's prevarications and follow his actions to try and determine where he's taking us. During his first two years in office, Obama went on a massive spending spree: first a $700 billion bailout; then a $787 billion stimulus program; then Obamacare, estimated by the Congressional Budget Office to cost $1.76 trillion over the next decade. In 2010, Obama and the Democrats suffered a serious rebuke in the midterm election. This, however, has not changed Obama's priorities in the slightest. If he had the power, he would keep spending with reckless abandon. The Republicans, however, now control the House of Representatives and they have been blocking Obama. Under pressure to address the deficit, Obama set up the Bowles-Simpson deficit reduction commission. The commission released a report that showed how to remove $4 trillion in red ink over the coming decade. It bowed neither to the orthodoxy of left nor right, advocating Social Security and Medicare cuts (while protecting low-income beneficiaries), trimming defense and social programs, and raising tax revenues by reforming the tax code, closing loopholes, and lowering rates. Obama's reaction? He ignored the commission's findings, even though they could have provided bipartisan political cover for him to do things that would make a real dent in the national debt. The commission offered Obama the chance to strike a "grand bargain" with the Republicans, but Obama declined the offer.

In August 2011, the credit rating of the United States was lowered by Standard & Poor's from AAA to AA+. This is the first time the United States had lost its AAA rating since the agency first granted it in 1917. The S & P, along with other credit agencies like

Fitch and Moody's, had all warned the Obama administration and Congress that without a serious approach to reducing the deficit, the country faced a downgrade. Instead of taking this chastening advice, Obama officials attacked the S & P. Obama fatuously said that no matter what "some agency" might say, "we've been and always will be a triple-A country."[7] So Obama has yet to show any real concern with the debt. In an election year, admittedly, he realizes he must appear to be concerned. Thus Obama offers deficit reduction measures that are largely symbolic and almost comically ineffective. His Buffett Rule, for example, would only cover a small number of wealthy Americans and raise, according to the Tax Foundation, "insignificant revenue."[8]

How, then, could America erase its annual deficit if the president and Congress were serious about doing it? One way is through tax increases. The Tax Foundation is blunt about how severe these would have to be. In order to balance the budget next year, the government would have to impose on all Americans earning $200,000 a year or more the Barack Obama Sr. tax rate: 100 percent. The Tax Foundation says this would raise $1.5 trillion and balance the budget: "It may be economically ruinous, but at least this proposal would solve the problem."[9] The other way is to reduce government spending. Here the government would have to impose a one-third across the board spending cut. It's drastic, but businesses do it all the time when they are in comparable straits. Certainly a family facing debt proportionate to that of the United States would have no choice but to alter its spending habits and modify its lifestyle.

Of course, neither of these two drastic approaches—the 100 percent tax rate or the 30 percent spending cut—is likely to be adopted, no matter who is elected this year. Deficits, therefore, are likely to continue and the only questions are: How big? And with what effect? America could afford to run deficits of the Reagan and even Bush magnitude as long as the economy was growing at a steady pace. But Obama's economy is virtually stagnant; its growth is anemic at best. Moreover, Obama's deficits are unsustainable, even as Obama jubilantly tells donors, "We're not even halfway there yet," with his promise of yet more big spending programs. Not even halfway there? Obama seems to be saying that he intends to keep going the same way he has been; indeed, he wants to speed up the pace. Thus we have the unpleasant task of considering what deficits of the Obama magnitude will do to the American economy over the next four years.

First, a $20 trillion national debt will force the government to print vast quantities of new money. Running the presses at the national mint is not exactly how the government does it—the Federal Reserve has more sophisticated techniques to achieve the same result—but printing money is a perfectly reasonable way to summarize what the government is actually doing. It is solving the problem through inflation. So imagine that the government prints $20 trillion. Hey, now we can pay off the national debt! Yes, but we have also put $20 trillion of new money into circulation. This will dramatically raise prices, causing inflation rates far worse than anything America endured in the mid to late 1970s.

"We haven't experienced real inflation," Nina Easton writes in *Fortune*, "in more than a generation."[10] Only older Americans are likely to recall grocery items with multiple stickers because the prices kept going up from month to month. Still, we may recall the double-digit inflation of the 1970s with fond nostalgia. Our debt levels suggest that in the future we may be facing banana republic levels of inflation—the kind of triple-digit runaway inflation typically experienced in countries like Peru and Argentina—except that today the banana republics are doing far better than we are, with higher growth rates and lower inflation risks. Today the only

countries that have runaway inflation are places like Haiti and Zimbabwe, and how humiliating it would be for us to be in their position. Inflation not only drives up prices, it also reduces the value of
work and savings. It also wipes out the value of the dollar, making
dollar bills worth less and less. A high rate of inflation makes the
dollar essentially worthless, just as Third World currencies used to
be, just as Confederate money had little or no purchasing power
after the Civil War.

Second, debts in the $20 trillion range will force upon foreign
lenders two separate recognitions: the recognition that they can now
push us around, and the recognition that the United States is never
going to pay that money back. Consider what would happen if we
owe China several trillion dollars, and the Chinese decide to take
over Taiwan. Sure, we can fight, but as one wag put it, "We'd have
to borrow the money from China to wage that war." But in reality
there might not be a war. Both the Chinese and the Americans know
that the international game has changed. We are no longer indisput-
ably in charge; we can object, but it's no longer the case that what
America says goes. In fact, America now has to keep China happy
instead of China having to keep America happy. Debtors are the ones
who have to kowtow to creditors, not the other way around. Thus
we may be headed for a world in which America has to reluctantly
accept a lot of bad outcomes over the next several decades because
we are no longer the economic superpower that we used to be.

It will also become clear to countries like China that America
just doesn't have the funds to pay back the debt. We can print money
and give the foreigners more of our dollars, but they are smart
enough to realize that these dollars are buying them less and less.
So they are going to start by demanding much higher interest rates
on the money they are lending us. That's not good, because it means
that the government is going to have to pay more interest to service

the debt; that drives the annual deficit up even further. Moreover, at some point not long from now, foreign countries are going to dispense with the dollar as the universal currency and pick an alternative: perhaps the Chinese yuan, or more likely a basket of currencies that hold their value better than the currency of the United States. Already China is taking steps in this direction. The Chinese government has encouraged its exporters and foreign firms exporting to China to move away from dollar transactions and start pricing their goods in yuan. On December 25, 2011, China and Japan reached an agreement to stop using dollars and instead use their own currencies in trade and financial transactions. Economist Arvind Subramanian predicts that the yuan "could become the premier reserve currency by the end of this decade, or early next decade."[11]

Once the dollar ceases to be the international currency, then we are in trouble. Now it's no use printing more dollars to pay the foreigners, since the foreigners won't be willing to accept dollars as payment. They will demand to be paid in the new currency, and America will have to turn over assets, goods, and services in order to obtain sufficient amounts of the new currency. This is the point at which the lenders can say: if you can't pay, then we are going to demand that you sell us your major companies, or give us a portion of the real estate in the country, or sell us the national parks.

Third, with $20 trillion in debt, Americans are going to see a sharp decline in their standard of living. We will become poorer as other nations become richer. Our stock market will keep falling as theirs keeps rising. And the effects will be felt across the country. People who are used to going on vacation to Europe are going to have to vacation near their homes, or camp in the backyard. Indeed, it will be more common to see foreigners vacationing in America than to see Americans vacationing abroad. Americans will have to become accustomed to eating at home rather than eating out. If things get bad enough, families may have to ration how often they eat meat. Indeed, Americans will have to endure the unfamiliar sight of Chinese, Brazilian, and Indian visitors occupying the best tables in the best American restaurants. Designers won't bother to have stores in New York or Los Angeles, preferring venues like Rio de Janeiro, Seoul, and Beijing. Americans will start going abroad to study, and find that they may have to learn Mandarin Chinese or Hindi in order to improve their job prospects; the best jobs, after all, will be found elsewhere. Moreover, American popular culture will lose its global appeal, since America will cease to be associated with what is new and rich and cool. Even more significant, the average size of the American home, which has been growing since World War II, is likely to start shrinking. Homeownership will become a luxury, even for one and two-bedroom homes. Renting will become the norm. We may even see families have to share apartments and living spaces, the way that they did when I was growing up in India. The number of homeless may surge, and the government may no longer be able to afford facilities to shelter or feed them. Beggars and panhandlers, who are now a rare sight in a few cities, may begin to appear all over the country. Unemployment will reach levels not seen since the Great Depression, and Americans will be accustomed to seeing what we now see mainly in foreign countries: lots of people with nothing to do, just standing around. For the first time in American history, children will grow up and be worse off than their parents. How can they not be? They are saddled with $20 trillion in debt with no benefits to show for it, and this is money they will have to pay back.

All of this may seem like a nightmare scenario, yet there is nothing dreamlike or imaginary about it. Some of it is already happening, as suggested by a recent headline in the *Wall Street Journal*, "Foreigners Snap Up Properties in the U.S." The newspaper reports that America is seeing "a property-buying binge by Asians, Canadians, Europeans, and Latin Americans" who are increasingly convinced that "America is on sale." We read that "in Manhattan, foreign buyers, led by Russians and Ukranians, are setting records by buying apartments at some of the city's high-end addresses. In Miami, Brazilians and Venezuelans have helped soak up a glut of condos in glass towers overlooking Biscayne Bay, while in Arizona, Canadians are snapping up foreclosed properties they hope to rent out at a profit."[12] Expect all of this to accelerate; it is the logical outcome of continuing down the Obama path. Now, one might say, Obama can't be this stupid. Surely he recognizes that debt of this magnitude cannot go on forever, and as economist Herbert Stein once put it, "If something cannot go on forever, it will stop." There may be some who hold that Obama will correct his course in the second term, and his irresponsible spending will then stop. One reason for thinking this is that if America goes down, it won't be the rich alone who suffer. It will also be the middle class and the poor. Therefore whatever his anti-colonial philosophy, why would Obama pursue policies that harm ordinary and even poor people in America?

The answer to this question is provided in a recent article in *Foreign Policy*, revealingly titled, "We Are the 1 Percent." The article points out that there is indeed a large discrepancy in America between the rich and the poor. But there is an equally large discrepancy between the American standard of living and that of the rest of the world. In other words, Americans who are middle class or even poor by our standards are well-off by world standards. Consider this: the average American household is, according to the article, "scraping by on $55 per person per day." But the global average "is about a fifth of that," about $10 a day. To be in the top 1 percent globally, all you need is an income of $34,000 a year.

We find in the article a supreme irony. Many of Obama's supporters rail against the top 1 percent, fancying themselves in the lowly 99 percent, and this may be true as far as they are concerned. But it is not true as far as Obama is concerned. When he talks about the 1 percent and the 99 percent, he is using a global basis of comparison. So by Obama's measure, the vast majority of Americans are counted as rich; indeed, as the *Foreign Policy* article accurately points out, "if you live in the West, you probably are that 1 percent."[13] Given his anti-colonial mindset, Obama might be supremely indifferent if middle class, lower middle class, and even poor Americans are hurt by his policies, because they too are part of the neo-colonial affluent class; they too owe global reparations; and therefore they too must pay their fair share to achieve global justice through economic leveling.

Obama's goal is to raise up the standard of living in the rest of the world while lowering the standard of living in the United States. This is admittedly a challenging task. Americans currently make up 5 percent of the world's population, but we consume a quarter of the world's resources and products. From my point of view, and probably that of most Americans, this is not inherently unjust. Americans use more because they produce more. But this is not how anti-colonialists see it. For them, America has more because America has stolen this wealth from others, and America must now give it back. This means that Obama will not consider his job finished until America consumes a much smaller fraction of the global economy, or until the American standard of living is comparable to that of the rest of the world.

In fact, Obama seems content to burden our children and grandchildren, who never voted for him, with trillions of dollars of debt that he has accumulated, without them receiving any benefits from it. Again, we may see this as grossly unfair, but from the anti-colonial perspective these future generations are still the beneficiaries of inherited privileges. In a sense, they are in possession of "stolen goods." So they are not entitled to the bigger homes and more expensive cars and healthier meals and superior education that they are getting, and this becomes part of their unfair stock of capital that Obama can reduce by saddling them with a huge pile of debt. If debt produces not just decline but collapse, then these "luxuries," or the benefits of being an American, may not even be there for future generations. I believe that Obama is very clear-eyed about all this. He knows it may take a catastrophe, or a series of catastrophes, to bring about such a fundamental change in the American way of life. Debt is the device he is using to precipitate those catastrophes. And when they occur, and when America has been brought down to the same level as everyone else, then Obama can feel deep satisfaction that, as a consequence of his singular efforts, his country has paid for its colonial sins and settled its debt to the rest of the world.

CHAPTER FOURTEEN

BIG DADDY

He believed in his own talent and singularity;
he felt sure that the usual rules would not apply.[1]
—Jodi Kantor, *The Obamas*

S o far we have seen that Obama, while calling on others to
fulfill their obligations to the needy, doesn't help the needy
in his own family or community. Poor George Obama is on
his own. Obama's aunt can continue to sell coal on the street until
she earns enough to get her teeth fixed. The Obama school can live
on promises; who needs actual cash for books or teacher salaries?
Put this down to rank hypocrisy; Obama wouldn't be the first political leader to call upon others to do what he won't do himself. What
we haven't emphasized thus far, however, is how Obama chastises
others for extravagance while indulging himself extravagantly.
"Everyone must sacrifice for the greater good," Obama said in 2009.
Again, in 2011, Obama said the nation's problems could easily be
solved "if everybody took an attitude of shared sacrifice."[2] Clearly

"everybody" does not include Obama, who lives well by any standard and is not notable for making any obvious personal sacrifices.
In a sense, the rules of frugality are for "the people" rather than for
their leaders. Obama has become, like many Third World anti-
colonial rulers, something of a Big Daddy.

I'll explain what I mean by Big Daddy, but first I must answer an
objection to my premise. Media reports suggest that it is Michelle
rather than Barack who is the driver of the Obamas' lavish lifestyle.
She has been called a North American Evita Peron, and America's
answer to Marie Antoinette, spending $10 million in taxpayer money
for her vacations and putting on a public display of magnanimity
by bagging groceries at a food bank—while wearing a pair of $540
Lanvin sneakers.[3] Michelle has been blasted for everything from her
Princeton thesis to her subsequent employment history. Of her thesis—now available on the web—the writer Christopher Hitchens
wrote, "To describe it as hard to read would be a mistake; the thesis
cannot be 'read' at all, in the strict sense of the term. This is because
it wasn't written in any known language."

Michelle's thesis was about being black at Princeton. Here is the
type of passage that accounts for Hitchens's disdain: "By actually
working with the Black lower class or within their communities as
a result of their ideologies, a separationist may better understand
the desparation [*sic*] of their situation and feel more hopeless about
a resolution as opposed to an integrationist who is ignorant to their
plight."[4] Alas, the grammar is wrong; the tenses are garbled. People
are ignorant "of" the plight of the lower class, not ignorant "to" their
plight. And "desparation" should be spelled "desperation." As Hitchens would surely have pointed out, these are not mere typos; they
reflect an estranged relationship with the English language. Moreover, they appear not in an off-the-cuff transcript but in a thesis that
is supposed to reflect the culmination of one's college career.

Remarkably Michelle graduated with honors at Princeton and was admitted to Harvard Law School. And subsequently Michelle was hired by the University of Chicago to run "programs for community relations, neighborhood outreach, volunteer recruitment, staff diversity, and minority contracting" with a salary of $316,000 a year.

All this may be true, but so what? Michelle Obama is surely not the first mediocre student to graduate from an Ivy League school, or to benefit from her racial background and political connections. If they taught her little at Princeton and yet graduated her with honors, that's an indictment of Princeton; if she was admitted to law school with substandard preparation, that tells you something about the admissions policies of Harvard Law School. And what's the big deal about Michelle's spending habits—she can afford $540 sneakers.

So I'm going to lay off Michelle and focus on Barack Obama, who poses a different and much more serious problem. With Obama, we don't get Michelle's familiar sense of racial entitlement; rather, we see the kind of personal arrogance that was characteristic of his father. Barack Obama Sr. was convinced that he was a genius, and that Kenya needed him, and ultimately that his genius was unrecognized by petty, unimportant people. President Obama displays some of that same narcissism. His favorite word is "I." This was evident in his speech announcing the Bin Laden killing. "And so shortly after taking office, I directed ... I met repeatedly with my national security team.... Finally, last week, I determined.... Today, at my direction...." And so on. With so many uses of the personal pronoun by Obama, one is a little surprised to discover that he was not actually the one who pulled the trigger. Like his father, Obama displays indignation when his great achievements are not appreciated. Of the business community, he says, "I saved these guys when the economy was falling off a cliff. Now I get nothing but their venom." Obama even wants the group he calls greedy, selfish, and fat cats to appreciate how much he has done for them.[5]

One of Obama's lines from the 2008 campaign was "we are the ones we have been waiting for." This seems to imply that the country has been longing for a savior and now he's here. Warned by his political advisers that his party faced a debacle in the 2010 midterm election comparable to the debacle that Clinton faced in 1994, Obama dismissed the comparison: "Well, the big difference between here and '94 was that you've got me." Well, the Democrats suffered big losses in 2010, comparable to their '94 rout, so having Obama didn't help much.

Further examples of Obama's self-esteem abound. Obama has inserted himself into the biographical accounts of other presidents on the White House website. Thus, for example, in the section on President Franklin Roosevelt, we read, "On August 14, 1935, President Roosevelt signed the Social Security Act. Today the Obama administration continues to protect seniors and ensure Social Security will be there for future generations." In a recent interview with Steve Kroft of CBS, Obama noted that "I would put our legislative and foreign policy accomplishments in our first two years against any president with the possible exceptions of Johnson, FDR, and Lincoln." Here Obama places himself in the very top rank of presidents, with just three "possible" exceptions.[6]

My own favorite incident revealing Obama's estimate of himself occurred in India, when the president spoke at a business roundtable in Mumbai. Bhupendra Kansagra, a Kenyan entrepreneur of Indian origin, was speaking, and Obama was trying to guess where his remarks were headed.

> **Kansagra:** Welcome, Mr. President, to India. As a fellow Kenyan, I'm very proud to see that you have made …
> **Obama:** [laughing] Made something of myself?

> **Kansagra:** … India the focus of your drive for exports
> out of the U.S.[7]

I asked psychologist Paul Vitz about the source of Obama's narcissism, and he suggested it comes from Obama's sense of abandonment as a child. Abandonment creates a void, and narcissism is one way to fill the void. Lacking appreciation from his parents, the child becomes his own supplier of praise and recognition. There is a whole literature on this, I understand, but I haven't bothered to read it. What interests me is not so much the psychological basis for Obama's narcissism as the ideological basis for it. Where does Obama get this idea that he is above the normal standards that apply to everyone else?

We can get some insight about this by looking at several prominent African leaders over the past few decades. I am thinking of men such as Idi Amin in Uganda, Jean-Bedel Bokassa in the Central African Republic, Mobutu Sese Seko in Zaire, and Kamuzu Hastings Banda in Malawi. Some of these guys were freedom fighters in the heady colonial days, but over time anti-colonialism became their pretext for looting the country and blaming their country's problems on the former rulers. Moreover, they did not hesitate to make passionate speeches about poverty while they themselves lived like kings. Banda, for instance, lived in a 300-room presidential palace and traveled with a troupe of female dancers who entertained him wherever he went. Amin gave himself innumerable military medals and titles such as Conqueror of the British Empire and True Heir to the Throne of Scotland. Mobutu owned a fleet of Mercedes Benzes and insisted that all government officials wear lapel badges carrying his portrait.

Perhaps the best living example of this genre is the dictator Robert Mugabe in Zimbabwe. Mugabe fought in the revolutionary war against the British, yet since assuming power he has shown little concern for the welfare of his people. Instead he has enriched himself and his supporters. Mugabe treats Air Zimbabwe as his personal airline. He used state funds to build a $25 million palace for himself, expertly decorated by his wife Grace, who is locally called "First Shopper" for her numerous European shopping sprees. Invoking the legacy of British rule, Mugabe routinely confiscates the land of white farmers for his cronies. Yet while Mugabe lives high on the hog, Zimbabwe today is a failed state, with widespread poverty, malnutrition, and disease. Life expectancy has fallen nearly fifteen years, from sixty to forty-five. The African writer and Nobel laureate Wole Soyinka writes about "the corruption, venality, hypocrisy, and megalomania of much of the Third World leadership," noting both "their arrogant neglect of, and alienation from, the people they are meant to serve" and "the contrast of their lifestyles with that of the productive majority."[8]

Obama, too, displays some of these traits. The London *Daily Mail* reports that Obama likes to travel in style. Shortly after being elected he took his wife to a Broadway show. The trip from Washington to New York required two planes, two helicopters, extra planes for security, and closing the streets for a presidential motorcade through the city. Obama said he had promised his wife the treat, and he seemed unbothered by the fact that American taxpayers paid for the whole trip, except the $60 Broadway tickets, which the Obamas paid for themselves. The *Daily Mail* also reported that when the Obamas vacationed on Martha's Vineyard, renting a $50,000-per-week farmhouse for the occasion, Obama and his wife took separate jets, even though they arrived only a few hours apart. Evidently convenience for the Obama family was, in their view, worth the cost to the American taxpayer. While the White House customarily displays around a dozen Christmas trees, the Obama White House in 2011 featured thirty-seven trees, including one that was flown in from

Wisconsin for the purpose. More recently the *Daily Mail* reveals that the Obamas fly in a personal trainer from Chicago each week for their workout regimen; apparently there are not adequate trainers in the nation's capital. All presidents deserve time off, but Obama has set a record for a single presidential term in taking seventeen vacations stretching over seventy-four days and involving more than a hundred rounds of golf.[9]

Now several points are worth noting here. First, very little of this is reported in the United States. Obama worshippers in the media ignore Obama's excesses, and when reports from abroad surface, they dismiss and pooh-pooh them. Second, while the Obamas are permitted to use government funds for legitimate purposes, such as White House expenses, official travel, and so on, previous presidents, like Bush and Reagan, took vacations at their own ranch, or at Camp David. The Obamas' preferred venues are beachfront villas in Hawaii or ski cottages in Vail or mansions in Martha's Vineyard. Third, what makes the Obamas' lifestyle especially galling is that they regularly portray themselves as ordinary folks, struggling with the same difficulties as the rest of us; yet they are reveling while much of the country is in economic distress.

Still, for me this is all a side issue. My real interest is elsewhere. In his classic work, *Imagined Communities*, Benedict Anderson reflected on the anti-colonial leaders who had come to power in many Third World countries. He offered this observation about them: "One should ... not be much surprised if the revolutionary leaderships, consciously or unconsciously, come to play lord of the manor."[10] Now that's an arresting statement. Why is this behavior unsurprising? And how do the new leaders themselves make this transition?

We can gain some insight into this topic by examining Obama's June 2011 press conference in which he railed against the owners of corporate jets. Six times he singled them out for attack, according to the subsequent news report in *USA Today*. And what was Obama's purpose? He was attacking a tax break that allows corporate jet owners to depreciate their planes two years faster than commercial jet owners. As Obama well knew, the actual benefit to the Treasury from eliminating the tax break would be minimal. Yet Obama clearly conveyed by his remarks how much he disdains these fat cats. A few days later, the legal scholar Richard Epstein pointed out a little anomaly. Obama himself travels on a jet. It's called Air Force One. "For those who are not up on the details," Epstein wrote, "Air Force One is not a single plane, but it is a code for whatever jet the president flies at any given time. In fact, there are two specially equipped Boeing 747s capable of whisking the president and his entourage away at a moment's notice anywhere around the globe." Air Force One, Epstein added, comes with an operating cost of between $60,000 and $181,000 per hour. That's not counting all the planning and support services involved. To rub it in, Epstein writes, "Just think of the number of college scholarships and food inspection programs this nation could fund if it had the moral courage to make the president fly first class commercial on international long hauls, take Amtrak for shorter trips, and use Skype for critical one-on-one negotiations."[11]

Epstein is being sarcastic. He is not calling for Obama to stop using Air Force One. His point is that just as the president may have good reason for using a corporate jet, even one that costs tens of thousands of dollars per hour, so too corporate jet owners may have good reason for owning and flying in private planes. I would also add that corporate jet owners may get modest tax breaks, but in general they are paying for their own planes, while we are the ones who are paying for Obama's plane. Most striking about Obama's attitude is not that he detests corporate fliers—whom he portrays as the illegitimate beneficiaries of tax breaks—but that he seems totally oblivious to his own 100 percent flying subsidy.

Now why is that? One way to answer this question is to think of Obama himself as the CEO of a big corporation: the Federal Government. The Federal Government is the largest corporation in America. Has it been performing well? Actually, it has been performing miserably. It is drowning in waste, incompetence, and debt. If it were a private corporation it would long ago have gone bankrupt and shut its doors. In the private sector, there is predictable outrage when CEOs whose companies are doing badly nevertheless get lavish bonuses, perks, and benefits. How, then, can Obama justify appropriating rewards to himself when his corporation has accumulated $5 trillion of debt on his watch? By ordinary standards Obama seems like a shameless hypocrite for doing what he faults other CEOs for doing. Our error, however, may be to use ordinary standards in evaluating Obama. Let's remember that he judges himself by his own standard, the anti-colonial standard. By that standard, Obama is succeeding. He seeks to increase the size of his corporation and reduce the power of the other corporations, and he has done that. He intends to use debt to level the gap between American affluence and global want, and he has done that also. Once again, Obama is doing all this not because he wants what's bad for America. He wants what's good for America, but he has a very different view of what's good for America than most Americans do.

What I find most problematic about Obama playing lord of the manor is not that it leads to extravagance and waste—although it does—but that it leads to the arrogance of power. David Brooks addressed the issue of how Obama views his own power in a recent column, "The Pragmatic Leviathan." Brooks recalls that when he was in college he read Thomas Hobbes's great work, *Leviathan*. "On the cover was an image from the first edition of the book, published in 1651. It shows the British nation as a large man. The people make up the muscles and flesh. Then at the top, there is the king, who is the head and the mind." Brooks sees an analogy here to Obama: "He has come to seem like the sovereign on the cover of *Leviathan*—the brain of the nation to which all the cells in the body and the nervous system must report and defer."[12]

In other words, Obama is the Indispensable One and we are his subordinates. Or, to use a term drawn from the colonial and anti-colonial literature, Obama is the Big Daddy. The Big Daddy is the Great Leader who makes our problems his own and takes it upon himself to solve them. Solving them is obviously supremely challenging, and therefore who can begrudge the Big Daddy a special set of privileges that are not available to anyone else? No wonder that Obama feels comfortable in asking of others what he doesn't ask of himself. Don't they realize that they are not like him? Big Daddy operates by his own rules, living above the normal restraints, even in some cases above the law. America seems to be the only Western country today that is being ruled by a Big Daddy.

One of Obama's Big Daddy traits is that he surrounds himself with "czars": there is an auto czar and a border czar, a climate czar and a domestic violence czar, an energy czar and a technology czar, an Afghanistan czar and a Mideast czar, a regulatory czar and a stimulus czar, a science czar and a pay czar. What's with all these czars? Do we live in czarist Russia? I think Obama relishes the idea of czars because they suggest administrative officials who are accountable to no one but him. He is the Supreme Czar and they are the Little Czars. Together they will tell the rest of us little people how we should live.

It may seem unfair to brand Obama an autocrat on the Russian model. But Obama has repeatedly shown that he has an autocratic streak. On at least two occasions, he has shown that if he doesn't like a law, he just doesn't enforce it. Recently Obama said that he would selectively apply the immigration laws so that if illegal immigrants came here as children, and pose no security threat, they will not be deported or prosecuted. Now if this is a wise policy, Congress should make the necessary change to the immigration laws. But instead of urging Congress to change the law, Obama implements the parts of the law he wants to and ignores the parts that he wants to. In a similar vein, Obama announced that his administration will not enforce the Defense of Marriage Act (outlawing gay marriage) because he doesn't think it is constitutional. Now the Defense of Marriage Act was passed with overwhelming majorities in both Houses of Congress and signed into law by President Clinton. It has withstood all legal challenges so far, and obviously it is the Supreme Court, not Obama, that determines the constitutionality of legislation. It seems obvious that we cannot have a president who enforces only the laws he agrees with, and yet this is precisely the president we do have.[13]

Behind such policies there is an attitude, captured in Obama's recent remark, reported in the *New York Times*: "Mr. Obama has told people that it would be so much easier to be the president of China." Ah yes. That's because the president of China is basically a dictator. He doesn't have to answer to Congress, and he is largely unaccountable to public opinion. He just does what he wants, and I'm sure he has lots of little czars to help him execute his grand designs. Obama so desperately seeks this kind of power that he blurts out one of the most imprudent remarks of his presidency, and the *New York Times* obligingly buries it in the last line of a long article on Obama's Middle East policy.[14]

When I served in the Reagan White House, I enjoyed listening to the band play "Hail to the Chief." Yet Reagan always emphasized

that the White House was the people's house, and that he worked
for the American people. With Obama, however, we have a leader
who fancies himself as the overlord of America. His attitude, not
dissimilar from that of his father, is less one of a democratic leader
than one of a Third World dictator or hereditary tribal chief. He
harbors grand visions of himself as the savior, setting right the problems not only of America, but also of the world. If we re-elect him,
we are choosing to be governed by a man who has become a legend
in his own mind, a law unto himself, America's Big Daddy. Under
those circumstances, "Hail to the Chief" takes on a totally different
connotation.

CHAPTER FIFTEEN

SURVIVING OBAMA

On this earth one place is not so different from another.[1]

—Barack Obama, *Dreams from My Father*

The most dangerous man in America currently lives in the White House.

He's dangerous not because he wants to do what's bad for America. He's dangerous because what he thinks is good for America is actually very bad for America. Here's a way to think about it. Imagine if we were in charge of the Los Angeles Lakers. We hired a coach, who began to call plays for the team to lose. He did so not because he hated the Lakers, but because he thought it was wrong for the Lakers to win so much. He didn't like the dominance of the Lakers, believing it would produce hubris in the team and was also unfair to the other teams. If we had such a coach, there is little doubt that we would not renew his contract. But we would also ask ourselves how we hired this guy in the first place.

How did we get Obama? Are the American people to blame for putting him in? I don't think so. People didn't know Obama, so they voted for him based on what he told them. He appealed to their hopes and aspirations, and they were noble hopes and aspirations. So the public was deceived. Obama was no ideological centrist, no unifier—he never intended to be. He had a completely different agenda all along, one that he knew even most Democrats would not support. So Obama has, from the beginning, disguised his true ideology and his true agenda. Only an investigation of his background and an examination of his actions have helped us to ferret him out.

So now we know him. Or at least we know a lot more about him. We can see where he came from, and we can understand what he is doing. And while we can project, based on his current actions, where he is likely to go in the next four years, we cannot really know what he has in store for America. Presidents don't always reveal themselves in their first term; they have to build constituencies and focus on re-election. Only after Obama is re-elected will he be truly free to move in whatever direction he chooses, unconstrained by public opinion. In ways that we have foreseen and ways that we have not, he can complete the job of remaking America.

How should we respond to Obama? We shouldn't despise him; I don't. In some ways, I feel sorry for him. He is a victim of the most terrible parental abandonment. He responded to that abandonment with a certain creativity and determination. He's a fractured soul, still seeking, as he admits in his book, to be worthy of his father's love. He discovered that his father was a profoundly flawed man, and he knew it would not be good to copy his personality. So he embraced what he thought was the best of his father: the anti-colonial ideology. That ideology was supported by his mother, a profoundly flawed woman. Throughout his life Obama sought surrogate fathers or mentors who could reinforce and develop his anti-colonial worldview. That worldview is now embedded in his psyche.

I understand Obama's deep attachment to anti-colonialism. Colonialism was a brutal system, which came about because of the immense military superiority of Europe to non-Western cultures. The English writer Hilaire Belloc summarized the European advantage:

> Whatever happens, we have got
> the Maxim Gun, and they have not.[2]

Once the Europeans established their domination, they did not hesitate to use force in order to maintain it. Sometimes the gun was used on pretexts that were whimsical, even recreational. The British explorer Henry Morgan Stanley, for instance, reported that as he piloted his boat *Lady Alice* across Lake Tanganyika, "the beach was crowded by infuriates and mockers.... We perceived we were followed by several canoes in some of which we saw spears shaken at us." So Stanley got to work: "I opened on them with the Winchester Repeating Rifle. Six shots and four deaths were sufficient to quiet the mocking." Another British explorer, Richard Burton, once remarked that Stanley "shoots Negroes as if they were monkeys."[3]

One of Obama's first acts as president was to remove a Winston Churchill bust from the White House. Churchill was a lifelong colonialist. He was a cavalry officer with the Malakand Field Force fighting on the northwest frontier of India. He rode with Lord Kitchener at the Battle of Omdurman in the Sudan. He championed British rule in India and scorned Gandhi as a troublemaker and a fraud. And when Churchill was re-elected in the 1950s, he suppressed the Mau Mau insurrection in Kenya, which resulted in the arrest of Obama's father Barack Sr., and the detention and torture of his grandfather Onyango Obama.[4] So President Obama has good reason to hate Winston Churchill.

Churchill viewed colonialism purely from the point of view of the colonizer, but colonialism was hard on the people who lived under it. My grandfather was routinely humiliated by his British superiors, and when, many years later, I wanted to come to America, he recommended that I not go: "It's full of white people." I can see why Obama's own grandfather might feel this way; he was, after all, held in a detention camp by the British. Obama and I are the descendants of these colonial subjects. We have not suffered, but we have the knowledge of the suffering, and the scar can do the work of the wound. Yet I believe that if we are honest with ourselves, we have to admit that while colonialism was bad for our grandfathers, it has been pretty good for their children and grandchildren.

Let's pause to consider why this is so. Our authority for this inquiry is, of all people, Muhammad Ali. When Ali returned to America, having won the heavyweight title against George Foreman in Zaire, he was asked by a reporter, "Champ, what did you think of Africa?" Ali replied, "Thank God my granddaddy got on that boat!" Ali was being his usual outrageous self, but his point is a provocative one. Ali is saying that slavery was very hard for his ancestors but nevertheless it was the transmission belt that brought him into the orbit of Western civilization. Had there been no slavery, had Ali been born in Zaire instead of America, his life would be very different, much poorer, much less free.

The same is true of colonialism. It was the transmission belt that brought black and brown and yellow people into the orbit of Western prosperity and Western freedom. Actually, it brought them into the modern world. As Kishore Mahbubani puts it in *The New Asian Hemisphere*, "Modernity is a gift from the West to the rest of the world."[5] When I survey my own life—my ability to speak English, my Western education, my moral commitments to democracy and civil liberty and human dignity and individual rights—I realize how much of this is the consequence of two and a half centuries of British rule in India. Paradoxically, Winston Churchill and what he represents have far more to do with what I most cherish than Gandhi and what he represents. If I had the chance, I'd move the Winston Churchill bust back into the Oval Office.

None of this is intended as a simple-minded defense of colonialism. The British didn't come to India or Kenya to give the native people all these wonderful gifts. Colonialism was not based on philanthropy; it was a form of conquest and occupation. When the British came to India and Kenya, they came for selfish reasons: they came to rule and to benefit from that rule. Nevertheless, in order to rule effectively the British introduced Western ideas and Western institutions to the subject peoples. Eventually those people used British ideas of self-determination and freedom to combat British rule. As a native-born Indian, I have to say that even our freedom was a consequence of what we learned from our Western captors. And I came to America to study and work because I viewed it as the apex of Western civilization. So here is the paradox. I am a Third World guy who has embraced America, and Obama is an American who has embraced a Third World ideology.

Still, it is not enough to describe Obama as an anti-colonialist without specifying what kind of an anti-colonialist he is. Actually there are two types of anti-colonialism. One is anti-colonialism of the free market, pro-American type. The American revolution represented that type of anti-colonialism. India today represents the same desire to be free of foreign rule, and yet to adopt a pro-American, free market approach. Even in Kenya, the first president, Jomo Kenyatta, stressed that he wanted to get rid of British rule but he was pro-Western and wanted to preserve property rights and free markets.

This is clearly not the anti-colonialism of Obama. Rather, he adopted his father's brand of anti-colonialism, which can be described as socialist in economics and anti-American in foreign policy. This is a particular type of anti-colonialism that developed in the twentieth century. Obama is not alone in this camp; a whole bunch of Third World rulers, from Idi Amin in Uganda to Julius Nyerere in Tanzania to Robert Mugabe in Zimbabwe, shared the same ideology. Not that it worked out in those countries; it hasn't worked anywhere. Yet Obama seems to be relentlessly implementing it in America, perhaps in the expectation that it can work here for the first time.

So far I haven't bothered to defend free markets and show that they are the best way to generate wealth. The world already knows this, and the Third World now knows it as well as the West. More than once Obama has raised the question: why is South Korea now forty times richer than Kenya, when both countries were at the same level at the time of Kenya's independence in the early 1960s? We know the answer to that question: Kenya went the socialist road and South Korea went the capitalist road. Sure, there are important cultural differences between the Kenyans and South Koreans. We can, however, demonstrate the superiority of capitalism by comparing North Korea and South Korea. Same people, same culture. Yet North Korea remains desperately poor while South Korea is a comparatively rich country. Another example is my own native country of India. India tried socialism for nearly a half-century after independence, and now for the past two decades it has been trying free market capitalism. Once again, the results are in: capitalism is working and socialism failed miserably. The Indians didn't figure this out by reading Adam Smith; they figured it out by watching what capitalism has done for living standards in China. Today in India and China there is no more debate between capitalism and socialism; the issue is settled. Ironically, Obama reviles the very free market capitalism that is helping the developing world overcome poverty and become rich.

Obama's depreciation of Pax Americana—of America's outsized influence—is equally delusional. Contrary to Obama's view, America is not a colonizing nation. America is not like the British and the French. Nor are we like the Roman Empire. Sure, America has intervened in several countries over the last few decades. So here's my question: if we invaded those countries, why don't we own them? The reason is that America moved in and America moved out. Nor did we steal the resources of those countries. Iraq is a case in point. America did not benefit financially from its occupation of Iraq. On the contrary, the war in Iraq was a costly expedition. And from the beginning America encouraged free elections in Iraq, so the Iraqi people could choose their own government. America turned the keys to the oilfields over to the Iraqis, so that they could do what they want with their oil. Even when America has used massive force, as against Germany and Japan in World War II, that force was accompanied by a desire to put something better in place of what was destroyed. Thus America introduced democratic institutions to both countries, and invested huge amounts of money in rebuilding Europe after the war. What other empire would do these things? What would the twentieth century have been like if it were not for America? Far from being an empire of looting, America has proved to be an empire of ideals, an "empire of liberty."[6]

I know that many Americans are weary of war and ready to get out of faraway places like Afghanistan. During the second half of the nineteenth century, there was a lively debate between two British politicians, Benjamin Disraeli and William Gladstone, over the future of the British Empire. Disraeli was the champion of empire, and he defended the British Empire in terms of national greatness. England had to choose, he said, between "a comfortable England," isolated and ordinary, or being "a great country, an imperial country, a country where your sons, when they rise … obtain not merely the esteem of their countrymen, but command the respect of the world."

Gladstone took up Disraeli's challenge, and defended what he was not ashamed to call Little England. He said, in effect: Let's forget about empire. Let's forget about the world. Let's just live on our little island, and tend to our vegetable gardens, and grow our petunias. Let's not try to be special, because we aren't. Let's just enjoy what we have over here.[7] I don't want to directly compare Gladstone and Obama—there are too many cultural and historical differences to take into account. I do think that Obama's philosophy can be neatly summed up as: Little America. He wants to shrink America, to diminish America, to downsize America. What makes Gladstone different from Obama is that even as prime minister, Gladstone did not actually liquidate the British Empire. Ultimately the British Empire was destroyed by two world wars. By contrast, Obama is diminishing American prosperity and influence. Little America is a realizable goal for Obama in a way that Little England was not for Gladstone.

We cannot hope or wait for Obama to change course; he cannot change course. If he could have, he would have. Look at it this way. Obama could have assured his re-election this year by moving to the center, as Bill Clinton did after the 1994 midterm debacle. Obama faced a similar debacle in 2010, so why has he refused to do what any other politician would have done under the circumstances? For most people this question is unanswerable, but we know the answer. He simply can't bring himself to do it, because if he did, the Great One would be disappointed. His mentors would be disappointed. Obama would become a sellout, like Lolo and Onyango and George. His mom sent him home from Indonesia to avoid this. This is who he became and this is the Obama we are stuck with.

I realize that our problem may be bigger than Obama. There may be some Americans who share Gladstone's outlook: they are tired of America being a world power; they too would like to go back to their vegetable gardens. First Lady Michelle Obama has already planted her vegetable garden, and she's urging other Americans to do likewise.[8] Between these people and Obama there is a secret: he is pursuing decline, and they want decline. How much decline has Obama achieved in four years? I would estimate that he has achieved about 40 percent decline. I get this number from the 40 percent wealth decline that Americans have seen over the past five years.[9] If Obama gets a second term, and can achieve a further 40 percent reduction in the net worth of Americans, he would have presided over a stunning two-thirds decline in the wealth of America. Basically America at that point would cease to be a first world country, and its wealth would be comparable to that of the rest of the world. Similarly, Obama has moved America from the world's sole superpower to a world increasingly shaped by other countries: China, Russia, Brazil, India, and the Islamic countries. In another four years, Obama can complete the transition from an America-dominated world to the kind of multi-polar world that preceded the age of European discovery and conquest.

For me, this is a strategy of national suicide. For me to see America shrunk, downsized, and diminished would be to see my childhood ambitions crushed, my decision to come to America invalidated, my lifelong love for America bitterly disappointed. I don't want to see this happen. I have faith in the good sense of Americans, and believe that if most people realize who Obama really is, they will not give him a second term. Earlier we didn't know him; now we do. Whether he realizes his agenda is ultimately not up to him—it's up to us. Still, Obama is hoping that he can once again cajole a majority of Americans into voting for their own decline and impoverishment. He needs them to keep him in office, although ultimately he isn't concerned about what they think of him. Ultimately he answers to the verdict of his own conscience. How gratifying it would be for Obama to have accomplished his permanent remaking of America by 2016, and to hear as he leaves office, from a voice inside his head: Well done, good and faithful servant.

NOTES

CHAPTER 1

1. Barack Obama, Inaugural Address, January 20, 2009, http://www
    .whitehouse.gov/blog/inaugural-address.
2. Brett Arenda, "IMF Bombshell: Age of America nears end," April 25,
    2011, http://articles.marketwatch.com/2011-04-25/commen
    tary/30714377_1_imf-chinese-economy-international-monetary
    -fund; Arvind Subramanian, "The Inevitable Superpower," *Foreign
    Affairs*, September/October 2011, http://www.foreignaffairs.com/arti
    cles/68205/arvind-subramanian/the-inevitable-superpower; Stephen
    M. Walt, "The End of the American Era," *National Interest*, October
    25, 2011, http://nationalinterest.org/article/the-end-the-american
    -era-6037.
3. Federal Reserve Board, "Changes in U.S. Family Finances from 2007
    to 2010," *Federal Reserve Bulletin*, June 2012, http://www.federalre
    serve.gov/pubs/bulletin/; Robert Frank, "America Lost 129,000 Mil-
    lionaires in 2011," CNBC, May 31, 2012, http://www.cnbc.com
    /id/47631154/America_Lost_129_000_Millionaires_in_2011; James
    Surowiecki, "No End in Sight," *The New Yorker*, April 30, 2012, p. 23;
    Jeff Bergner, "What a Difference Four Years Makes," *Weekly Standard*,
    June 18, 2012, p. 18.

4. "Nuclear Summit: Barack Obama Tells Russia's Dmitry Medvedev More Flexibility After Election," *Reuters*, March 26, 2012.

5. Frantz Fanon, *The Wretched of the Earth* (Grove Press, 1963), pp. 102–3.

6. Kwame Nkrumah, *Neocolonialism: The Last Stage of Imperialism* (International Publishers, 1965).

7. Chinweizu, *The West and the Rest of Us* (Vintage Books, 1975), p. 406.

8. Ali Mazrui, *Cultural Forces in World Politics* (James Currey, 1990), p. 106; Edward Said, *Culture and Imperialism* (Alfred A. Knopf, 1993), pp. xxii–xxiii; Aimé Césaire, *Discourse on Colonialism* (Monthly Review Press, 2000), p. 77.

9. Frantz Fanon, *Black Skin, White Masks* (Grove Press, 2008), p. 193; Albert Memmi, *The Colonizer and the Colonized* (Beacon Press, 1991), pp. 127, 147, 151; Chinweizu, *The West and the Rest of Us*, p. 137.

CHAPTER 2

1. Barack Obama, *The Audacity of Hope* (Three Rivers Press, 2006), p. 11.

2. Charles Krauthammer, "The Perfect Stranger," *Washington Post*, August 29, 2008, http://www.washingtonpost.com/wp-dyn/content/article/2008/08/28/AR2008082802852.html.

3. "Charlie Rose Show: A Conversation with Tom Brokaw," October 30, 2008, http://www.charlierose.com/view/interview/9330.

4. James Fallows, "First Families," *New York Times Book Review*, June 17, 2012, p. 10; Jonathan Alter, *The Promise* (Simon & Schuster, 2010), p. viii; Richard Cohen, "Who is Barack Obama?" *RealClearPolitics*, July 20, 2010, http://www.realclearpolitics.com/articles/2010/07/20/barack_obama_introduce_yourself_106374.html; Bill Keller, "Fill in the Blanks," *New York Times*, September 18, 2011, http://www.nytimes.com/2011/09/19/opinion/filling-in-the-blanks.html?pagewanted=all; David Maraniss, *Barack Obama: The Story* (Simon & Schuster, 2012), p. xxi.

5. Barack Obama, *Dreams from My Father* (Three Rivers Press, 2004), pp. 3, 210; Sasha Abramsky, *Inside Obama's Brain* (Portfolio Press, 2009), p. 33; Janny Scott, "Obama's Account of New York Years Often Differs from What Others Say," *New York Times*, October 30, 2007,

http://www.nytimes.com/2007/10/30/us/politics/30obama.html
?pagewanted=all; David Maraniss, "Becoming Obama," *Vanity Fair*,
June 2012, p. 145.

6. Peter Firstbrook, *The Obamas* (Crown Publishers, 2010), p. 169; Sally
Jacobs, *The Other Barack* (Public Affairs, 2011), p. 25.

7. Nick Pisa, "Barack Obama's 'Lost' Brother Found in Kenya," *London
Telegraph*, August 20, 2008, http://www.telegraph.co.uk/news/world
news/barackobama/2590614/Barack-Obamas-lost-brother-found-in
-Kenya.html; David McKenzie, "Behind the Scenes: Meet George
Obama," CNN, August 22, 2008, http://articles.cnn.com/2008-08-22
/politics/bts.obama.brother_1_half-brother-kenyan-father-barack
-obama?_s=PM:POLITICS.

8. David Cohen, "Barack Obama's Broken Promise to African Village,"
London *Evening Standard*, July 25, 2008.

9. See, e.g., Jesse Washington, "Many Insisting That Obama Is Not
Black," *Huffington Post*, July 29, 2010, http://www.huffingtonpost
.com/2008/12/14/ap-many-insisting-that-ob_n_150846.html.

10. Ishmael Reed, cited in David Remnick, *The Bridge* (Alfred A. Knopf,
2010), p. 534; Amy Goodman, Cornel West interview, November 19,
2010, http://www.democracynow.org/2010/11/19/cornel_west_on
_charles_rangel_bush; Rick Cohen, "Cornel West Says Obama Policies
Have Racist Effects," *NPQ*, November 23, 2010, http://www.nonprof
itquarterly.org/index.php?option=com_content&view=article&id=7
481:cornel-west-says-obama-policies-have-racist-effects&catid
=155:nonprofit-newswire&Itemid=986.

11. Isabel Wilkerson, "Race to the Bottom," *New Republic*, March 1, 2012,
pp. 10–11; Brian Montopoli, "Maxine Waters: Why Isn't Obama in
Black Communities?" CBS News, August 17, 2011, http://www
.cbsnews.com/8301-503544_162-20093711-503544.html; Scott Wilson,
"Obama, the loner president," *Washington Post*, October 7, 2011,
http://www.washingtonpost.com/opinions/obama-the-loner-presi
dent/2011/10/03/gIQAHFcSTL_story.html.

12. Maureen Dowd, "Spock at the Bridge," *New York Times*, March 1,
2009, http://www.nytimes.com/2009/03/01/opinion/01dowd.html;
Jacob Weisberg, "Only Connect!" *Slate*, January 23, 2010, http://www
.slate.com/articles/news_and_politics/the_big_idea/2010/01/only_con
nect.html; James Kloppenberg, *Reading Obama* (Princeton, NJ:
Princeton University Press, 2011).

13. Frank Rich, "Obama's Original Sin," *New York Times Magazine*, July 3, 2011, http://nymag.com/news/frank-rich/obama-economy /presi dents-failure/; Robert Kuttner, "What Now for the Democrats?" *Huffington Post*, December 5, 2010, http://www.huffingtonpost.com /robert-kuttner/what-now-for-the-democrat_b_792301.html; AP, "Obama, Democrats Losing Labor Union Support," *Huffington Post*, September 4, 2011, http://www.huffingtonpost.com/2011/09/04 /obama-democrats-labor-unions_n_948319.html; Ron Suskind, *Confidence Men* (New York: HarperCollins, 2011).

14. Jonah Goldberg, "What Kind of a Socialist is Barack Obama?" *Commentary*, May 2010, p. 9.

15. Stanley Kurtz, "Romney, Obama, and Socialism," *National Review*, September 23, 2011, http://www.nationalreview.com/corner/278158 /romney-obama-and-socialism-stanley-kurtz#.

16. "The Candidates and Repeal," *Weekly Standard*, January 2-January 9, 2012, p. 10.

17. Noemie Emery, "Over-Rated," *Weekly Standard*, October 10, 2011, p. 24; Fred Barnes, "Obama's Learning Curve," *Weekly Standard*, December 27, 2010, p. 11; Edward Klein, *The Amateur* (Regnery, 2012), p. 71; Brett Stephens, "Is Obama Smart?" *Wall Street Journal*, August 9, 2011.

18. Kevin Hassett, "Manchurian Candidate Starts War on Business," Bloomberg, March 9, 2009, http://www.bloomberg.com/apps/news? pid=newsarchive&sid=amhpOT5rlR1Y.

19. Dorothy Rabinowitz, "The Alien in the White House," *Wall Street Journal*, June 9, 2010, http://online.wsj.com/article/SB10001424052 7487033026045752942316313187278.html.

20. Obama, *The Audacity of Hope*, pp. 8–9; Sean Wilentz, "The Mirage," *New Republic*, November 17, 2011, p. 25.

21. Stephen Cohen and J. Bradford DeLong, *The End of Influence* (Basic Books, 2010), pp. 6, 14, 143; Erica Werner, "Obama Promotes Modest American Dream," *Seattle PI*, February 21, 2012, http://www .seattlepi.com/news/article/Obama-promotes-modest-American -dream-3345306.php.

22. Export-Import Bank of the United States, "Ex-Im Bank Board Approves $2.84 Billion Export Financing for Colombian Refinery Project," May 19, 2011, http://www.exim.gov/pressrelease_print .cfm/0BF22A51-A985-1648-515C22E229E893C6/.

23.   Zach Carter, "Trans-Pacific Partnership: Key Senate Democrat Joins
      Bipartisan Trade Revolt Against Obama," *Huffington Post*, May 23, 2012,
      http://www.huffingtonpost.com/2012/05/23/trans-pacific-partnership-ron
      -wyden_n_1540984.html; Zach Carter, "Congress Revolts On Obama Plan
      That Would Ban 'Buy American,'" *Huffington Post*, May 3, 2012, http://
      www.huffingtonpost.com/2012/05/03/obama-trade-congress-buy
      -american_n_1475277.html; Zach Carter, "Obama Trade Document
      Leaked, Revealing New Corporate Powers and Broken Campaign
      Promises," *Huffington Post*, June 13, 2012, http://www.huffingtonpost
      .com/2012/06/13/obama-trade-document-leak_n_1592593.html.

24.   Dan Voorhis, "Hawker Beechcraft Loses Out on Big Air Force Con-
      tract," *Wichita Eagle*, November 18, 2011, http://www.kansas
      .com/2011/11/18/2108059/hawker-beechcraft-said-air-force.html;
      Zachary Goldfarb, "Obama's Support for Export Industry Leads to
      Clash of U.S. Interests," *Washington Post*, February 19, 2012, http://
      www.washingtonpost.com/business/economy/obamas-support-for
      -export-industry-leads-to-clash-of-us-interests/2012/02/16/gIQA
      le2YJR_story.html.

25.   Eyder Peralta, "WikiLeaks: Japan Rebuffed Idea of U.S. Apology for
      Hiroshima," National Public Radio, October 12, 2011, http://www
      .npr.org/blogs/thetwo-way/2011/10/12/141276162/wikileaks-japan
      -rebuffed-idea-of-u-s-apology-for-hiroshima; Richard Halloran, "Will
      Obama Apologize for Hiroshima & Nagasaki?" *RealClearPolitics*,
      November 15, 2009, http://www.realclearpolitics.com/arti
      cles/2009/11/15/will_obama_apologize_for_hiroshima_naga
      zaki_99166.html; Tim Edwards, "Falklands: Obama Under Fire for
      Failing Britain," *The Week*, February 26, 2010, http://www.theweek
      .co.uk/politics/16331/falklands-obama-under-fire-failing-britain; Nile
      Gardiner, "Barack Obama's unwelcome Jubilee Present to Britain,"
      London *Telegraph*, June 5, 2012, http://blogs.telegraph.co.uk/news
      /nilegardiner/100162290/barack-obamas-unwelcome-jubilee-present
      -to-britain-washington-reaffirms-oas-resolution-calling-for-falklands
      -negotiations-with-argentina/.

CHAPTER 3

1.   Barack Obama, *Dreams from My Father*, p. 220.
2.   Ibid., pp. xv, 430.

3.   See, e.g., Howard Kurtz, "White House Rips Forbes over Obama Cover Story," *Washington Post*, September 17, 2010, http://www.washington post.com/wp-dyn/content/article/2010/09/16/AR2010091606921.html; Michael Calderone, "Robert Gibbs Questions Accuracy of Forbes' Obama Piece," Yahoo! News, September 17, 2010, http://news.yahoo .com/blogs/upshot/robert-gibbs-questions-accuracy-forbes-obama -piece.html; Maureen Dowd, "Who's the Con Man?" *New York Times*, September 14, 2010, http://www.nytimes.com/2010/09/15 /opinion/15dowd.html; interview with Joe Biden, *Rachel Maddow Show*, MSNBC, September 15, 2010; Media Matters, "D'Souza's The Roots of Obama's Rage Rooted in Lies," October 4, 2010, http://media matters.org/research/201010040030; David Frum, "Gingrich: Obama Wants Whitey's Money," FrumForum.com, September 13, 2010, http:// www.frumforum.com/gingrich-obama-wants-whiteys-money/; Alex Pareene, "Newt Gingrich on Obama the 'Kenyan Anti-Colonial' Con Man," *Salon*, September 13, 2010, http://www.salon.com/2010/09/13 /newt_dsouza_obama_kenyan_con/; Ryan Chittum, "Forbes' Shameful Piece on Obama as the 'Other,'" *Columbia Journalism Review*, September 13, 2010, http://www.cjr.org/the_audit/forbes_shameful_obama _dinesh_dsouza.php?page=all.

4.   Jodi Kantor, "In Law School, Obama Found Political Voice," *New York Times*, January 28, 2007, http://www.nytimes.com/2007/01/28 /us/politics/28obama.html?pagewanted=all.

5.   Tom Shachtman, *Airlift to America* (St. Martin's Press, 2009), p. 236; John Oywa, "My Life With Obama Senior," Kenya *Standard*, November 11, 2008; Obama, *Dreams from My Father*, pp. 209, 348; Sally Jacobs, *The Other Barack*, pp. 148–49; Sally Jacobs, "A Father's Charm, Absence," *Boston Globe*, September 21, 2008, http://www.boston.com /news/politics/2008/articles/2008/09/21/a_fathers_charm_absence/; Jon Meacham, "On His Own," *Newsweek*, August 22, 2008.

6.   Kevin Merida, "The Ghost of a Father," *Washington Post*, December 14, 2007, http://www.washingtonpost.com/wp-dyn/content/arti cle/2007/12/13/AR2007121301784.html; Meacham, "On His Own"; David Mendell, *Obama* (Harper, 2007), p. 40; Obama, *Dreams from My Father*, p. 220; Barack Obama, *The Audacity of Hope*, p. 205; Auma Obama, *And Then Life Happens* (St. Martin's Press, 2012), p. 153.

7.   Obama, *Dreams from My Father*, p. 114.

8.   Ibid., p. 129.

9.   Ibid., pp. 216–17, 220.

10. Ibid., pp. 128–29.

11. David Remnick, *The Bridge*, pp. 51–52; Jacobs, *The Other Barack*, p. 167; Merida, "The Ghost of a Father"; Edmund Sanders, "So Alike and Yet So Different," *Los Angeles Times*, July 17, 2008, http://articles .latimes.com/2008/jul/17/world/fg-obamadad17; Obama, *Dreams from My Father*, pp. 66–67.

12. Jacobs, *The Other Barack*, pp. 84–86, 148, 188.

13. Ibid., pp. 210, 246–47.

14. Ibid., pp. 200, 214, 231.

15. Ibid., pp. 108, 114–15; "First African Enrolled in Hawaii Studied Two Years by Mail," *Ka Leo O Hawaii*, October 8, 1959; Janny Scott, *A Singular Woman* (Riverhead Books, 2011), pp. 85–87.

16. Jacobs, *The Other Barack*, p. 206.

17. Obama, *Dreams from My Father*, pp. 305, 310, 323, 372.

CHAPTER 4

1.   Kristen Scharnberg and Kim Barker, "The Not-so-simple Story of Barack Obama's Youth," *Chicago Tribune*, March 25, 2007, http:// articles.chicagotribune.com/2007-03-25/news/0703250359_1_barry -obama-sen-barack-obama-stories.

2.   Barack Obama, *Dreams from My Father*, p. 53.

3.   Jake Tapper, "Life of Obama's Childhood Friend Takes Drastically Different Path," ABC News, April 3, 2007, http://abcnews.go.com /GMA/story?id=3045281&page=1#.T9ieTOxn2uI; David Maraniss, *Obama: The Story*, p. 290.

4.   Obama, *Dreams from My Father*, pp. xi, 50.

5.   Janny Scott, *A Singular Woman*, p. 7.

6.   Tim Jones, "Barack Obama: Mother Not Just a Girl from Kansas," *Chicago Tribune*, March 27, 2007, http://www.chicagotribune.com /news/politics/obama/chi-0703270151mar27-archive,0,2623808 .story; Scott, *A Singular Woman*, pp. 95, 119; Jonathan Martin, "Obama's Mother Known Here as Uncommon," *Seattle Times*, April 8, 2008, http://seattletimes.nwsource.com/html/politics/2004334057 _obama08m.html.

7.   Janny Scott, "Obama's Mother—An Unconventional Life," *New York Times*, March 14, 2008; Janny Scott, "A Free Spirited Wanderer Who

Set Obama's Path," *New York Times*, March 14, 2008, http://www
.nytimes.com/2008/03/14/us/politics/14obama.html?pagewanted=all;
Scott, *A Singular Woman*, p. 81.

8. Sally Jacobs, *The Other Barack*, pp. 118, 121, 125; Scott, *A Singular
    Woman*, p. 75.

9. Obama, *Dreams from My Father*, p. 125; Scott, *A Singular Woman*,
    p. 97.

10. Obama, *Dreams from My Father*, p. 273.

11. Norimitsu Onishi, "Obama Visits a Nation That Knew Him as
    Barry," *New York Times*, November 8, 2010, http://www.nytimes
    .com/2010/11/09/world/asia/09indo.html?pagewanted=all.

12. Obama, *Dreams from My Father*, pp. 35–39, 41.

13. Ibid., p. 47.

14. Scott, *A Singular Woman*, pp. 125–27, 253.

15. Obama, *Dreams from My Father*, p. 46.

16. Ibid., pp. 47, 50.

17. Scott, *A Singular Woman*, pp. 6, 247.

18. Ibid., pp. 294–96, 336.

19. Ibid., pp. 145, 188, 249, 292; S. Ann Dunham, *Surviving Against the
    Odds* (Duke University Press, 2009), pp. 9, 14, 19, 267.

CHAPTER 5

1. "Bill Ayers to University Students: America's 'Game is Over' and
    'Another World is Coming,'" the *Blaze*, May 2, 2012, theblaze.com.

2. Barack Obama, *Dreams from My Father*, p. 220.

3. Tim Cavanaugh, "D'Souza Puts Obama on Couch, Discovers Male
    Elektra Complex," *Reason*, September 12, 2010, http://reason.com
    /blog/2010/09/12/dsouza-puts-obama-on-couch-dis; Shelby Steele,
    "Obama and the Burden of Exceptionalism," *Wall Street Journal*,
    September 1, 2011, http://online.wsj.com/article/SB1000142405311
    19047874045765326231761155 58.html; Shelby Steele, "A Referen-
    dum on the Redeemer," *Wall Street Journal*, October 26, 2010, http://
    online.wsj.com/article/SB10001424052702304173704575578363243
    019000.html.

4. Tim Cavanaugh, "D'Souza Puts Obama on Couch, Discovers Male
    Elektra Complex," *Reason*, September 12, 2010, reason.com; Shelby
    Steele, "Obama and the Burden of Exceptionalism," *Wall Street Jour-*

nal, September 1, 2011, online.wsj.com; Shelby Steele, "A Referendum on the Redeemer," *Wall Street Journal*, October 26, 2010.

5. David Remnick, *The Bridge*, pp. 96–97.

6. Frank Marshall Davis, *Sex Rebel* (Greenleaf Classics, 1968), pp. 14, 77; Obama, *Dreams from My Father*, p. 77.

7. Frank Marshall Davis, *Livin' the Blues* (University of Wisconsin Press, 1992), pp. 315, 321; Frank Marshall Davis, "Frankly Speaking," *Honolulu Record*, January 12, 1950.

8. Haunani-Kay Trask, *From a Native Daughter: Colonialism and Sovereignty in Hawaii* (University of Hawaii Press, 199), pp. 3, 79, 171.

9. Davis, *Livin' the Blues*, p. 323; John Edgar Tidwell, ed., *Writings of Frank Marshall Davis* (University of Mississippi Press, 2007), pp. 93, 96.

10. Frank Marshall Davis, "How Our Democracy Looks to Oppressed Peoples," *Honolulu Record*, May 19, 1949; Paul Kengor, "Obama's Surrogate Anti-Colonial Father," October 14, 2010, http://spectator.org/archives/2010/10/14/obamas-surrogate-anti-colonial; Davis, *Livin' the Blues*, p. 277.

11. Edward Said, *Orientalism* (Vintage, 1978), p. 3.

12. Edward Said, *Culture and Imperialism* (Alfred A. Knopf, 1993), pp. 25, 30; Obama, *Dreams from My Father*, p. 103.

13. Edward Said, *The Question of Palestine* (Vintage Books, 1992), pp. xxi, 37, 143; Edward Said, *The Politics of Dispossession* (Vintage Books, 1995), pp. xv, xxvii, 31, 70, 82, 138, 178; Stanley Kurtz, "Edward Said, Imperialist," *Weekly Standard*, October 8, 2001, p. 35.

14. Obama, *Dreams from My Father*, pp. 276, 437; Elise O'Shaughnessy, "Harvard Law Reviewed," *Vanity Fair*, June 1990.

15. Remnick, *The Bridge*, p. 185.

16. Roberto Mangabeira Unger, *The Left Alternative* (Verso, 2005), pp. xix, 128, 134–35, 143, 146, 148, 164; Roberto Mangabeira Unger, *Free Trade Reimagined* (Princeton University Press, 2007), pp. 2, 197; Roberto Mangabeira Unger, *What Should Legal Analysis Become?* (Verso, 1996), pp. 108, 161, 165; Roberto Mangabeira Unger and Cornel West, *The Future of American Progressivism* (Beacon Press, 1998), pp. 30, 93.

17. Bonnie Kavoussi, "Roberto Unger, Obama's Former Harvard Law Professor, Says the President 'Must Be Defeated,'" *Huffington Post*, June 16, 2012, http://www.huffingtonpost.com/2012/06/16/roberto-unger-obama_n_1602812.html.

18. James Cone, *Black Theology and Black Power* (Seabury Press, 1969), p. 111; James Cone, *A Black Theology of Liberation* (Orbis Books, 1990), p. xvii

19. Jeremiah Wright, "Confusing God and Government," April 13, 2003, http://www.blackpast.org/?q=2008-rev-jeremiah-wright-confusing -god-and-government.

20. Interview with Jeremiah Wright, *Bill Moyers Journal*, PBS, April 25, 2008, available at http://www.pbs.org/moyers/journal/04252008 /watch.html.

21. Jeremiah Wright (speech, National Press Club), April 28, 2008, chicagotribune.com.

22. Edward Klein, *The Amateur*, pp. 39, 43, 50; Remnick, *The Bridge*, p. 533.

23. Ben Smith, "Ax on Ayers," *Politico*, February 26, 2008, http://www .politico.com/blogs/bensmith/0208/Ax_on_Ayers.html.

24. Marcia Froelke Coburn, "No Regrets," *Chicago*, August 2001, chicago mag.com; Dinitia Smith, "No Regrets for a Love of Explosives; In a Memoir of Sorts, a War Protester Talks of Life With the Weathermen," *New York Times*, September 11, 2001, http://www.nytimes.com /2001/09/11/books/no-regrets-for-love-explosives-memoir-sorts-war -protester-talks-life-with.html?pagewanted=all; Ayers, *Fugitive Days*, p. 295.

25. Ayers, *Fugitive Days*, pp. 67, 114, 126, 143, 145–46, 162, 164, 265; Bernardine Dohrn, Bill Ayers, and Jeff Jones, eds., *Sing a Battle Song* (Seven Stories Press, 2006), pp. 170, 315.

CHAPTER 6

1. Barack Obama, *Dreams from My Father*, p. 406.

2. Amilcar Cabral, *Return to the Source: Selected Speeches by Amilcar Cabral* (Monthly Review Press, 1973), p. 64.

3. David Anderson, *Histories of the Hanged* (New York: W. W. Norton, 2005).

4. Maraniss, *Barack Obama: The Story*, pp. 54–56.

5. Obama, *Dreams from My Father*, p. 426.

6. Jacobs, *The Other Barack*, pp. 15, 20, 30; Tom Shachtman, *Airlift to America* (St. Martin's Press, 2009), p. 5; Peter Firstbrook, *The Obamas*, pp. 134, 151; Obama, *Dreams from My Father*, p. 410.

7. Firstbrook, *The Obamas*, pp. 152, 160; Jacobs, *The Other Barack*, pp. 21, 31.

8. Obama, *Dreams from My Father*, pp. 369, 397, 400, 407, 410, 414, 417; Firstbrook, *The Obamas*, p. 159.

9. Obama, *Dreams from My Father*, p. 406.

10. Mark Obama Ndesandjo, *Nairobi to Shenzhen* (Aventine Press, 2010), pp. 7, 172–73.

11. Obama, *Dreams from My Father*, pp. 341–42.

12. Ibid., pp. 343–44; Auma Obama, *And Then Life Happens* (St. Martin's Press, 2012), p. 201.

13. John Vause, "Obama Brothers Meet in China," CNN, November 18, 2009, http://articles.cnn.com/2009-11-18/politics/obama.half .brother_1_president-obama-chinese-president-hu-jintao-big -brother?_s=PM:POLITICS.

14. George Obama, *Homeland* (Simon & Schuster, 2010), p. 18; Obama, *Dreams from My Father*, pp. 431–32.

15. George Obama, *Homeland*, p. 273.

16. "Remarks of the President at the National Prayer Breakfast," February 2, 2012, http://www.whitehouse.gov/the-press-office/2012/02/02 /remarks-president-national-prayer-breakfast; David Mendell, *Obama: From Promise to Power*, p 227.

17. George Obama, *Homeland*, p. xx.

18. Ibid., pp. 170, 192, 237, 249.

CHAPTER 7

1. Saul Alinsky, *Rules for Radicals* (Vintage Books, 1989), p. 12.

2. Sanford Horwitt, *Let Them Call Me Rebel: Saul Alinsky, His Life and Legacy* (Vintage Books, 1992).

3. Alinsky, *Rules for Radicals*, pp. 184–96.

4. Ibid., pp. ix, 25, 30–31, 36.

5. Jennifer Senior, "Dreaming of Obama," *New York Magazine*, September 24, 2006, http://nymag.com/news/politics/21681/.

6. Obama, *Dreams from My Father*.

7. Scott Whitlock, "Chris Matthews Swoons Again," *Newsbusters*, March 4, 2011, http://m.newsbusters.org/blogs/scott-whitlock/2011/03/04 /chris-matthews-swoons-again-everything-obamas-done-has-been -good-cou.

8.   Shelby Steele, *A Dream Deferred* (HarperCollins, 1998), p. 119.
9.   Shelby Steele, *White Guilt* (HarperCollins, 2006), pp. 24, 34–35.
10. Shelby Steele, *A Bound Man* (Free Press, 2008), pp. 76, 78.
11. Ibid., pp. 77–79, 85.
12. Ibid., p. 87.
13. Ibid., p. 86, 89, 95.
14. Ibid., p. 99; Barack Obama, *Dreams from My Father*, pp. 94–95.
15. Shelby Steele, "Obama's Unspoken Re-Election Edge," *Wall Street Journal*, May 25, 2011, http://online.wsj.com/article/SB100014240527 48704569404576299241421694066.html; Steele, *A Bound Man*, p. 116.
16. Mendell, *Obama: From Promise to Power* (Harper, 2008), p. 7.

CHAPTER 8

1.   Barack Obama Sr., "Problems Facing Our Socialism," *East Africa Journal*, July 1965.
2.   Ibid.
3.   Editorial, "The Buffett Alternative Tax," *Wall Street Journal*, September 20, 2011, http://online.wsj.com/article/SB1000142405311190419 4604576580800735800830.html; Editorial, "Mr. Obama and the Buffett Rule," *New York Times*, April 11, 2012, p. A-20.
4.   Scott A. Hodge, "White House's Own Data Contradicts Claims on Buffett Rule," *Tax Foundation*, April 12, 2012, http://taxfoundation .org/blog/white-houses-own-data-contradicts-claims-buffett-rule.
5.   Eduardo Porter, "The Case for Raising Top Tax Rates," *New York Times*, March 28, 2012, p. B-1, B-6.
6.   Transcript: Obama and Clinton Debate, ABC News, April 16, 2008, http://abcnews.go.com/Politics/DemocraticDebate/story?id =4670271&page=1#.T9YDh-xn2uI.
7.   "Too Big Not to Fail," *Economist*, February 18, 2012, pp. 22–24; Paul Sperry, "1,000 Small Banks May be Shut Down Due to Dodd-Frank," *Investor's Business Daily*, May 23, 2011, p. 1.
8.   "Now What?" *Economist*, March 27, 2010, p. 13.

CHAPTER 9

1.   "Obama Camp Spies Endgame in Oregon,"AFP, May 16, 2008.

2.   "Barack Obama's Inaugural Address," *Salon*, January 20, 2009, salon
      .com; Carl Lavin, "Obama's Oil Spill Speech: Full Text," *Forbes*, June
      15, 2010, http://www.forbes.com/sites/energysource/2010/06/15
      /obamas-oil-spill-speech-full-text/.

3.   John Broder, "Obama Oil Drilling Plan Draws Critics," *New York
      Times*, March 31, 2010, http://www.nytimes.com/2010/04/01/science
      /earth/01energy.html?pagewanted=all; John Broder and Clifford
      Krauss, "U.S. Taking Step to Open Drilling in Arctic Ocean," *New York
      Times*, August 5, 2011, p. A-1.

4.   John Broder and Dan Frosch, "U.S. Delays Decision on Pipeline Until
      After Election," *New York Times*, November 10, 2011, http://www
      .nytimes.com/2011/11/11/us/politics/administration-to-delay-pipeline
      -decision-past-12-election.html; Deborah Solomon and Laura Meck-
      ler, "Obama Says No, for Now, to Canada Pipeline," *Wall Street Jour-
      nal*, January 10, 2012, p. A-2; Theophilos Argitis and Jeremy Van
      Loon, "Obama's Keystone Denial Prompts China to Look to China
      Sales," Bloomberg, January 19, 2012, http://www.bloomberg.com
      /news/2012-01-19/canada-pledges-to-sell-oil-to-asia-after-obama
      -rejects-keystone-pipeline.html.

5.   Adam White, "Powering Down," *Weekly Standard*, November 21,
      2011, p. 15; Joe Nocera, "Poisoned Politics of Keystone XL," *New York
      Times*, February 7, 2012, p. A-31.

6.   "Obama's Speech on Climate Change," *New York Times*, September
      23, 2009, http://www.nytimes.com/2009/09/23/us/politics/23obama
      .text.html?pagewanted=all; "He Who Pays the Paupers," *Economist*,
      November 5, 2011, p. 90; Walter Russell Mead, "The Politics of Cli-
      mategate," *American Interest*, January-February 2010, p. 125; The
      White House, "Remarks by the President at the Summit of the Amer-
      icas Opening Ceremony," April 17, 2009, http://www.whitehouse.gov
      /the_press_office/Remarks-by-the-President-at-the-Summit-of-the
      -Americas-Opening-Ceremony.

7.   "Obama Underwrites Offshore Drilling," *Wall Street Journal*, August
      18, 2009, http://online.wsj.com/article/SB10001424052970203863204
      574346610120524166.html.

8.   "Lawmakers, Executives Slam Obama for Boosting Brazil's Offshore
      Drilling," Fox News, March 23, 2011, http://www.foxnews.com
      /politics/2011/03/23/lawmakers-execs-slam-obama-boosting-brazils
      -offshore-drilling/; Kelly Hearn, "China gets jump on U.S. for Brazil's

oil," *Washington Times*, January 19, 2012, http://www.washington
times.com/news/2012/jan/19/china-gets-jump-on-us-for-brazils-oil/.

9. "U.S. Backs $1 B Loan to Mexico for Oil Drilling Despite Obama
Moratorium," *Fox News*, September 11, 2010, http://www.foxnews
.com/politics/2010/09/11/backs-b-loan-mexico-oil-drilling-despite
-obama-moratorium/; Terence Jeffrey, "U.S. Gov't Agency Plans $2.84
Billion Loan for Oil Refinery in Colombia," CNS News, April 18, 2011,
http://cnsnews.com/news/article/us-govt-agency-plans-284-billion
-loan-oil-refinery-colombia; Export-Import Bank of the United States,
"Ex-Im Board Approves $2.84 Billion Export Financing for Colom-
bian Refinery Project," May 19, 2011, http://www.exim.gov/press
release.cfm/0BF22A51-A985-1648-515C22E229E893C6/.

10. Steve Forbes, "News Flash! Positive Change Coming," *Forbes*, September 12, 2011, p. 14; Daniel Halper, "Obama Warned that His
Policies Would Bankrupt Coal Power Plant Owners," *Weekly Standard*,
May 11, 2012, http://www.weeklystandard.com/blogs/obama
-warned-his-policies-would-bankrupt-coal-power-plant-owners
_644384.html.

CHAPTER 10

1. Council on Foreign Relations, "Obama's Speech at the Nuclear Security Summit, April 2010," April 13, 2010, http://www.cfr.org/prolif
eration/obamas-speech-nuclear-security-summit-april-2010/p21889.

2. Mary Beth Sheridan and Scott Wilson, "In Nuclear Summit, Obama
Seeks Global Help in Sanctioning Iran," *Washington Post*, April 13,
2010, http://www.washingtonpost.com/wp-dyn/content/arti
cle/2010/04/12/AR2010041201495.html.

3. Jonathan Alter, *The Promise* (Simon & Schuster, 2010), p. 425; Charles
Krauthammer, "Obama's nuclear strutting and fretting," *Washington
Post*, April 6, 2010, http://www.washingtonpost.com/wp-dyn/content
/article/2010/04/15/AR2010041504663.html.

4. David Sanger and William Broad, "U. N. Agency Says Iran Data Points
to A-Bomb Work," *New York Times*, November 9, 2011, p. A-1.

5. Michael Winter, "A.P.: Pentagon drafts plans for cuts in U.S. nuclear
arsenal," *USA Today*, February 14, 2012, http://content.usatoday.com
/communities/ondeadline/post/2012/02/ap-obama-weighing-deep
-cuts-in-us-nuclear-arsenal/1#.T9Y1zuxn2uI.

6. "Obama Prague Speech on Nuclear Weapons: Full Text," *Huffington Post*, May 6, 2009, http://www.huffingtonpost.com/2009/04/05/obama -prague-speech-on-nu_n_183219.html.

7. Thomas Donnelly and Gary Schmitt, "A Path to Security," *Weekly Standard*, April 2, 2012, p. 9.

CHAPTER 11

1. Douglas Feith and Seth Cropsey, "The Obama Doctrine Defined," *Commentary*, July 2011, http://www.commentarymagazine.com /article/the-obama-doctrine-defined/.

2. Pew Annual Religion and Public Life Survey, "Religion, Politics and the President: Growing Number of Americans Say Obama Is a Muslim," August 19, 2010.

3. Conor Friedersdorf, email query to the author, May 2, 2011.

4. Cited in Bruce Lawrence, ed., *Messages to the World: The Statements of Osama Bin Laden* (Verso, 2005), p. 59; "Full text: Bin Laden's 'letter to America,'" *The Guardian* (London) November 24, 2002, http://www .guardian.co.uk/world/2002/nov/24/theobserver.

5. Barack Obama, *The Audacity of Hope*, p. 304.

6. Transcript, "Obama announces the death of Osama Bin Laden," CNN, May 2, 2011, http://articles.cnn.com/2011-05-02/world/bin.laden .announcement_1_qaeda-bin-afghan-border?_s=PM:WORLD.

7. Barack Obama, "Remarks by the President on a New Beginning," Cairo Univeristy, June 4, 2009, http://www.whitehouse.gov/the-press -office/remarks-president-cairo-university-6-04-09.

8. V. I. Lenin, *Imperialism: The Highest Stage of Capitalism* (Pluto Press, 1996), http://www.pewforum.org/Politics-and-Elections/Growing -Number-of-Americans-Say-Obama-is-a-Muslim.aspx.

9. Obama, *The Audacity of Hope*, p. 294; Associated Press, "Obama: U.S. Troops in Afghanistan Must Do More than Kill Civilians," Fox News, August 14, 2007, http://www.foxnews.com/story/0,2933, 293187,00.html.

10. "Sources: Obama Administration to Drop Troop Levels in Iraq to 3,000," Fox News, September 6, 2011, http://www.foxnews.com/politics /2011/09/06/sources-obama-administration-to-drop-troop-levels-in -iraq-to-3000/; Max Boot, "Losing Iraq?" *Weekly Standard*, September 19, 2011, pp. 10–11.

11. Federick Kagan, Kimberly Kagan, and Marisa Cochrane Sullivan, "Defeat in Iraq," *Weekly Standard*, November 7, 2011, pp. 25–32.

12. Bob Woodward, *Obama's Wars* (Simon & Schuster, 2010), p. 247.

13. The White House, "Remarks by the President on the Way Forward in Afghanistan," June 22, 2011, http://www.whitehouse.gov/the-press-office/2011/06/22/remarks-president-way-forward-afghanistan.

14. Dexter Filkins and Mark Landler, "Afghan Leader is Seen to Flout Influence of U.S.," *New York Times*, March 30, 2010, p. A-1; Ken Dilanian, "Karzai Remarks About Taliban Give White House Pause," *USA Today*, April 7, 2010, p. 6-A; Ahmed Rashid, "How Obama Lost Karzai," *Foreign Policy*, March–April 2011, pp. 71–76.

15. Julian Borger and Jon Boone, "Taliban leaders held at Guantanamo Bay to be released in peace talks deal," *The Guardian*, January 3, 2012, http://www.guardian.co.uk/world/2012/jan/03/taliban-leaders-guantanamo-bay-deal; "The World This Week," *Economist*, January 28, 2012, p. 6.

16. The White House, "Remarks by the President in Address to the Nation on the Way Forward in Afghanistan and Pakistan," December 1, 2009, http://www.whitehouse.gov/the-press-office/remarks-president-address-nation-way-forward-afghanistan-and-pakistan.

17. "Seven killed in Kabul in bomb, grenade attack on heels of Obama's Afghanistan visit," CBS News, May 2, 2012, http://www.cbsnews.com/8301-202_162-57425744/7-killed-in-kabul-in-bomb-grenade-attack-on-heels-of-obamas-afghanistan-visit/.

18. Ryan Lizza, "The Second Term," *The New Yorker*, June 18, 2012, p. 55; Bing West, "Groundhog War," *Foreign Affairs*, September-October 2011, p. 171.

19. Barack Obama, "A New Beginning"; Ian Buruma, "Is Israel a Normal Country?" *The Globe and Mail*, July 12, 2010, http://www.theglobeandmail.com/commentary/is-israel-a-normal-country/article1386938/; Edward Said, *The Question of Palestine*, p. 69.

20. "Ties between Israel and U.S. 'worst in 35 years,'" BBC News, March 14, 2010, http://news.bbc.co.uk/2/hi/8567706.stm; The White House, "Remarks by the President on a New Beginning"; Mark Landler and Steven Lee Myers, "Obama Seeks End to the Stalemate on Mideast Talks," *New York Times*, May 20, 2011, pp. A-1, A-9.

21. Thomas Friedman, "Israel's Best Friend," *New York Times*, March 7, 2012, p. A-27.

CHAPTER 12

1.   Barack Obama, "Remarks by the President on a New Beginning lecture," Cairo University, June 4, 2009.

2.   Fawaz Gerges, *Obama and the Middle East* (Palgrave Macmillan, 2012), p. 152.

3.   Walter Russell Mead, "The Dreamer Goes Down For The Count," *American Interest*, May 25, 2011, http://blogs.the-american-interest.com/wrm/2011/05/25/the-dreamer-goes-down-for-the-count/.

4.   Laura Kasinof and David Sanger, "U. S. Shifts to Seek Removal of Yemen's Leader, an Ally," *New York Times*, April 3, 2011, http://www.nytimes.com/2011/04/04/world/middleeast/04yemen.html?pagewanted=all.

5.   "Islamists and Secularists at One," *Economist*, November 26, 2011, p. 58.

6.   Fawaz Gerges, *The Far Enemy* (Cambridge University Press, 2005); Ayman al-Zawahiri, "The Way To Jerusalem Passes Through Cairo," *Al Mujahideen*, April 1995.

7.   Ayman al-Zawahiri, "Knights Under the Prophet's Banner," *Asharq al-Awsat*, December 2001.

8.   Mona El-Naggar, "Banned Group Urges Egyptians to Vote on Sept. 7," *New York Times*, August 22, 2005, p. A-7.

9.   David Corn, *Showdown* (William Morrow, 2012), p. 218; Ryan Lizza, "The Consequentialist," *The New Yorker*, May 2, 2011, p. 55.

10. "'We've Never Seen Such Horror': Crimes Against Humanity by Syrian Security Forces," Human Rights Watch, June 1, 2011; "In Syria, Accounts of Widening Torture," *Wall Street Journal*, May 28, 2011, http://online.wsj.com/article/SB100014240527023036548045763410 30013131512.html.

11. The White House, "A Statement by President Obama on Syria," April 22, 2011, http://www.whitehouse.gov/blog/2011/04/22/statement -president-obama-syria; Steven Lee Myers, "U. S. and Allies Say Syria Leader Must Step Down," *New York Times*, August 19, 2011, p. 1; Charles Levinson and Gregory White, "America Exits Syria as Russia Makes Push," *Wall Street Journal*, February 7, 2012, p. 1; AP, "Obama: Syria Military Intervention Premature," *Huffington Post*, March 14, 2012, http://www.huffingtonpost.com/2012/03/14/obama-syria-mili tary-intervention_n_1345070.html; Associated Press, "Officials:

Obama ramps up aid to Syrian opposition," *Townhall*, April 13, 2012, http://www.townhall.com/news/politics-elections/2012/04/13/offi cials_obama_ramps_up_aid_to_sign_opposition..

12. Max Boot, "Assad Must Go," *Weekly Standard*, December 5, 2011, pp. 8–9; Lee Smith, "Free Syria," *Weekly Standard*, March 5, 2012, pp. 8–9.

13. Helene Cooper, Mark Landler, and David Sanger, "In U. S. Signals to Egypt, Obama Straddled a Rift," *New York Times*, February 12, 2001, http://www.nytimes.com/2011/02/13/world/middleeast/13diplomacy .html?pagewanted=all.

14. David Kirkpatrick, "From U.S. and Tahrir Square, Pressures Converge on Egypt's Military," *New York Times*, November 26, 2011, p. A-9.

15. David Kirkpatrick, "Egypt Lifts a Border Blockage, Along with the Hopes of Gazans," *New York Times*, May 29, 2011, p. A-1; David Kirkpatrick, "In Shift, Egypt Extends Hand to Israel's Foes," *New York Times*, April 29, 2011, p. A-1; Ethan Bronner and Isabel Kershner, "Fatah and Hamas Announce Outline of Deal," *New York Times*, April 27, 2011, http://www.nytimes.com/2011/04/28/world/middle east/28mideast.html?pagewanted=all; Matt Bradley and Joshua Mit-nick, "Egypt Cancels Israel Natural Gas Deal," *Wall Street Journal*, April 28, 2012, p A-7.

16. Associated Press, "Obama Administration Warns Egypt's Military Leaders to Hand Over Power or Risk Losing US Aid," *Washington Post*, June 18, 2012, http://www.washingtonpost.com/politics/pentagon -is-concerned-about-egyptian-militarys-latest-moves-but-hopeful-of -transition/2012/06/18/gJQAFAvZlV_story.html.

17. Haleh Esfandiari, "Iran: The State of Fear," *New York Review of Books*, April 7, 2011, p. 31; Lara Setrakian, "Iran President Tells Obama to Back Off," ABC News, June 25, 2009, http://abcnews.go.com/Interna tional/story?id=7932217#.T9ZZg-xn2uI; Ryan Lizza, "The Consequen-tialist"; Charles Krauthammer, "Hope and Change—But Not for Iran," *Townhall*, June 29, 2009, http://townhall.com/columnists/charleskraut hammer/2009/06/19/hope_and_change_-_but_not_for_iran/page/full/.

18. Jonathan Alter, *The Promise*, p. 355.

19. Middle East Media Research Institute, "Muslim Brotherhood Figure and Former Spokesman in the West: Establish a Global Islamic State," June 24, 2011, http://www.thememriblog.org/blog_personal /en/38783.htm.

CHAPTER 13

1. Branko Milanovic, *The Haves and the Have-Nots* (Basic Books, 2011), p. 117.

2. David Remnick, *The Bridge*, p. 265.

3. Barack Obama, *The Audacity of Hope*, p. 188.

4. Mark Knoller, "National Debt Has Increased More Under Obama than Under Bush," CBS News, March 19, 2012, http://www.cbsnews.com/8301-503544_162-57400369-503544/national-debt-has-increased-more-under-obama-than-under-bush/; Terrence Jeffrey, "Obama on Pace to Borrow $6.2 Trillion in One Term—More Than All Presidents from Washington Through Clinton Combined," CNS News, January 13, 2012, cnsnews.com; Brian Riedl, "Zero Hour," *American Legion*, September 2011, pp. 26–32.

5. Dennis Cauchon, "Real Federal Deficit Dwarfs Official Tally," *USA Today*, May 18, 2012, http://www.usatoday.com/news/washington/story/2012-05-18/federal-deficit-accounting/55179748/1.

6. The White House, "Remarks by President Obama and President Clinton at a Campaign Event," New York, June 4, 2012, http://www.whitehouse.gov/the-press-office/2012/06/05/remarks-president-obama-and-president-clinton-campaign-event; Jim Kuhnhenn, "Obama on the Defensive on Spending, Debt," AP, May 26, 2012, http://news.yahoo.com/obama-defensive-spending-debt-163810353.html.

7. "Looking for Someone to Blame," *Economist*, August 13, 2011, p. 25.

8. David Logan, "Warren Buffett's Proposed Tax Hikes Would Provide Insignificant Revenue," The Tax Foundation, August 21, 2011, taxfoundation.org.

9. Ibid.

10. Nina Easton, "Add This to Obama's List of Economic Woes: The Specter of Inflation," *Fortune*, May 23, 2011, p. 77.

11. Barry Eichengreen, "The Once and Future Dollar," *American Interest*, May/June 2012, p. 13; Arvind Subramanian, cited in Sebastian Mallaby and Olin Wethington, "The Future of the Yuan," *Foreign Affairs*, January/February 2012, p. 135.

12. Nick Timiraos, "Foreigners Snap Up Properties in the U.S.," *Wall Street Journal*, June 12, 2012, pp. A-1, A-4.

13. Charles Kenny, "We're All the 1%," *Foreign Policy*, March/April 2012, p. 24.

CHAPTER 14

1.   Jodi Kantor, *The Obamas* (Little, Brown and Company, 2012), p. 18.

2.   Jim Hoft, "Michelle Obama Takes Aspen Ski Vacation a Month After Hawaiian Beach Vacation," *Human Events*, February 18, 2012, http://www.humanevents.com/2012/02/18/michelle-obama-takes -aspen-ski-vacation-a-month-after-hawaiian-beach-vacation/; Dave Boyer, "Obama Calls for Shared Sacrifice," *Washington Times*, August 17, 2011, http://www.washingtontimes.com/news/2011/aug/17/prep ping-debt-plan-obama-calls-shared-sacrifice/.

3.   "Michelle Obama Wears $540 Sneakers To Food Bank," *Huffington Post*, May 30, 2009, http://www.huffingtonpost.com/2009/04/29 /michelle-obama-wears-silv_n_193138.html; Kantor, *The Obamas*, pp. 240–42.

4.   Michelle LaVaughn Robinson, "Princeton-Educated Blacks and the Black Community" (Princeton University, 1985), published under the heading "Michelle Obama Princeton Thesis," obamaprincetonthesis .wordpress.com.

5.   The White House, "Remarks by the President on Osama Bin Laden," May 2, 2011, http://www.whitehouse.gov/the-press-office/2011/05/02 /remarks-president-osama-bin-laden; David Corn, *Showdown* (William Morrow, 2012), p. 49; Jonathan Last, "American Narcissus," *Weekly Standard*, November 22, 2010, p. 25.

6.   John Hinderaker, "Obama Places Himself on the Continuum of Greatness," Powerline Blog, December 20, 2011, http://www.powerline blog.com/archives/2011/12/obama-places-himself-on-the-continuum -of-great ness.php; Andrew Malcolm, "Narcissism Update," *Investor's Business Daily*, May 16, 2012, http://news.investors.com/article /611592/201205160808/obama-inserts-his-own-name-into-online -presidential-biographies.htm?p=full; M. J. Lee, "Blogs Bash Obama's Historic Claim," *Politico*, December 20, 2011, http://www.politico .com/news/stories/1211/70684.html.

7.   "American Narcissus (cont.)," *Weekly Standard*, December 27, 2010, p. 2.

8.   Wole Soyinka, *Art, Dialogue and Outrage* (Pantheon Books, 1993), p. 210.

9.   David Gardner, "How Obamas' romantic £120 trip to Broadway racked up a £45,000 bill," London *Daily Mail*, June 1, 2009, http:// www.dailymail.co.uk/news/article-1189893/How-Obamas-romantic

-120-trip-Broadway-racked-45-000-bill.html; Andrew Malcolm, "As Americans Struggle, the Obamas Make Do with 37 Christmas Trees," *Investor's Business Daily*, December 12, 2011, http://news.investors .com/article/594258/201112120812/obama-white-house-christmas -trees.htm?p=full; "Obama Gets into the Swing of Things on His Martha's Vineyard Vacation," London *Daily Mail*, August 20, 2011, http://www.dailymail.co.uk/news/article-2027541/Obama-golfs -Marthas-Vineyard-increasing-personal-debt-ceiling.html; "Meet the White House personal trainer that the Obamas fly in from Chicago—and even share with their staff," London *Daily Mail*, March 1, 2011, http://www.dailymail.co.uk/news/article-1361575 /Meet-White-House-personal-trainer-Obamas-fly-Chicago-share -staff.html.

10. Benedict Anderson, *Imagined Communities* (Verso, 2006), p. 160.

11. Richard Epstein, "Would We Ever Ground Air Force One?" *Defining Ideas*, a Hoover Institution Journal, July 5, 2011, http://www.hoover .org/publications/defining-ideas/article/84536.

12. David Brooks, "The Pragmatic Leviathan," *New York Times*, January 19, 2010, http://www.nytimes.com/2010/01/19/opinion/19brooks.html.

13. Julia Preston and Helene Cooper, "After Chorus of Protest, New Tune on Deportations," *New York Times*, June 17, 2012, http://www.nytimes .com/2012/06/18/us/politics/deportation-policy-change-came-after -protests.html?_r=1&ref=illegalimmigrants; Marc Ambinder, "Obama Won't Go to Court Over Defense of Marriage Act," *National Journal*, February 24, 2011, http://www.nationaljournal.com/obama-won-t -go-to-court-over-defense-of-marriage-act-20110223.

14. Mark Landler and Helene Cooper, "Obama Seeks a Course of Pragmatism in the Middle East," *New York Times*, March 10, 2011, http:// www.nytimes.com/2011/03/11/world/africa/11policy.html.

CHAPTER 15

1. Barack Obama, *Dreams from My Father*, p. 437.

2. Hilaire Belloc, *The Modern Traveller* (London, 1898), p. vi.

3. Adam Hochschild, *King Leopold's Ghost* (Houghton Mifflin, 1998), pp. 49–50.

4. Helene Cooper, "On the World Stage, Obama Issues an Overture," *New York Times*, April 3, 2009, http://www.nytimes.com/2009/04/03

/world/europe/03assess.html; Richard Toye, *Churchill's Empire* (Macmillan, 2010).

5.   Kishore Mahbubani, *The New Asian Hemisphere* (Public Affairs, 2008), p. 17.

6.   The term is Jefferson's. Thomas Jefferson to James Madison, April 27, 1809.

7.   James Morris, *Heaven's Command* (Harvest Books, 1973), pp. 382–83.

8.   Marian Burros, "Obamas to Plant Vegetable Garden at the White House," *New York Times*, March 19, 2009, http://www.nytimes.com/2009/03/20/dining/20garden.html.

9.   Binyamin Appelbaum, "For U.S. Families, Net Worth Falls to 1990s Levels," *New York Times*, June 12, 2012, p. A-1; Reuters, "Americans Suffered Record Decline in Wealth During Recession," *Huffington Post*, June 11, 2012, http://www.huffingtonpost.com/2012/06/11/americans-suffered-record_n_1587387.html.

INDEX

Z